Student
Characteristics
and Teaching

Student Characteristics and Teaching

Jere E. Brophy
Michigan State University

and

Carolyn M. Evertson
University of Texas at Austin

with
Linda M. Anderson, Michigan State University
Michael C. Baum, Illinois State University
and
John Crawford, Canyon Landing, Incorporated
and University of New Mexico

New York and London

Longman Inc., New York, 19 West 44 St., New York, N.Y. 10036
Associated companies, branches, and representatives
throughout the world.

Developmental Editor: Lane Akers
Editorial and Design Supervisor: Judith Hirsch
Cover Design: Dan Serrano
Manufacturing and Production Supervisor: Robin B. Besofsky
Composition: Eastern Graphics
Printing and Binding: BookCrafters Inc.

Manufactured in the United States of America

9 8 7 6 5 4 3 2 1

Library of Congress Cataloging in Publication Data

Brophy, Jere E
    Student characteristics and teaching.

    Bibliography: p.
    Includes index.
    1. Students—Attitudes. 2. Students—Psychology.
3. Teachers—Attitudes. I. Evertson, Carolyn M.,
1935-   joint author. II. Title.
LB3605.B74   371.8'1   80-23741
ISBN 0-582-28152-0

Contents

Preface

In recent years, there has been a flurry of research on the dynamics of teacher-student interaction. Much of this began with the publication of Rosenthal and Jacobson's (1968) *Pygmalion in the Classroom,* with its exciting conclusion that teacher expectations for student achievement could function as self-fulfilling prophecies. This study led many investigators, ourselves included, to conduct research on teacher expectations and related topics.

At first, our focus was on understanding the mechanisms that mediate teacher expectation effects. We wanted to see if teachers taught high expectation students in ways that would maximize their learning, and low expectation students in ways that might minimize theirs. In several studies, we showed that this sometimes was the case, and identified some of the ways that teacher expectation effects are produced.

In the process, we became intrigued with individual differences. These included differences in the degrees to which teachers were affected by their own expectations, as well as differences in students that affected the formation of teacher expectations. We also became interested in teacher attitudes toward students. Again, there were individual differences in students that led to these teacher attitudes in the first place.

The Student Attribute Study described in this book was a large-scale investigation designed to study individual differences in students by identifying student attributes associated with contrasting teacher expectations, attitudes, and behavior. The data were analyzed to address the following questions: What attributes of students do teachers use to develop contrasting expectations or attitudes? Are the teacher perceptions substantiated by real differences in student characteristics and behavior? Which student attributes are most likely to be associated with particular expectations or attitudes? To what extent is differential teacher behavior appropriately based on real student differences, and to what extent is it based on unsubstantiated teacher perceptions that could be considered inappropriate?

As you will see, a variety and large amount of data were collected to address these questions. Many results were predictable, although often surprising and fascinating in their depth and complexity. Other results provided surprises, showing that teachers sometimes are unusually patient with students who appear unusually exasperating, overly hostile toward students who do not seem to deserve such treatment, and so on. The book raises questions about a variety of topics, but one thing is certain: it will convince you that student differences must be taken into account in thinking about and making prescriptions for ideal teacher-student interaction.

Readers should note that this book constitutes only a summary of the major findings of the study, and not a complete presentation. To facilitate presentation and discussion of the findings we consider to be most important and interesting, we have included only a subset of the variables addressed in the study and simplified the presentation of the results. Also, coding categories and other methodological procedures have been summarized rather than presented in complete detail.

Readers desiring more complete information about the design, methodology, analysis procedures, or results of the study can find them in the final report (Brophy, Evertson, Anderson, Baum, and Crawford, 1980) and in several smaller technical reports referenced at appropriate places in the book.

The authors wish to thank the following people, all of whom played key roles in one or more aspects of the Student Attribute Study: Connie Anderson, Cynthia Coulter, Bucky Evertson, Carol Greenhalgh, Janet Honea, Carol King, Jane Ogden, Georgia Reed, Dr. Kathleen Senior, Gael Sherman, Mike Tebeleff, Ann Turney, and Cicely Wynne, who collected data as classroom coders; Jim Blackwell, John Brozovsky, Paul Cockreham, Mary Jane Leahy, and Wally Washington, who assisted in data preparation or analysis; Dr. Jeanne Martin, who critically reviewed earlier drafts and made substantive suggestions for revision; and Beatrice Mladenka, Gwen Newman, June Smith, and Sidney Weaver, who assisted in manuscript preparation.

The study was supported in part by the National Institute of Education, Contract OB-NIE-78-0216, the Research and Development Center for Teacher Education, University of Texas at Austin. In addition, a portion of Anderson and Brophy's time was supported by the National Institute of Education, Contract 4-0-76-0073, the Institute for Research on Teaching, Michigan State University. The opinions expressed herein do not necessarily reflect the position or the policy of the National Institute of Education and no official endorsement by that office should be inferred.

Part 1

Overview and Rationale
for the Study

1

Introduction: Teacher Reactions to Students

Susie Smith makes a grand entrance on her first day at Lincoln School. She is confidently escorted to Mrs. Barnett's classroom by her chic, well-dressed mother. Mrs. Smith introduces herself to Mrs. Barnett with considerable poise and charm, and then proudly presents Susie, who beams and displays her well-stocked school box. After a few minutes of pleasant conversation, Mrs. Smith bids Susie goodbye, reminding her that she will pick her up after school and that Mrs. Barnett will take charge of her in the meantime. Susie confidently says goodbye to her mother and then asks Mrs. Barnett where she should sit.

Mrs. Barnett is beaming throughout all of this, too. With Susie's home background, maturity, social skills, and confidence, she looks like a sure bet to be a class leader and high achiever. Working with Susie probably will be a pleasure.

Sally Jones gets off to a very different kind of start. First, her mother does not come with her, and no one introduces her to Mrs. Barnett. Instead, her older brother, a boy with whom Mrs. Barnett had problems two years ago, brings Sally to the door and tells her to "get on in there." He then runs off to his own class, leaving Sally standing frightened, confused, and alone at the doorway. Mrs. Barnett waits to see what will happen, hoping that Sally will come in and introduce herself. Instead, she remains where she is, looking increasingly con-fused and afraid. Fearing that Sally may run away or panic, Mrs. Barnett decides to go to her.

Sally seems startled when Mrs. Barnett greets her, and she never does look her in the eye or relax. She gives her name upon request, but only after some hesitation. Mrs. Barnett tries to put her at ease by telling her that she is happy to have her in the class and that she has a seat all picked out for her. Sally listens and follows as she is led to her seat, but she remains incommunicative and anxious.

Throughout all of this, Mrs. Barnett is concerned and somewhat depressed. She is concerned about Sally, fearing that this first-day-of-school trauma may leave lasting scars, and aware that her usually successful techniques for putting new children at ease have not worked in this case. She is depressed because she notes that Sally has arrived without any of the supplies she is supposed to have, and that she shows the same lack of readiness for school and uneasiness around Mrs. Barnett that her brother showed two years ago. Mrs. Barnett felt natural and relaxed with Susie, but she feels vaguely tense and uncomfortable around Sally.

When Mr. Thompson first looked over the roster for his tenth-grade homeroom class, he was delighted to see that Don Davis was included on it. Discussions with ninth-grade teachers and contacts with ninth graders the previous year had indicated that Don was one of the best all around students in the grade. He excelled academically and was a popular and respected leader among the students. These qualities made him especially desirable, because he would be a positive influence on the class as well as a pleasure to work with personally.

However, Mr. Thompson was surprised and disheartened when school began and he got a look at the "new" Don. He could hardly believe it was the same boy. This formerly respectful student had developed a macho complex, complete with exaggerated hip talk, affected mannerisms and clothing, and an antagonistic, almost defiant attitude toward teachers. Worse yet, he was heavily into alcohol and dope, and he was still a strong influence on classmates. Suddenly, one of Mr. Thompson's anticipated resources had become a trouble spot.

It is November, and Joan Richards is reviewing her records and making notes in preparation for a round of conferences with the parents of each of her students. This year, the school administration decided to cut the number of report card gradings in favor of individualized conferences with parents. The idea was to give parents and teachers opportunities to meet one another and to see that parents got richer and more extended feedback than report cards gave. Joan was looking forward to this, although she had never done it before. She wasn't sure what to tell some of the parents, especially the parents of students who were doing very poorly or misbehaving regularly. Perhaps it was because she was thinking mostly about these students that she had difficulty making notes for a talk with the parents of Julie Wilson.

She began in the usual way, with a general characterization of Julie's progress (average) and classroom conduct (good). However, when she tried to add more, she couldn't think of a single thing to say! Joan suddenly realized that she didn't really know Julie at all, even though Julie had been in her class for ten weeks now and even though she knew most of the other students quite well. She couldn't recall a single conversation with Julie, didn't know much about Julie's interests or background, and didn't know who her friends were. In many ways, it was as if Julie had not been there at all!

In the process of preparing notes, Joan discovered something else about herself and her students: she very much liked and enjoyed some of them, did not have strong feelings one way or another about many of them, and, she had to admit, she couldn't stand a few of them. She found this somewhat surprising, because she had not been aware of these feelings before, at least not in any systematic way. She began to wonder if these feelings affected her classroom behavior. Did she show special favoritism toward the students that she liked? Did she pick on the ones she disliked? Was it professional for her to have strong reactions to certain students?

Upon reflection, Joan realized that in most cases she could point to good reasons why she liked or disliked certain students. So, she decided that it was perfectly natural, not unprofessional, to like some kinds of students and dislike other kinds. However, she realized that she needed to make sure that her feelings did not interfere with her fairness and objectivity in dealing with students. This might be difficult, because the students that she liked and disliked probably were aware of her feelings.

Joan was bothered by certain things that didn't hang together well. If she had developed strong feelings about certain students, and if this was natural, why didn't she have clear-cut feelings about all of her students? Also, although she could point to the reasons why she liked certain students and disliked others, she couldn't give reasons in some cases. Obviously, things were not so simple as they seemed at first.

Out of curiosity, math teacher Bill Robinson was looking at his students' scores on standardized math tests and their scores on a group intelligence test given earlier in the year. He was not surprised to see a general correspondence. Students with high IQs did relatively well in math, and vice versa. However, he became intrigued with certain exceptions. Several students didn't do nearly so well on the math test as Bill would have expected from their IQ scores. The math scores of these students seemed appropriate at the time, because they reflected the students' general performance in his course and his own assessment of their knowledge of the subject matter. However, these discrepancies with IQ scores suggested that they might be underachievers who had not been working up to their potentials. Also, Bill was surprised to see that some students who did well in math had lower IQs than he would have guessed. Did this mean that they were overachievers, making up in persistence and effort what they lacked in native ability? How might Bill go about answering these questions? What would he do with the information if he did answer them to his satisfaction? Should he try to answer them at all?

These vignettes are fictional but typical of the experiences of teachers in respect to their own expectations and attitudes about students. Mrs. Barnett's experiences with Susie and Sally on the first day of school illustrate that important individual differences among students often are obvious at a glance. Many students make strong first impressions on teachers in the first few moments they are with them, even if the teachers know nothing about them beforehand. These first-day-of-school experiences, along with the reactions of Mr. Robinson to his students' math and IQ scores, illustrate the kinds of expectations for student performance that teachers form and some of the factors involved in forming them.

The other vignettes illustrate how teachers have not only expectations but also attitudes toward their students. Sometimes these are very strong, as in the case of the students that Joan Richards strongly liked and disliked. Note that she could give clear reasons for her positive and negative reactions toward certain students, but not all. Apparently, she liked or disliked some students for reasons that were not obvious. Even she herself did not know what was involved here, although she was aware of her feelings. In addition, the chances are that she had strong feelings about a few other students without even realizing it. The students themselves as well as their classmates might have recognized this, even if Joan did not.

On the other hand, some students not only do not engender strong feelings in their teachers; they make little or no impression at all. Julie Wilson was such a student. After ten weeks in her class, Joan knew virtually nothing about her and had no special feelings toward her.

Teacher expectations and attitudes toward students usually are stable, because they usually are based on stable student attributes. However, there are exceptions. Students sometimes change between or even within school years. Occasionally, as in the case of Don Davis, such changes can be dramatic and can produce dramatic changes in teacher expectations and attitudes.

Although most teacher expectations and attitudes are based on identifiable student characteristics, some are difficult to explain or justify. For example, teachers sometimes believe that students can do better than they are doing, or that they are doing as well as they can and are not really as bright as their IQ scores suggest. Such teachers have well-defined ideas about the levels of performance that should be expected from different students, based on their own assessments of student ability. Sometimes these teacher assessments are remarkably accurate, more so than IQ scores or other "objective" data. In other cases, however, they are incorrect. As is discussed in the next chapter, teacher expectations may cause student performance instead of merely reflecting it. Likewise, teachers' attitudes toward students (discussed in chapter 3) are reflected in and may set the tone for their daily interactions.

Because of the potential impact of teachers' expectations and attitudes on students' life in classrooms, knowledge about how expectations and attitudes form and are maintained is important. Therefore, one focus of this book will be on the factors teachers take into account in forming expectations and attitudes.

A second major focus is on the dynamics of teacher-student interactions as they reflect teachers' expectations and attitudes. To explain the various patterns of interactions, it becomes necessary to consider the nature of the classroom and the roles played by the teacher and students.

There is a large body of literature in social psychology on such topics as impression formation and change, interpersonal perception, and group dynamics. Since this research presumably applies to people in general, theoretically it applies to the dynamics of teacher-student interaction in classrooms. However, application often is difficult in practice. One reason is that much of social psychology is based on laboratory research using strangers brought together for a brief contact in an artificial experimental situation. Because the laboratory situations are so artificial, their results need to be replicated in naturalistic situations.

In the case of teacher-student interaction, there is another reason why naturalistic classroom research is needed. Existing social psychology is mostly the study of relationships among peers: adults dealing with adults, and to a lesser extent, children dealing with children. When adults are dealing with children or youth, as in the classroom, an age and status differential is present which affects the relationship to some degree.

Furthermore, teacher-student interaction takes place among individuals operating within well-defined roles. Teachers are the classroom authority figures, charged with initiating and conducting instruction. They spend a great deal of time with their students, but role demands focus most interactions on matters directly related to instruction.

Similarly, students' interactions with teachers are somewhat different from their interactions with adults generally. They know that they will be dealing with teachers each school day, that teachers will help them learn but also evaluate their learning and assign grades, and that teachers are authority figures who may reward or punish their achievement or conduct.

In summary, the teacher and student roles focus and also limit teachers' and students' perceptions of and interactions with one another. Students deal with teachers primarily as teachers, and only secondarily as adults with individual personalities. Teachers deal with students primarily as students, and only secondarily as unique, individual children or youths. Sometimes, the dynamics of teacher-student relationships are just special cases of more general interpersonal dynamics. Often, however, the status and age differential involved and/or the teacher and student roles produce effects that are unique to classrooms. Thus, to some degree, this book contains information about social psychology as it applies to classrooms, but mostly it concerns the social psychology of teacher-student relationships that are unique to classrooms.

OVERVIEW OF THE BOOK

Part 1 reviews three lines of research that led up to the Student Attribute Study: studies of teacher expectations, teacher attitudes, and student effects on teachers. Part 2 describes the study and presents data about classroom interaction patterns and descriptions of students perceived in different ways by their teachers. Part 3 presents discussion of the findings by distinguishing between students' success in meeting student role demands and students' personal attributes. The teacher attitude data are also discussed here, as are the meanings of various classroom interaction measures when they are used to study teacher expectations and attitudes.

2

Teacher Expectations

Social psychologists typically divide impressions of and reactions to others into beliefs, expectations, and attitudes. *Beliefs* are statements thought to be true whether or not they are. Certain beliefs concern other people, and these beliefs often form the basis for expectations and attitudes relating to other people. If you believe certain people to be completely honest, you will expect them to tell you the truth. If you value honesty, you also will have a positive attitude toward them. You would have contrasting expectations and attitudes about people whom you believe to be dishonest.

Expectations are explicit or implicit predictions. When they concern other people, they involve predictions about how they will behave. Most research and writing about teacher expectations has focused on expectations for students' achievement, although many other teacher expectations are important, too. These include, among others, expectations concerning student effort and care in completing assignments, and expectations concerning student classroom conduct and acceptance of teacher authority (Good and Brophy, 1978).

Expectations vary in strength, or the degree of certainty with which they are held. Some are merely weak hunches, not even strong enough to qualify as real predictions. Expectations like these are typical when little reliable information is available or when situations are so complex or unpredictable that confident expectations are impossible. Other expectations are true predictions, made with varying degrees of confidence. Some are held with absolute certainty, because they are based on repeated experience or highly reliable information. We are all sure that the familiar cycle of day and night will continue for the rest of our lives, and that two and two always equal four. Rigid, powerful expectations like these usually are well grounded in reality, although it is possible to develop strong expectations that are not justified by objective facts.

Expectations about other people are essentially cognitive or intellectual pre-dictions about what they will do. In contrast, *attitudes* are affective or emotional reactions to others. They are described by such terms as positive versus negative, liking versus disliking, or approving versus disapproving. Some attitudes are common, because people tend to react similarly to particular behavior by others. Most people enjoy being treated with courtesy and respect but dislike being treated with rudeness or hostility. Other attitudes are more limited or even unique to those who hold them. It is not unusual to find different people holding contrasting attitudes toward the same behavior. For example, some react very positively to people who avoid flattery and always "tell it like it is." Others prefer pleasant illusions to brutal truths.

As with expectations, attitudes can vary from extremely vague and weak to extremely clear and strong. Also, clear, strong attitudes usually are understandable reactions to particular behavior, but it is possible to form strong attitudes toward people without being able to point to the reasons for them (or at least without being able to give convincing reasons). Regardless of the facts, beliefs, expectations, and attitudes tend to support one another. We all have a need for consistency among our beliefs, expectations, and attitudes. This need for consistency predisposes us to attend to information selectively, in order to make our beliefs, expectations, and attitudes as consistent with one another as possible. We may even use defense mechanisms to avoid becoming aware of information that would introduce conflict or provide disconfirmation, if the need to sustain a particular false impression is strong enough (Festinger, 1957; Bem, 1970).

When our impressions and perceptions are accurate, our beliefs develop systematically as we acquire more information. Expectations and attitudes form as experience teaches us what can be predicted and how we feel about certain experiences. Here, beliefs, expectations, and attitudes accurately reflect our experiences and preferences. In fact, they could be predicted by someone who knew what experiences we would encounter and what preferences we had developed.

The situation is different with unjustified beliefs, expectations, or attitudes, especially when they are held strongly and in combination with one another. When rigid but inappropriate expectations or attitudes develop, the person usually is not aware of the problem. Except for people with serious adjustment problems who cannot or will not face reality, awareness of discrepancies between expectations or attitudes and objective facts leads to change, usually rapid change. Incorrect expectations or attitudes are adjusted to fit the facts, as they are newly perceived, so that consistency is maintained. Thus, awareness is the key to the formation and maintenance of accurate expectations and attitudes, in teachers and in people in general (Good and Brophy, 1978).

However, sometimes selective perception occurs and defense mechanisms are invoked when there is discrepancy between facts and beliefs, expectations or attitudes. Consistency needs operate so that if any one of these three types of impressions is held strongly the other two types may be affected. We may use defense mechanisms to insure that only safe or acceptable information comes to our attention. We may remain unaware of contradictory information, even when it is obvious to everyone else.

Thus, if for some reason we develop a strong negative attitude toward certain people, we may support this attitude by developing negative expectations about their probable behavior and a generally negative set of beliefs about them. Our attitude could cause us to see only their bad qualities, to believe bad things about them that are not even true, or both. Similarly, a strong but mistaken belief about people can cause us to develop expectations and attitudes about them that are compatible with our belief, and strongly held but erroneous expectations can cause us to develop consistent attitudes and belief systems.

In summary, beliefs, expectations, and attitudes are very responsive to our need for consistency, sometimes at the expense of objective truth. When interpersonal impressions exist that are strong and resistant to change, the stage is set for *self-fulfilling prophecies*. People usually need consistency not only among their beliefs, expectations, and attitudes, but also between these internal events and external behavior. Our behavior toward others usually is consistent with our impressions of them, even where these impressions are false. If we systematically treat people as if they were something other than what they are, eventually they may begin to conform to our expectations, even though these expectations were incorrect initially. This is how expectations (and beliefs and attitudes as well) can function as self-fulfilling prophecies.

SELF-FULFILLING PROPHECIES

Pygmalion in the Classroom (Rosenthal and Jacobson, 1968) created interest in the possibility that teachers' expectations for student achievement might function as self-fulfilling prophecies, causing students to achieve what teachers expect them to achieve. This was the first widely publicized application to education of the concept of self-fulfilling prophecies, although the concept itself had been around for a long time. The general idea that prior possession of a belief, expectation, or attitude could help make it come true has been part of folk wisdom extending back at least to the Bible. Furthermore, the concept of self-fulfilling prophecy was labeled and defined by Merton (1948) long before the recent flurry of interest in it. The concept is worth considering, both to appreciate its complexities and to see its applications and limits. Merton used bank failures as an example, and this still is one of the best illustrations of the concept. Imagine what would happen if persistent rumors were spread claiming that a bank was about to go bankrupt. Let us say that the bank was in fine financial condition, so that the rumors were completely false when they began. However, suppose that many of its depositors believed the rumors and, worse yet, acted on them by withdrawing their money and putting it in a "safer" bank. In time, the bank's financial position would deteriorate, and bankruptcy would result.

This is a classical self-fulfilling prophecy. The initial belief was false, but enough people acted on it to make it come true. The behavior that made it come true was based directly on the belief itself, but note that the outcome stemmed from behavior, not mere belief. If the depositors had not acted on the rumor (or if they had investigated and found that it was false) the prophecy would not have been fulfilled.

Teachers' impressions of students can act as self-fulfilling prophecies in the classroom. If teachers believe that certain students are bright and others are dull, they may teach in ways that help confirm these beliefs. Bright students may get called on more often and be given more challenging work, for example, so that they end up achieving more. Other students who are capable of the same achievement may not fulfill their potential because they do not get opportunities to learn about or work on certain things. If this happens because their teachers don't think they can handle the work and don't even attempt to verify their beliefs, reduced achievement will have occurred as a result of teacher beliefs and expectations influencing teacher behavior that creates self-fulfilling prophecies.

The Oak School experiment described by Rosenthal and Jacobson (1968) in *Pygmalion in the Classroom* was an attempt to demonstrate that teachers' expectations for student achievement can function as self-fulfilling prophecies. They claimed that teachers who had been led to expect unusually good performance from certain students did get unusually good performance from those students, and that this was because of what they expected. Their study has been exposed to a variety of criticism (see Elashoff and Snow, 1971), leading many to reject it.

Initial doubts about the reality of teacher expectation effects were fueled not only by criticism of *Pygmalion in the Classroom,* but also by several replication attempts that failed. Also, a study by Fleming and Anttonen (1971) showed that teachers did not even believe inflated IQ scores, let alone act on them. These replication failures are still relevant today, not for dismissing the reality of teacher expectation effects but for providing perspective about them, especially concerning teachers' reliance on credible information.

A great many other studies have demonstrated that teacher expectations can have self-fulfilling prophecy effects, especially when preexisting, natural expectations rather than artificially induced (and false) expectations are related to student outcomes. For example, Palardy (1969) related teacher expectations concerning sex differences in reading achievement to scores on reading achievement tests. Several months prior to the study, he gave a questionnaire to some first-grade teachers, asking them questions about a variety of issues. One question concerned sex differences in first-grade reading achievement. Using responses to this questionnaire item, Palardy identified one group of teachers who clearly expected girls to do better than boys and another group who expected no sex differences at all. Then he matched five pairs of teachers, one from each group, according to sex, race, teaching experience, type of school in which they taught, and textbook used for teaching reading in the first grade. At the end of the next school year, he compared the reading achievement scores of their students. Notice that this study did not involve any actual treatment at all. The teachers did not interact with the researcher and did not even know that the reading achievement of their students was being studied.

The data provide convincing evidence for expectation effects. Comparisons of boys' and girls' reading achievement scores (adjusted for IQ) showed no differences among teachers who expected no differences. However, scores were higher for girls in the classes of teachers who expected girls to do better than boys. Furthermore, the scores for girls in the latter classes were similar to the scores for both boys and girls in the former classes, but the scores for boys were lower. Thus, both groups of teachers got the sex differences they expected, although the group who expected no sex differences also got better results overall. Given the clever design of this study, the careful matching of teachers on relevant characteristics, and the adjustment of student reading scores for IQ, it is difficult to attribute the results to anything other than teacher expectations.

Doyle, Hancock, and Kifer (1972) obtained similar results in a study of the effects of teachers' expectations concerning both sex and IQ. Working in schools where IQ tests were administered in the first grade routinely, they asked first-grade teachers to estimate their students' IQs shortly before the tests were given. Although their estimates correlated highly with measured IQ, the teachers systematically overestimated the IQs of girls and underestimated the IQs of boys. These differences between teacher estimates and the actual scores proved to be important.

First, reading tests given at the end of the school year showed that students whose IQs had been overestimated by their teachers had higher reading achievement scores than their IQs predicted, and students whose IQs were underestimated by their teachers had lower achievement scores than their IQs predicted. Thus, in both sexes, students for whom teachers had relatively high expectations did better than students for whom teachers had relatively low expectations. These interesting student data were supplemented by differences among teachers that provide more evidence that the results were attributable to teacher expectations. The teachers were divided into high and low groups according to whether they generally overestimated or generally underestimated their students' IQs (regardless of sex). Comparisons revealed that students of overestimators generally achieved more than students of underestimators, even when achievement scores were adjusted for IQ. This suggests that teacher expectations can affect the achievement levels of entire classes, not just those of individual students.

Naturalistic studies such as these show such effects more regularly than experimental ones where false information is provided, but teacher expectation effects are not always obtained even in the naturalistic studies. Nevertheless, the weight of the evidence from both types of studies suggests that teacher expectation effects are real and can occur, although they do not occur necessarily or always and they differ in strength and type of outcome (Brophy and Good, 1974; Braun, 1976; Good, 1980).

The remainder of this chapter examines the mechanisms by which self-fulfilling prophecies can affect student achievement. First is presented research on teachers' behavior toward students for whom they held different expectations for achievement. The second section discusses teachers' perceptions of student characteristics in different expectancy groups. Both lines of research are relevant to the Student Attribute Study, which examined links between teacher perceptions of student characteristics and behavior toward students who were perceived differently.

TEACHER BEHAVIOR AS A MEDIATOR OF EXPECTANCY EFFECTS

While some researchers were concentrating on whether or not teacher expectations could function as self-fulfilling prophecies, others already convinced that they could designed studies to find out how the process worked. Such information is needed in order to give teachers and future teachers useful suggestions about how they can use positive expectation effects to their advantage and minimize undesirable negative expectation effects. In addition, the widespread tendency to spread myths about teacher expectation effects, and in particular the tendency to portray them as mysterious or magical, underscores the need for analysis of the processes involved.

Rosenthal and Jacobson (1968) provided no such information, because their study did not involve any observation of the teachers. Beez (1968) did provide some information about the processes involved. This was an experimental study in which students taking graduate education courses were asked to tutor Head Start children. Tutoring involved teaching the children words printed on cards. All tutors received the same 20 cards. They were asked to teach their Head Start child as many words as they could in a single ten-minute session.

The Head Start children were assigned randomly to experimental and control groups. Half of the tutors were led to believe that they were assigned a high ability child, and the other half were led to believe that they were assigned a low ability child. The tutors had not seen the children previously, and they only interacted with them for ten minutes, so most of them apparently believed this information. At any rate, clear-cut expectation effects were obtained.

Children taught by tutors with high expectations learned an average of about six words, while those taught by tutors with low expectations learned an average of only about three words. Thus, in this case, the experimental group learned roughly twice as much. Furthermore, observational data from this study showed that the difference was due to expectation effects. Tutors with high expectations tried to teach more than tutors with low expectations. The children in the high group learned more mostly because they were taught more.

Also, the tutors in the low group spent more time explaining the meanings of the words and providing multiple examples, and they spent more time on nonteaching activities. As we will see, this behavior is typical under low expectancy conditions. Finally, interview and questionnaire data obtained from the tutors after the experiment showed that the information was believed and acted upon. Tutors led to have high expectations rated their children higher, not only on achievement but also on social competence and general intellectual ability. They thought that the difficulty level of the task was just about right for the students. In contrast, tutors led to have low expectations rated their students lower on the rating scales and saw the task as much too difficult. In summary, the Beez study provides a convincing demonstration that expectations can have self-fulfilling prophecy effects, and that these can be quite potent under certain conditions.

Beez showed expectation effects on both student achievement and teacher behavior. Certain studies show effects on one but not the other, either because only one is measured, or because effects show up in only one area (usually teacher behavior). For example, Kester and Letchworth (1972) studied the interactions of 23 teachers with 150 average ability seventh graders who had been identified to the teachers as being especially bright. Observational data revealed that compared to their behavior toward control students teachers spent more time with the "bright" students, talked with them more often, and generally were more supportive of them. These effects were enhanced when the "bright" students responded by initiating more and showing more support of the teachers.

This study revealed a general change in teacher behavior toward students identified as bright, and also a more specific and extreme change in patterns of reciprocal interaction with these students. They responded to better teacher treatment by becoming more positive in their own interactions with the teachers. These data demonstrate how teacher expectations can affect teacher behavior, and how teacher behavior can affect student behavior.

Impetus for research designed specifically to investigate the processes mediating teacher expectation effects was provided by a study by Brophy and Good (1970b). Following Merton (1948), Brophy and Good assumed that if expectation effects were real, they would be produced by systematic teacher behavior, not merely by teacher expectations. These assumptions were developed into an explicit model for explaining expectation effects (paraphrased from Brophy and Good, 1970b):

1. Early in the year, teachers form differential expectations for student performance.

2. Consistent with these differential expectations, teachers behave differently toward different students.

3. This differential teacher behavior communicates to each individual student something about how he or she is expected to behave in the classroom and perform on academic tasks.

4. If teacher treatment is consistent over time, and if students do not actively resist or change it, it will likely affect student self-concept, achievement motivation, level of aspiration, classroom conduct, and interactions with the teacher.

5. These effects generally will complement and reinforce the teacher's expectations, so that students will conform to these expectations more than they might have otherwise.

6. Ultimately, this will make a difference in student achievement and other outcomes, indicating that teacher expectations can function as self-fulfilling prophecies.

This model, stressing that teacher expectation effects should be mediated through observable behavior, provided direction about potentially profitable research relating to these mediating processes. In the first of a series of studies, Brophy and Good (1970b) began by attempting to demonstrate the middle stages of the model, relating preexisting teacher expectations to differential teacher treatment of different students and differential student response to this treatment. It is obvious that teachers have different expectations for different students, so there was little point in demonstrating this. However, it did seem worthwhile to see if these differential expectations led teachers to treat individual students systematically and predictably in ways that seemed likely to produce expectation effects.

Combining common sense considerations with what research was available, Brophy and Good hypothesized that differential teacher expectations could be revealed by such measures as time spent with students, amount and difficulty level of material taught, and positive and negative affect (emotion). Differential patterns of patience, determination, and expectations of ultimate success versus resignation to ultimate failure and a tendency to give up easily would indicate self-fulfilling effects in teacher behavior. Once a list of promising behaviors to investigate was compiled, existing classroom observation systems were examined. Unfortunately, none were appropriate for the purpose at hand.

The problem was that almost all classroom coding systems up to that time were keyed to the teacher. If student behavior was coded at all, it typically was coded for students as an undifferentiated group rather than separately for individual students. Consequently, in order to get the individual student data that the research required, the Dyadic Interaction Observation System was developed (Brophy and Good, 1970a). A major feature of the system was its focus on dyadic interactions between teachers and individual students. Each student's interactions with the teacher were coded and tabulated separately, so that different teacher interaction patterns with different students could be identified and analyzed.

Another important feature was that interactions initiated by teachers were coded separately from interactions initiated by students, and events occurring in sequence were coded with the sequence retained. This made it possible to separate interaction patterns due to teacher behavior from those due to student behavior.

These features are central to research in classrooms. First, because the model specified different teacher behavior toward different students, classroom observations had to be tabulated separately for each student if this aspect of classroom interaction was to be studied at all. Also, knowledge of the initiation and sequencing of interactions is vital to the interpretation of the meaning of any differences observed. Simple frequency counts are ambiguous without this information.

For example, suppose that a teacher criticizes Jim only once during ten hours of classroom observation, but criticizes Bill 15 times. Is the teacher showing favoritism toward Jim and/or picking on Bill? We cannot answer only on the basis of the frequency of criticism because we do not know how Jim and Bill act in the classroom or about the quality of their work. If they are similar, the teacher probably is favoring Jim and/or picking on Bill. However, if Jim is a talented and well-motivated student who does good work and seldom misbehaves, and if Bill is lacking in both talent and motivation so that he rarely does work and constantly is causing trouble, the differential teacher behavior is quite understandable.

In fact, it is possible that the teacher is more likely to criticize Jim than Bill for a given reason but that this tendency doesn't show up because Jim practically never gives the teacher reason to criticize him. Meanwhile, Bill gives reason so often that he virtually insures frequent criticism. This is just one of many examples that could be given to show that observational data from the classroom often are ambiguous in meaning and thus difficult to interpret. We will return to this point many times in discussing situations where different conclusions would be drawn depending upon how data are interpreted.

For the moment, though, let us return to the Brophy and Good (1970b) study of how teacher expectation effects work. Achievement expectations held by four first-grade teachers were measured by asking these teachers to rank their students according to general achievement. The instructions deliberately were vague, to encourage teachers to rank on the basis of general impressions rather than specific test scores. The data were collected early in the spring, so that the teachers had had ample time to interact with their students and form impressions about their ability and achievement potential. The rankings were used to identify six high expectation students and six low expectation students (three boys and three girls) in each classroom. Then, the classrooms were observed for two mornings and two afternoons each, and teacher interactions with these 12 students were recorded.

This study revealed many differences between the high and low expectation groups, some of which could be interpreted as indicating self-fulfilling prophecy effects, and some of which could not. The latter group of findings included the following: high expectation students raised their hands more often when teachers asked questions; they initiated more private interactions with the teachers; they were criticized for misbehavior less often; they gave correct answers more often; they had fewer problems in reading during reading group; and they received more praise and less criticism. All of these differences are consistent with the idea that the teachers were acting on their differential expectations so as to produce self-fulfilling prophecy effects. However, none of these group differences shows this convincingly. Each difference could have resulted entirely from differences between the groups of students rather than from discriminatory teacher behavior.

However, in addition to these ambiguous differences, there were differences on measures that took into account student behavior and seemed to imply self-fulfilling prophecy effects. First, teachers were more likely to praise correct answers and less likely criticize wrong answers or failures to respond when interacting with high expectancy students, even though these students responded successfully more often. Thus, the praise and criticism differences appeared not only in frequency counts but in the percentages of correct answers followed by praise and the percentages of failures followed by criticism. This indicates that the teachers were least likely to praise and most likely to criticize the very students who most needed patience and encouragement.

Another indication was the degree to which teachers paid attention to student answers and gave specific feedback in response to them. Teachers failed to give feedback to high expectation students only about 3 percent of the time, but they failed to give feedback to low expectation students almost 15 percent of the time. Thus, the teachers were least likely to give feedback to the students who needed it most.

A third indication came from data on teacher persistence in seeking correct answers from students. When a student failed to answer a question or could not read a word in reading group, teachers were much more likely to try to elicit the answer by repeating the question, giving a clue, or providing some other kind of help if the student was a high expectation student. When faced with such failure situations involving low expectation students, they were more likely to give the answer or to call on someone else than to persist in trying to get the answer. Teachers were more persistent in seeking improved responses from high expectation students, but more likely to give up easily when dealing with low expectation students.

These data indicate that teachers were responding to their differential expectations by systematically treating high and low expectation students differently. Furthermore, the differences observed suggest that high expectation students were being taught in ways likely to maximize achievement, but that low expectation students were being taught in ways likely to minimize it. The findings indicate some of the ways that teacher expectations can function as self-fulfilling prophecies (when they do).

These general results were not always replicated in subsequent studies, although some teachers showed similar patterns in the studies that did not replicate the group differences for the sample as a whole (Brophy and Good, 1974). In any case, this study and later ones identified several mechanisms mediating teacher expectation effects, and studies conducted by others identified additional factors. Eventually, Rosenthal (1973) developed a four-factor theory of positive expectation effects, combining the findings of several investigators. He suggests that rather than trying to avoid expectations teachers should project positive expectations and thus get better results than they might otherwise. According to Rosenthal, teachers will maximize positive expectation effects on students if they:

1. Create particularly warm social-emotional relationships with these students (climate).
2. Give these students more feedback about their performance (feedback).
3. Teach these students more (and more difficult) material (input).
4. Give these students more opportunities to respond and to ask questions (output).

Rosenthal's four-factor model does seem to bring together many of the findings concerning expectation effects. However, there are many more specific findings. Brophy and Good (1974) included the following among teacher behaviors that often are associated with low expectations:

1. Waiting less time for low expectation students to answer questions.

2. Prematurely giving up on low expectation students when they fail to answer questions correctly (giving them the answer or calling on someone else rather than trying to elicit the answer from them).

3. Rewarding inappropriate behavior of low expectation students (praising marginal or even wrong answers or poor work, something that tends to discourage such students if they become aware of it).

4. Criticizing low expectation students more than high expectation students in parallel situations, and/or criticizing their misconduct but not their poor academic work.

5. Failing to praise low expectation students in situations where other students typically are praised (in particular, failing to notice and praise hard work or improved performance that has resulted from persistent effort).

6. Failing to give low expectation students feedback concerning the correctness of their responses or their work, or failing to give them feedback sufficiently specific to be useful.

7. Calling on low expectation students less often.

8. Calling on low expectation students only for easy questions.

9. Paying less attention to low expectation students except when they are misbehaving (thus missing chances to provide reinforcement by attending to good work), and failing to monitor what these students are doing and provide feedback regularly and quickly.

10. Segregating low expectation students in seating patterns, placing them farthest away from the teacher.

11. Generally expecting and demanding less, and less difficult, work from low expectation students.

12. Allowing other students to call out answers if the original respondent hesitates (this enables the brighter and more motivated students to get most of the public response opportunities, and it may demoralize those slower students who are trying to respond and/or reinforce those slower students who are trying to avoid responding).

Brophy and Good, noting that there were individual differences among teachers in whether or not expectation effects appeared, and in the kinds and degree of such effects when they did appear, suggested that teachers could be broadly classified into three types:

1. *Proactive teachers.* These teachers stay aware of their expectations and keep them flexible, so that they change as students change. Positive expectation effects like those suggested by Rosenthal are most likely in their classrooms, especially for low achievers.

2. *Reactive teachers.* These teachers simply react to student behavior. Their

expectations are shaped by students and not vice versa. They show few if any expectation effects, although many measures will reveal that high achievers have better experiences in their classrooms than low achievers.

3. *Overreactive teachers.* These teachers have strong and relatively rigid expectations so that they are less likely to change expectations if students change, and most likely to have expectation effects. Some of these will be desirable, if the teachers have high (but not too high) expectations for students that purely reactive teachers would be less impressed with. However, undesirable expectation effects are most likely in the classrooms of overreactive teachers, who may make little effort to teach low achievers because they have rigid, low expectations for them.

These "pure types" are stereotypic, of course. Most teachers vary in the strength and flexibility of expectations they hold for different students. This is a major focus of the book.

TEACHER PERCEPTIONS OF STUDENTS

The research reviewed in the preceding section focused on behavioral measures that reflected teacher expectations. Another important line of research that suggests how self-fulfilling prophecies occur (although in a less direct way) is work on teachers' perceptions of students for whom they hold different expectancies.

Nash (1973) found that teacher perceptions of students tend to be global halos, combining achievement and personal attributes. Disliked students may be seen as duller than they actually are. Ryan (1958) and Stevenson, et al. (1976) also reported strong halo effects in teachers' ratings. Student achievement level is generally at the core of these halo perceptions: teachers think well of high achievers and usually share mutually satisfying patterns of interaction with them.

Most investigations of teacher perceptions reveal that teachers like students and enjoy working with them, but primarily within the teacher role. Their perceptions of students focus on matters relating to the student role. Jackson (1968) noted this in interviewing teachers who had been nominated as outstanding. He found these teachers to be warm and student oriented, but mostly focused on their own roles as teachers (not socializers or parent surrogates) and on their students as learners (not individual personalities or peer group members).

Morrison and McIntyre (1969) found similar data in interviews with teachers in Britain. Most teacher reactions fell into three major clusters: pupil achievement, general classroom behavior and attitudes toward the teachers, and peer relationships. There were many more comments about the first two areas than about the third. They also found that younger teachers were more concerned about classroom behavior, while older teachers were more concerned about student achievement. This probably means that more older teachers had developed satisfactory methods of handling classroom organization and discipline, so that they could focus their concerns on instructional matters (Fuller, 1969).

The things that teachers mentioned most frequently provide clues about the student attributes they attend and react to in forming expectations and attitudes toward students. The nine that occurred most frequently were, in order, general student ability, carelessness, laziness, talkativeness, cooperativeness, persistence, courtesy, ability to use language, and originality. Obviously, all of these are directly related to the teacher and student roles. More purely social or personal student characteristics were ranked much lower. The teachers did notice such traits as social confidence, sociability, and peer popularity, but their perceptions concentrated on matters related to teaching and learning.

Accuracy of Teacher Perceptions

Studies concerned with the accuracy of teacher perceptions usually show teachers to be accurate about things that they are in a good position to judge (primarily student ability and student personal traits that show up in the classroom), but less accurate about other things, such as peer popularity or leadership status. Perceptions in the latter areas tend to show both halo effects (the effects of generally positive or negative impressions) and logical errors (the tendency to believe that students must be high or low on one attribute if they are high or low on another attribute believed to be connected with the first one). Thus, teachers generally overrate students they like and underrate students they don't like, and overrate high achievers and underrate low achievers when rating traits like peer popularity or leadership. Also, they may overlook adjustment problems in students who are doing well in school, presumably because of a logical error in reasoning (students doing well in school are assumed to be doing well generally).

In her study of relationships between teacher attitudes and classroom interactions, Jenkins (1972) found teachers to be more accurate about student behavior that required some response from them than about other student attributes. They were relatively accurate about success and failure in answering questions, carefulness and persistence at seatwork, paying attention, smiling at the teacher, initiation of private conversations, requests for help or evaluation of work, and frequency of hand raising.

In contrast, they were not very accurate about such things as time spent on seatwork assignments (as opposed to quality of seatwork), frowning at the teacher, failure to answer questions, behavior when another student had given a wrong answer, requests for permission, and reactions to work assignments (positive, neutral, or negative).

Jenkins' data also showed much halo effect. Frequently, teacher perception scores for particular behaviors correlated as highly with several measures of different behaviors as they did with the corresponding measure of "the right" behavior. For example, perceptions of student attention correlated higher with measures of other student behavior than they did with the measure of attention.

Teacher Perceptions and Achievement Expectations

These data from other investigators raised new questions about the accuracy of teacher perceptions and the relationships among teacher perceptions, teacher-student interactions, and student attributes. Our own work suggested that teacher impressions generally were accurate, but work by others sometimes did not. For example, several studies (reviewed in Brophy and Good, 1974) found statistically significant but relatively weak correlations between teacher estimates of student ability and scores on IQ or achievement tests. Meanwhile, we were finding that teachers were quite accurate even when they had little information to go on.

In our first study (Brophy and Good, 1970b), correlations between teacher rankings of expected achievement taken early in the spring and scores on achievement tests administered at the end of the year averaged .77. This is as high or higher than the correlations between the same test battery given two or three months apart would be, at their age level. In the follow-up study, correlations between teacher rankings of students in first grade and student scores on the Metropolitan Achievement Test administered in second grade generally were quite high, even for rankings made in September when students had been in school only about a month. These correlations averaged about .70, compared to .71 for the rankings made in November and .76 for those made in March. This led to curiosity about how teachers form achievement expectations, particularly how they form early impressions about students who are new to them and have not yet established a "track record" at the school.

This was investigated in a dissertation study by Willis (1972), in which first-grade teachers in a school system where there were no kindergartens were asked to rank their children on expected achievement after only three days of school (they also were asked to rank them again twice more later). The teacher rankings from the third day of school correlated about .60, on the average, with scores on the Metropolitan Readiness Test administered a few weeks later. A second set of rankings made after this test was given showed higher correlations (averaging about .79), indicating that the readiness test data or other information acquired during those weeks affected teachers' expectations somewhat. Even so, the teachers were remarkably accurate in their first impressions based upon minimal data. They also were flexible enough to change these first impressions when they appeared inaccurate.

In addition to gathering data about the accuracy of teacher achievement expectations Willis used questionnaire and interview techniques to try to find out what criteria the teachers used in making these judgments. Among teachers who filled out an adjective description questionnaire, the strongest correlates of achievement predictions were perceptions about children's attentiveness, self-confidence, maturity, and ability to work independently without constant supervision. Other perceptions which had significant but weaker correlations included getting along well with classmates, participating actively, obeying classroom rules, good self-control, physical attractiveness, and physical size. Note that the teachers gave more emphasis to the more reliable and rational criteria (those directly related to quality of work) than to such criteria as physical features or classroom conduct.

Another set of teachers was interviewed to get their free response observations and comments about students. These were coded into categories and analyzed. The data showed that students expected to do well were perceived as mature, healthy in their social-emotional development, compliant, ready for school, able to do assignments correctly, and high in general ability. Here again, primary emphasis was placed on observable and credible evidence of ability. Other perceived attributes that correlated with achievement expectations but not very strongly included race (whites were expected to do better than blacks), coming from an intact home, coming from a good family, independence in self-care, good attitudes or motivation, good classroom behavior, ability to perceive similarities and differences, ability to color or draw well, good motor coordination or writing ability, alertness, observational skills, general school readiness, ability to follow directions, and attention.

The questionnaire and interview data collected by Willis agree in suggesting that teachers are accurate in predicting student performance, probably because they use relevant cues in forming judgments.

A study designed along these same general lines was conducted by Moles and Perry (1975) in six first-grade classrooms in a large city. Although information about student achievement on standardized tests was not available, the investigators did interview the teachers concerning their expectations for student achievement and observed teacher-student interaction.

Teacher expectations were measured at the end of the second week of school by asking teachers to rank their students. This was repeated again in December. Other information collected included socioeconomic status indicators such as whether or not the student qualified for a free lunch, occupation of the family breadwinner, presence or absence of a father in the home, whether or not the mother worked, the child's sex, kindergarten performance as judged by report cards, parent involvement in the school as judged by teacher comments, early first-grade academic performance on a test of school readiness and achievement (the teachers did not see these data until after they had made both sets of achievement expectation rankings), and information about conduct in first grade based on observed reprimands for misbehavior and on teacher comments about the student during the interview. These data were correlated and analyzed with complex techniques designed to identify which factors were most basic in determining teacher expectations.

Several variables were correlated with teacher expectations in September after just two weeks of school. The most important of these were kindergarten performance (which was known to the teachers) and children's scores on readiness and early first-grade achievement tests (which were not). These findings necessarily are different from the Willis (1972) findings concerning correlates of initial expectations, because the teachers in her study did not have information on kindergarten performance. They did get access to test scores, but not until after their first expectation rankings. In any case, the two studies agree that teachers use the best information available to them.

Although it is impossible to tell from the data in this study, the fact that children's scores on the test administered by the investigators added a strong and separate contribution to the prediction of teacher expectations beyond that provided by the kindergarten performance of the children suggests that teachers were adjusting their expectations to take into account current information. Expectations obviously were not based only or even primarily on kindergarten performance. The fact that they were independently associated with scores on a test given about the same time suggests that the teachers were adjusting expectations based on kindergarten performance in ways that made them more accurate, probably by observing the kinds of predictors that the teachers in the Willis study observed.

Among the other variables studied, parental involvement and two SES (socioeconomic status) indicators were related significantly but weakly to teacher expectations, while sex and conduct were not related at all. The findings for sex are surprising, but those for conduct are not. The teachers in the Willis (1972) study stated that they tended to suspend judgment about conduct, ability to follow directions, and ability to work independently, because they knew that some students with little or no previous schooling take a while to settle down and adjust to school. Perhaps the teachers in the Moles and Perry (1975) study felt the same way.

The September data were compared with the December data to see if there were changes in associations with teacher expectations after the teachers had more experience with the students and had access to more information. This turned out to be the case. By December, the children's scores on the test of early first-grade performance were the best predictors of teacher expectations, and kindergarten performance still was a moderately strong predictor. SES and parental involvement measures no longer were significant predictors. However, sex now had a weak but significant relationship to expectations: girls were expected to achieve better than boys.

This finding again indicates that teachers base their expectations upon observable performance, and in particular upon the most reliable indicators available. The findings concerning sex suggest that teachers typically do not start out with clear-cut sex difference expectations [recall Palardy's (1969) study in which some teachers did expect girls to do better than boys but others did not], but that they develop differential expectations on the basis of differential behavior. If this differential behavior is related to student sex, a sex difference in expectations will show up eventually. As with some of the other data relating to sex (reviewed in chapter 4), this suggests that the sex difference is not related to sex as such, but instead is related to individual differences in student characteristics.

Taken together, these studies on the formation of expectations by first-grade teachers with little or no information other than what they can observe in the classroom indicate that they attend to relevant information, draw inferences appropriately, and develop generally accurate expectations. Furthermore, data on stability and change in expectations over time suggest that false early impressions usually are corrected. Teachers will use inefficient or questionable information to make predictions if no better information is available, but in realistic situations they tend to use the best information that they have. More recent experimental work by Shavelson, Cadwell, and Izu (1977) and by Borko, Cone, Russo, and Shavelson (1979) supports these conclusions.

3

Teacher Attitudes

Attitudes, along with beliefs and expectations, are impressions formed about people from observing and interacting with them. Expectations are predictions about their future behaviors, and attitudes are emotional reactions to them. Attitudes can be associated with self-fulfilling prophecies if they are strong and rigid enough. If we like people, we probably will treat them in ways likely to cause them to like us, and vice versa.

Silberman (1969) published a study of how teacher attitudes toward students are expressed in observable classroom behavior. His study was similar in conceptualization and design to the Brophy and Good (1970b) study of teacher expectations. Data about the relationship of teacher attitudes to teacher behavior in the Silberman study could be related to the Brophy-Good model for studying teacher expectation effects. Furthermore, the dyadic observation system used in the expectation research seemed equally applicable to attitude research, with minor alterations. These factors combined with interest in the questions Silberman was asking led to a replication and extension of his work by Good and Brophy (1972). Subsequent research relating to teacher attitudes conducted by the present authors and other colleagues eventually culminated in the Student Attribute Study described in this book.

Like research on teacher expectations, research on teacher attitudes has examined teacher behavior toward different groups of students as well as teacher perceptions of students for whom they report different attitudes.

TEACHER AND STUDENT BEHAVIOR
ASSOCIATED WITH TEACHER ATTITUDES

The inspiration for Silberman's (1969) study was an earlier study by Jackson, Silberman, and Wolfson (1969) on student saliency. In that study, 32 elementary school teachers were asked to name all of their students from memory. This proved to be very difficult for some teachers. Many required much time and help before they could remember all their students, even though they spent five hours a day with them and had been teaching them for many months.

Students named first were considered salient, and students named last were considered nonsalient. Once these students had been identified, the teachers were questioned about their attitudes and opinions concerning their most salient boy and girl and their least salient boy and girl. The teachers' comments were tape recorded and later analyzed for signs of emotional involvement with the students. Unsurprisingly, there were more signs of involvement in the teachers' comments about salient students than in their comments about nonsalient students. There also were more signs of involvement in their comments about boys, although more of these were negative ones indicating negative attitudes or disapproval. Teachers expressed fewer signs of involvement with girls, but gave a greater percentage of positive statements indicating approval or liking. These data fit with data from many other sources indicating that boys generally are more salient than girls but also are more likely to provoke negative reactions from teachers. These sex differences will be discussed in greater detail in the next chapter.

In analyzing the teachers' comments, Silberman noticed two common themes: the degree to which teachers liked or disliked students, and the degree to which teachers were concerned about students. This led to a follow-up study of teacher behavior toward four types of students:

1. *Attachment students.* These were students named when teachers were asked, "If you could keep one student another year for the sheer joy of it, whom would you pick?"

2. *Concern students.* These were students whom the teachers named when asked, "If you could devote all your attention to a child who concerns you a great deal, whom would you pick?"

3. *Indifference students.* These were students whom the teachers named when asked, "If a parent were to drop in unannounced for a conference, whose child would you be least prepared to talk about?"

4. *Rejection students.* These were students whom the teachers named when asked, "If your class was to be reduced by one child, whom would you be relieved to have removed?"

Silberman (1969) asked these questions of ten third-grade teachers, who named one student in response to each question. This yielded a total of ten students in each group, one in each class. Classes then were observed for 20 hours each, to see what these students were like and how the teachers interacted with them.

Attachment students generally were conforming and rewarding to the teachers. They often volunteered to answer questions, usually answered correctly, and made relatively few demands upon the teachers' energies. In general, they were model students. However, despite their excellent classroom behavior and even though the teachers nominated them as their favorites, there was little evidence of preferential treatment or overt favoritism. Teachers did not call on them more frequently despite their more frequent hand raising, and they did not interact with them more often. They did praise them more often, but this probably was due to their better general performance rather than to teacher favoritism.

In a later discussion, Silberman (1971) said that he thought he saw more subtle evidence of favoritism. For example, not only were attachment students praised more often, but Silberman thought they were praised more intensively and more publicly as if they were being held up as examples to their classmates. Also, although they were not called on more often, he believed that they were asked to share their ideas with the class more often. He also believed that they were criticized less harshly when they broke the rules.

Even if all this is true, it hardly constitutes the clear-cut favoritism connoted by a term like "teacher's pet." Remarks by some of the teachers suggest an explanation for this: they seemed to be aware of their attitudes toward these students but determined to avoid showing favoritism, because they did not want to be unprofessional or unfair. In summary, Silberman found little evidence of favoritism toward attachment students in his actual data, but he got the impression that these students were favored in subtle ways even though the teachers consciously tried to avoid favoring them at all.

The story was very different with students in the concern group. Teacher concern was overt and obvious. These children made extensive but appropriate demands on the teachers. They obeyed classroom rules and tried to do their assignments, but they were slow students who needed frequent help and supervision. Teachers responded by giving them more attention than other children, initiating contacts with them more often, and allowing them to approach them for help more freely. The teachers also seemed to consciously try to pay attention to their efforts and praise them when they did well. Thus, these children needed a lot of help, but the teachers were willing to provide it. Their concern was active and positive. However, sometimes they did express their attitudes openly by making statements like "I don't know what to do with you next."

The only thing that students in the indifference group had in common was the fact that they did not interact with the teachers very often. However, Silberman (1971) later stated his impression that teacher contacts with these students were less intense as well as less frequent. The teachers seemed to have briefer interactions with these students, and to be less emotionally involved when they did interact with them. The general impression was one of passive indifference. That is, the indifference students just were not noticed or thought about as much as the others. This differs from a more negative or active indifference involving a degree of rejection and deliberate avoidance or ignoring. In summary, the data and impressions about indifference students were what one would expect for students that teachers could hardly remember. However, they were disappointing in that they provided no clues as to why these students were the way they were or why the teachers reacted to them the way they did.

In contrast to their careful attempts to avoid showing favoritism toward attachment students, the teachers clearly and obviously showed hostility toward rejection students. Most of these students misbehaved often, which probably was a major reason for teacher rejection. Silberman described them as almost continually "under surveillance," and he described the teachers as quick to criticize or punish them for misbehavior. The teachers interacted with rejection students frequently, but this was due to the many interactions that occurred because teachers were trying to control misbehavior.

The teachers appeared to be conflicted about their attitudes toward rejection students, just as they were about attachment students. For example, these students received high rates of praise in addition to high rates of criticism, and Silberman thought that the teachers both praised and criticized these students in a public way, as if to hold them up as examples to the rest of the class. The teachers seemed to do this only in positive ways with attachment students, but in both positive and negative ways with rejection students.

The contrasting patterns of treatment of these four types of students were fascinating, although they raised more questions than they answered. What were the indifference students like, and why didn't the teachers become concerned about them? Why did the teachers take a special liking to the attachment students? Surely, they were not the only conforming and high achieving students. Was Silberman correct in his impression that the major difference between the concern and rejection groups was that the concern students were slow but conforming while the rejection students were mischievous? In what other ways might teachers behave differentially toward these four attitude groups? (Note that Silberman found few significant behavioral differences, although he had many impressions that seem plausible.)

This line of research was continued by Jenkins (1972). She conducted a similar study, using the same four questions to identify one student of each type in each of ten elementary classrooms and then observing in the classrooms and interviewing the teachers extensively.

The observational data from Jenkins' study revealed few differences among the four attitude groups. Of 22 student behaviors observed, only hand raising and student-initiated work interactions discriminated significantly among the groups. Attachment students were highest on these measures, and indifference students were lowest. The concern and rejection students were in between and not significantly different from each other.

Although this study produced many interesting interview findings, the observational part of it added little to Silberman's work, and it provided no additional information on the questions raised above. However, a larger study by Good and Brophy (1972) did provide some answers to these questions. In particular, it differentiated concern students from rejection students, and it identified more of the attributes of the four types of students.

The study replicated Silberman's procedures as closely as possible, although some modifications were introduced. First, to increase the number of students in the study, teachers were asked to nominate three students to each attitude group rather than only one. Second, Silberman interviewed the teachers in his study before taking observational measures, so that the teachers knew what variables were being studied. This could have led them to behave differently when being observed than they would have otherwise. For example, perhaps Silberman saw little favoritism toward attachment students partly because the teachers were aware of his interest in them and went out of their way to avoid favoring them. To eliminate this and related possibilities, Good and Brophy observed in the classrooms before interviewing teachers. Finally, both the Silberman study and the Jenkins study had been done in upper middle class suburban schools. To introduce more variation and take into account the possibility that school SES might make a difference, Good and Brophy included schools that contrasted in their student populations.

The schools and teachers already were included in a study of teacher expectation effects (Evertson, Brophy, and Good, 1973a). Three first-grade classes in each of three schools were observed for about 40 hours each. One school served a predominantly upper middle SES white population; the second served a predominantly lower SES white population; and the third served a predominantly lower SES black population. Teachers had been asked to rank their students on achievement in the fall and winter, but attitudes were not measured until spring, following data collection. Thus, teacher-student interaction could not have been affected by teacher awareness of our interest in teacher attitudes. The same was true of the classroom observers, who also did not know that teacher attitudes would be measured in the spring.

Silberman's (1969) four interview questions were used, with two differences. First, at the request of the school system, the rejection question was altered to "If your class was to be reduced by a few children, which would you have removed?" Second, teachers were asked to nominate three children in response to each question rather than just one. Behavioral data collected previously then were analyzed for differences among attitude groups. Analyses by school revealed no differences in patterns. Thus, the relationships between teacher attitudes and measures of classroom interaction were essentially the same across student SES and race. The findings generally replicated those of Silberman and Jenkins, although they were more numerous and provided a richer picture of these four student types and the kinds of interactions they had with their teachers.

Attachment students showed generally positive patterns. They were high achievers who actively sought out the teachers to initiate contacts with them, especially about work assignments. They were eager to respond to questions, but they did not call out answers or violate classroom rules often. They usually responded correctly when called on, had fewer errors per reading turn than other students, and were more likely than other students to make at least some kind of response even when they did not know the answer. It is easy to see why the teachers were attracted to these students, and why they enjoyed having them in their classrooms.

Nevertheless, as Silberman (1969) had found, the teachers did not systematically and overtly favor these children. Attachment students did receive more praise for good work and less criticism, but these differences clearly were related more to their higher achievement and better behavior than to teacher favoritism. The attachment students were not praised any more often per correct answer than their classmates were.

Another finding that replicated one reported by Silberman (1969) was that the teachers minimized their contacts with attachment students. They sought them out less frequently to discuss work and they called on them less frequently to answer questions. This may have reflected a desire to avoid showing favoritism, although it could have been recognition by the teachers that these students did not need much supervision and would come to them if they needed help.

There were a few indications that could be interpreted as subtle favoritism of attachment students, but no clear evidence of favoritism. For example, the attachment students received more reading turns than average, and they had higher percentages of process questions (which generally are more difficult questions, compared to other kinds). These data fit with Silberman's (1971) impression that teachers held up attachment students as positive examples to their classmates, although the same findings could have occurred even if such thoughts never crossed the teachers' minds.

The teachers could have asked attachment students to read more often because they were better readers and thus useful for maintaining a good pace during reading groups, and they could have asked them more difficult questions simply because they were more likely to be able to answer them. Similarly, the teachers gave detailed process feedback to attachment students less often, probably because they did not need it. All of these differences can be taken as subtle examples of favoritism, but they also can be explained more simply as due to teacher recognition that attachment students were among the more able students in the class.

Concern students were like attachment students in that they initiated many contacts with the teachers and were more likely to guess than remain silent when they did not know answers. However, they were mostly low achievers. They had fewer correct answers per response opportunity and more errors per reading turn. These data bear out Silberman's (1969) finding that concern students were low achievers who were highly dependent upon the teachers for direction and feedback. The data on teacher interactions with concern students also support Silberman's findings. The teachers showed their concern by interacting with these students often, giving them many more opportunities to answer questions in class discussions and reading groups, and seeking them out more frequently for private contacts about work or even procedural matters.

In addition to these differences in frequency of interaction, there were some interesting differences in quality of interaction. The teachers were more willing to spend time with concern students, providing them with feedback or explaining things over again if they failed to understand them the first time. Also, teachers were more willing to stay with concern students when they had failed to answer questions or read correctly. Rather than call on someone else or give the answer, they tended to try to elicit the answer from the concern students by giving them more time or by helping them with clues or hints.

Taken together, the data on concern students replicate and extend Silberman's findings that teachers show their concern and that their concern appears to be due to low achievement by these students. The teachers responded positively to them, even though they made unusually high demands upon their time and energy. They were willing to take the time to try to get points across to them or to elicit answers from them, and they went out of their way to interact with them often. In short, the teachers' concern seemed to be mostly concern about low achievement, and their response to this concern was obvious in their attempts to improve achievement through more frequent and intensive contacts and a conspicuous willingness to provide whatever help or direction was needed.

Most of these findings are consistent with Silberman's findings and impressions, although two of his impressions were not supported. There was no evidence that the teachers were going out of their way to praise concern students at every opportunity. Nor were they particularly quick to give concern students answers or unwilling to try to elicit answers from them. The data revealed no consistent differences in praise and criticism of concern students compared with their classmates, and, if anything, the teachers tended to push these students for better responses rather than to avoid pushing them. The Good and Brophy (1972) data suggest that the teachers were actively and seriously trying to teach the concern students, not expressing concern by lowering aspirations and substituting emotional support and reassurance for persistent teaching.

The Good and Brophy data were especially revealing in regard to indifference students. These students had very low rates of interaction with teachers, as Silberman (1969) had found. However, other data revealed additional differences. Several measures showed clearly that the low rates of interaction with teachers were due primarily to student avoidance of the teachers. Indifference students initiated fewer work and procedural contacts with the teachers, seldom called out responses, and were more likely to remain silent than to offer a guess when they did not know an answer.

Measures of classroom achievement and conduct indicated that indifference students were average, as a group. The teacher-student interaction data suggested that teachers responded to these students by avoiding them. They did not compensate by seeking them out more frequently. Indifference students were asked fewer direct questions than average, and the teachers initiated fewer private contacts with them.

These findings are unusual, because teachers typically compensate for individual differences in students (Brophy and Evertson, 1976). For example, if students do not come to teachers for help when they need it, teachers usually compensate by going to the students to check their work and provide help if necessary. Also, if students do not volunteer to answer questions by raising their hands, teachers tend to compensate by calling on them more often when they do not have their hands raised. Thus, the teachers' tendency to respond to student avoidance with avoidance of their own is unusual. It suggests a different interpretation of the dynamics relating to indifference students than the one given by Silberman (1969).

Silberman believed that indifference students were simply overlooked in a passive and presumably accidental fashion by teachers who were busy meeting the demands posed by more active and salient students. This version pictures indifference students as simply lost in the shuffle, not actively avoided or disliked. However, the teachers in the Good and Brophy study responded to student avoidance with avoidance of their own, rather than with compensatory increases in initiation of contact. This suggests the possibility that their indifference was more active, perhaps even rejecting.

This interpretation does not arise so much from direct data, which contained no positive elements of rejection (for example, indifference students were not criticized more or praised less than other students). However, the contrast with typical findings which indicate that compensatory teacher behavior is the norm suggests the possibility that the indifference students were conditioning the teachers to stay away from them! This will be discussed in more detail in the next chapter in connection with research on student effects on teachers.

The Good and Brophy data on rejection students bore out Silberman's description of these students as misbehaving. They initiated contacts with the teachers for procedural or work interactions often, called out answers without permission more frequently, and were especially likely to receive criticism for misbehavior. In general, they appeared to be overactive and aggressive, compared with their classmates.

Achievement measures showed no differences in rates of reading errors per reading turn or percentages of questions answered correctly in general class discussions, but rejection students did make more errors in responding to questions during reading groups. In general, though, the rejection students were characterized much more by misbehavior than by low achievement.

As with the concern students, teachers noticeably and consistently acted upon their attitudes toward rejection students. These students had fewer response opportunities than average, even though they called out answers more often and even though teachers asked them direct questions as often as they asked other students. This means that the difference in total response opportunities occurred because teachers were less likely to call on rejection students when they had their hands up, seeking to respond. Perhaps these students raised their hands less often, but the fact that they tended to call out answers suggests that the teachers might have been avoiding them. Also, the direct questions asked of these students may have been asked more to get their attention than to provide them with opportunities to respond.

Other data showed clearer evidence of teacher avoidance of rejection students. These students had fewer reading turns, and the teachers failed especially often to give them feedback after reading turns and responses to questions. Thus, when teachers did have public interactions with rejection students they tended to keep them brief and move on to someone else at the first opportunity.

The data from private interaction situations were very different. Teachers initiated more private work contacts with rejection students than average, so that they clearly did not try to avoid dealing with them in this context. However, rejection students were more likely to be criticized during these contacts. Taken together, these data provide a clear picture of what the rejection students were like and how the teachers reacted to them. Among other things, it seems obvious that the potential for undesirable self-fulfilling prophecy effects was greatest for the rejection students.

Data from the Good and Brophy (1972) study enriched the profiles of these four types of students regarding ways that teachers respond to them, although these data did not answer all questions. They strongly confirmed Silberman's (1971) impression that the major difference between concern and rejection students was the latter group's nonconforming misbehavior. They also confirmed his findings and impressions that teachers were quite obvious in showing concern and rejection.

However, the findings suggested a more positive picture of teacher responses to concern students than earlier data implied. The teachers appeared to act on their concern by mobilizing to do the best job they could to teach concern students as much as possible. Earlier findings and impressions had suggested that teachers reacted to concern students by sympathizing with them rather than by teaching them. The Good and Brophy data also elaborated the picture of indifference students, raising the possibility that teacher indifference is active avoidance, not just passive neglect. However, this was an indirect inference; no direct data support it. Thus, this study added much new information about indifference students, but also raised new questions.

The Good and Brophy (1972) study failed to add much to previous findings concerning attachment students. Again, glimmerings of favoritism appeared in subtle measures, but there was no solid evidence of favoritism of attachment students. This was true even though the teachers did not name attachment students until after the observational data were collected. Given the strong patterns for concern and rejection students and the new interpretations for indifference students, this only deepened the mysteries surrounding attachment students. Common sense suggests that attachment should be at least as strong as the other teacher attitudes, but observational studies failed to reveal much about attachment students and especially about how teachers interact with them.

A follow-up study conducted by Evertson, Brophy, and Good (1973b) used the same general procedures in six second-grade classrooms located in two of the same schools studied the previous year. The group differences that appeared in this study were similar to those in the first year, but there were fewer significant differences. The findings added no new information to what was available. In particular, the attachment students again were shown to be cooperative high achievers, but no evidence of overt teacher favoritism toward them was revealed.

The follow-up study supported Silberman's data and impressions about concern students, and conflicted to some degree with the Good and Brophy (1972) findings. As usual, high rates of teacher interaction with concern students were found. However, the concern students were especially likely to be praised for good behavior and criticized for misbehavior. The praise data fit Silberman's impression that teachers go out of their way to encourage and praise concern students.

The Good and Brophy (1972) finding that teachers pushed concern students for good responses and good work was not replicated. In fact, there was a tendency for the teachers to give the answers or call on someone else when these students did not answer correctly. Furthermore, when the teachers did try to elicit answers from concern students, they tended to provide a clue or some other kind of help rather than just allow more time or repeat the question. Thus, the follow-up data were closer to Silberman's initial data and impressions than they were to the Good and Brophy (1972) data. The second-grade teachers responded to concern students by interacting with them more frequently and trying to give them special help, but also by being somewhat less critical and demanding. Also, these teachers appeared to go out of their way to be encouraging when opportunities arose.

This is a clear conflict with the first-grade findings, and it is all the more remarkable because most of the concern students in the second-grade study were boys who misbehaved frequently in addition to having difficulty with their work. In many ways, the concern students in this study overlapped in their behavioral qualities with the typical rejection student. Even so, the teachers clearly responded to them with facilitative concern rather than rejection. Thus, the follow-up study not only failed to add anything of significance to previous findings, but it introduced discrepant findings and new and puzzling questions.

A dissertation study by McDonald (1972) was designed specifically to examine teacher interaction with attachment students. Fourteen elementary classrooms were involved. Each teacher was questioned about the degree to which she liked each of her students, and students were questioned about the degree to which they liked their teachers. The classes then were observed to see if interaction patterns were warmer when teachers and students liked each other than when they did not. Group differences were in the predicted direction on seven of ten measures, but none were statistically significant. Here again, classroom observation data revealed no favoritism toward attachment students. And, students who liked their teachers were no more warm toward them than students who disliked their teachers.

Nash (1973), although he did not collect systematic, low inference data, developed impressions of British teachers' reactions to favored and rejected students that are similar to the American findings regarding attachment and rejection students. He noted that favoritism usually is not revealed openly, but rejection is. The teachers he observed regularly underestimated the abilities of students they disliked, concentrated more on isolating them and minimizing the trouble they caused than on teaching them, and often tried to place them into special classes (and thus get rid of them).

Marland (1977), in an ethnographic study, identified several rules of thumb that teachers apparently tried to follow in the classroom. One of these was a general rule of compensation—if students don't volunteer, call on them; if students don't ask for opportunities to perform housekeeping chores, assign them; and so on. Other rules had to do with meeting special needs: extra patience and insurance of success when calling on shy or anxious students, extra monitoring of the progress of low achievers (many of whom would be called concern students). Interestingly, another rule was to suppress one's own (the teacher's) emotions, to avoid overt favoritism of preferred students, or hostile, rejecting responses to disliked students. Even so, Marland notes, teachers were especially careful to treat preferred students with respect and avoid any threat to their self-concepts. They were less protective with rejected students.

Finally, Brooks and Wilson (1978), in a study of classroom proxemics, found that teachers often worked at close quarters with concern students but tended to keep their distance from rejected students. Rejection, then, tends to show itself clearly, whereas attachment does not.

In combination, these studies revealed much information about the behavior of students who engender the attitudes of attachment, concern, indifference, or rejection in their teachers, and some information about how teachers interact with students toward whom they hold these attitudes. Many questions remained unanswered, however, particularly questions dealing with the dynamics of teacher interaction with attachment and indifference students.

For example, each study showed that attachment students were conforming high achievers. Teachers do not necessarily feel attachment toward all conforming high achievers, and they might occasionally feel attachment toward students who misbehave frequently. Thus, just as our expectation research led us to develop an increasing interest in student characteristics, so did our attitude research.

We also developed increasing curiosity about how teacher attitudes were expressed and how they interact with other factors. The picture was not completely consistent for any of the four groups. Five separate studies failed to find clear evidence of teacher favoritism of attachment students, or indeed of any systematic teacher behavior toward these students. However, impressionistic data and interpretations of some observed differences suggested that subtle favoritism might be revealed with other methods. The indifference students appeared to be simply lost in the shuffle in some studies, but other studies suggested that teacher indifference was more active, involving rejection and avoidance of these students. Studies agreed in showing that teachers exhibited concern about concern students, but there were conflicting findings about how teachers express this concern. Do they redouble their efforts to teach concern students, or do they substitute sympathy and reduced expectations for persistent teaching efforts? Finally, although the data on rejection students were the most consistent, there remained some doubt about whether teachers express rejection in clear and consistent ways, or whether they are conflicted about their rejection and vacillate between positive and negative interactions with rejection students.

TEACHER PERCEPTIONS AND TEACHER ATTITUDES

Willis and Brophy (1974) studied teachers' interview responses as they related to the teacher attitudes of attachment, indifference, concern, and rejection. The attitude data were collected at the end of the year, after the teachers had responded to the interviews. Equal numbers of boys and girls were nominated to the attachment group, but more boys were nominated to each of the other three groups, particularly the concern group. Data from the third interview taken in the spring were analyzed to see how the teachers described these four groups of students.

Boys in the attachment group were described as well clothed, physically immature, likely to wear glasses, unlikely to be unusually quiet, likely to be assigned as leaders or helpers, helpful with other children, likely to be busybodies, likely to know left from right and to be able to stay within lines on tablets, unable to draw well, not likely to be reading up to their ability, likely to volunteer information during discussions, likely to have a perceptual problem or learning disability, likely to have a generally positive pattern of conduct and social behavior, and likely to be high in general ability. These perceptions generally fit the stereotype of the attachment student as conforming and achieving, although there are interesting exceptions.

For example, the teachers saw these boys as busybodies, physically immature, likely to have physical problems, and not working up to their abilities. Even so, they responded to them with attachment, and the data even suggest some favoritism (allowing them to be leaders and helpers more often).

Girls in the attachment group were described as larger than average, more attractive than average, having interested and cooperative parents, likely to require glasses or have a visual impairment, having been to kindergarten, not knowing how to write their names, being creative and imaginative, being alert and close observers, liking stories, being able to work independently, being of generally high ability, coming from generally good families, and being high in expected achievement. In contrast to the data for boys in the attachment group, the data for girls are almost completely positive. However, they contain no hint of teacher favoritism.

Boys in the indifference group were described as more likely to have blond hair, to have blank eye expressions, to be physically immature, to be neat and clean, to have a working mother, to be reared by grandparents or substitute parents, to have uninterested or uncooperative parents, to need glasses or have visual impairments, to have speech impediments or use baby talk, to be sociometric loners, to be anxious to please, to be in poor health, to have negative attitudes toward school, to have failed to live up to the teachers' initial expectations of them, and to have poor verbal skills.

In many ways, these data suggest concern students rather than indifference students, although the teachers did perceive the indifference group boys as loners and as having negative attitudes toward school. They also perceived them as having failed to live up to the teachers' expectations for achievement, but this was true of the boys in the attachment group also. Taken together, these data provide more support for the suggestion that teachers do not particularly enjoy indifference students, but they provide no indication as to why not.

Girls in the indifference group were described as more likely to be nonwhite, not liking school, giving up easily on work assignments, lacking self-confidence, not being prepared for school, not knowing their colors and numbers, being creative and imaginative, having generally low ability, interacting infrequently with the teachers, and often presenting problems in their classroom behavior. As with the boys, these data on indifference group girls fit the previously reported indifference group findings to some extent, but they also contain elements more typically associated with the concern group and the rejection group. It is more clear in the case of the girls why the teachers would not enjoy interacting with them, although it is not clear why they responded to them with indifference rather than with concern or rejection.

The boys in the concern group were described as typically average in size, more likely to be reared by grandparents or older parents, likely to have a speech impediment or use baby talk, likely to be generally immature, active and vivacious, attention seeking, able to use and keep up with school supplies but dependent in schoolwork and in need of help from the teacher, in need of reassurance and approval, generally low in ability, needing readiness work, having positive attitudes toward school, poor in health, poor in social-emotional development, poor in oral and verbal skills, poor in independent work skills, and generally low in ability. These data quite clearly fit the picture of concern students as low ability students who are cooperative and conforming.

Girls in the concern group were described as likely to be nonwhite, likely to come from good homes and large families (although the large families were seen as causing problems for these children), likely to have speech impediments or use baby talk, dependent, quiet, lacking in confidence, needing supervision and help from the teacher, having generally positive attitudes toward school, and having poor verbal skills. These data are very similar to those for the boys. Again, they suggest a pattern of low ability, cooperation, and conformity.

The contrasts between the concern students and the indifference students provide clues about why the teachers did not respond more positively to the indifference students. First, concern students were notably positive in their attitudes toward school (and presumably toward the teachers), while indifference students were less positive or even negative. Second, concern students were conforming and compliant, but indifference students often caused behavior problems. Third, the data on indifference students suggest that they were turning off the teachers. They were described as having blank facial expressions, as being generally unresponsive, and as having poor attitudes toward school.

These teacher comments suggest that the concern and indifference students probably were conditioning the teachers like the children in the study by Yarrow, Waxler, and Scott (1971). Concern students apparently sought out the teachers and gave covert signals indicating that they enjoyed contacts with them. Indifference students apparently minimized contacts with the teachers and gave covert signals that they disliked such contacts. Apparently, the teachers responded by increasing their contacts with concern students and decreasing their contacts with indifference students, and by developing corresponding attitudes over time.

Boys in the rejection group were described as likely to be nonwhite, coming from intact families, immature and poorly adjusted, independent, loud, disruptive, not vivacious, not likely to be assigned as a leader or helper, not getting along well with others, talkative, not knowing similarities and differences, not knowing how to write their names, not knowing left from right or how to stay within lines, not able to use or keep up with school supplies, having weak reading abilities, needing extra help because of generally low ability, needing readiness work, likely to fail, having deteriorated in work since the beginning of the year, being either notably healthy or unhealthy, lacking in readiness skills, having poor verbal skills, being physically unattractive, providing frequent classroom behavior problems, generally lacking in school readiness, misbehaving during seatwork times, and being of generally low ability.

In short, the teachers' perceptions of these boys were unremittingly negative. Their statements included the admission that they did not allow these boys to act as helpers or leaders as often as the other students, and they contained no hint whatsoever of ambivalence or attempts to compensate. The negative halo effect produced by these boys was so strong that teachers described them as low in ability in several different ways, even though they did not differ significantly from their classmates on the Metropolitan Readiness Test. In this case, at least, strong negative attitudes distorted teacher perceptions of ability.

The girls in the rejection group were described as coming from less desirable families, being busybodies, not liking school, giving up easily, lacking self-confidence, being playful and mischievous, being unprepared for school, being poorly adjusted to school routines, not knowing colors and numbers, not knowing similarities and differences, being alert observers, not volunteering information in class discussions, not paying attention, being likely to fail, being able to do better than they were doing, having poor attitudes toward school, having poor school readiness, doing poor work, and having generally low abilities. Except for the statement that these girls were alert observers, these teacher perceptions are all negative, just as they were for the boys in the rejection group. Also, just as with the boys, these girls did not differ from their classmates in Metropolitan Readiness Test scores, despite frequent teacher statements about low ability.

The data on the rejection group from this study provide perhaps the clearest and broadest picture of rejection yet discussed. The rejection group students were seen almost completely negatively, even where the objective facts did not support these perceptions, and there was no indication at all that the teachers felt guilty or ambivalent about rejecting them. Furthermore, it is clear from the teachers' remarks that misbehavior in the classroom and generally negative attitudes toward school and teachers were the main reasons for rejection. Apparently, here as elsewhere, hostility breeds hostility.

Our study of six second-grade classrooms included teacher ratings of students' attributes and behavior in addition to the four attitude scales and the classroom observation data (Evertson, Brophy and Good, 1973b; Brophy and Good, 1974). The teachers rated the students in the attachment, concern, indifference, and rejection groups on 27 scales concerning classroom behavior, interaction with the teacher, and general personal attributes.

As might have been expected from previous data, significant correlations were obtained most frequently for student sex and for the rejection students. Fourteen of the 27 correlations were significant for sex, and they all indicated that the teachers perceived the girls more positively than the boys. Boys were seen as more restless, sassy, defiant, lazy, likely to make funny or irrelevant comments, likely to daydream, lacking in confidence, butting in with answers, fighting, defensive, needing to be pushed rather than encouraged (presumably because they were not achieving up to their potential), immature, and impulsive, compared to girls. The strongest correlations were for restlessness, daydreaming, and fighting. The general picture is one that should be familiar by now: these teachers saw boys as less motivated and less cooperative. Despite these perceptions, however, the classroom observation data from this study did not reveal teacher discrimination against boys.

The rejection students were seen even more negatively. The teachers described them as restless, cheating, making the teacher uncomfortable, sassy, defiant, lazy, making funny or irrelevant comments, daydreaming, lacking in imagination, butting in with answers, fighting, defensive, unhappy, messy, immature, avoiding eye contact, and impulsive. The strongest correlations were for restlessness, cheating, sassing the teacher, defiant, lazy, daydreaming, defensive, unhappy, and immature. Thus, the general picture is one of mutual hostility between the teachers and the rejection students, even though some of these students were seen as unhappy and immature.

In contrast, the data for attachment students were uniformly positive. They were described as unlikely to cheat, unlikely to be embarrassed in the classroom, making the teachers feel comfortable, unlikely to daydream, helpful, happy, attractive, unlikely to whisper, mature, and likely to make eye contact. Thus, the teachers saw these students as achieving and conforming, but also as mature and well adjusted.

Only six relationships were significant for the indifference students, although they provide an interesting picture. Teachers described these students as not very noticeable, unimaginative, unhappy, unattractive, likely to whisper rather than speak up, and likely to avoid eye contact. Thus, the indifference students were described as passive and shy, perhaps even insecure and troubled. Yet, the teachers reacted to them with indifference rather than concern.

Six relationships also were significant for concern students. Teachers perceived them as restless, likely to cheat, lacking in confidence, unimaginative, needing to be pushed rather than encouraged, and immature. Lack of confidence was the trait most strongly associated with these students. As expected, teacher perceptions focused on traits relating to poor academic performance. The only surprising finding was that teachers saw concern students as needing to be pushed rather than encouraged gently. This perception conflicts with the idea that concern students are hard working but limited in ability and thus dependent on the teacher for help. This and the fact that the concern students were seen as likely to cheat suggests that they were not so conforming as other studies suggested. Nevertheless, the teachers did respond to them with concern. Apparently, this was because these students presented problems only in the academic area; they did not sass or defy the teachers like the rejection students did.

Perhaps the greatest mystery was why the teachers did not react more positively toward the indifference students. The teachers themselves pictured these students as shy, unhappy, and generally in need of help. Part of the reason probably was that these students were relatively invisible, so that the teachers didn't notice them often even though they were aware of their problems. Another possibility is that the indifference students made the teachers uncomfortable, although the teachers did not report this.

This study confirmed certain earlier findings but contradicted others. At this point, it seemed clear that many teacher reactions to individual students were specific to the teachers and students involved. Still, there were enough common findings across studies to indicate that certain student characteristics were likely to produce predictable responses in teachers.

Studies by other investigators further compounded these problems in interpreting teacher perceptions and their relationship to student attributes. Garner and Bing (1973) studied interaction in first-grade classes in Britain, and identified several student groups or types. Although they were working independently of the lines of research described so far, one of their groups is described very similarly to the one we have been calling the attachment group, two others sound like rejection groups, and two others sound like indifference groups.

The two groups that sound like rejection groups (both had very high rates of disciplinary contacts with teachers) differed primarily in that one group was more interested in socializing than in learning and spent a lot of time talking and playing, whereas the other was seriously disobedient, defiant, and alienated. The latter group closely resembled the rejection groups seen in several studies conducted in the United States.

The two groups that sound like indifference groups (they had low rates of interaction with the teacher) contrasted in many ways. One group was characterized primarily by passivity. It corresponds closely to the indifference groups identified here. However, another group with very low rates of interaction with the teachers was composed of bright and well-behaved students capable of learning independently. Apparently, they had low rates of interaction with the teachers because they neither wanted nor needed them. This suggests that low rates of interaction with the teacher are common among indifference students, but that not all students who have low rates of interaction with their teachers are indifference students.

Power (1971) studied contrasting patterns of interaction with the teachers in four eighth-grade science classrooms. He also identified what appeared to be a rejection group. These students were low achievers and were generally alienated from school and from the teachers. They sat toward the rear of the classroom and were rarely called on. However, when they did interact with the teacher they were especially likely to be praised. This finding, suggesting possible guilt and compensatory behavior toward rejection students by the teachers, has appeared in some studies but not others

Powers also identified what looks like a concern group: students who were dependent and sensitive, low in achievement and apparently in ability, but nevertheless high in attitudes toward science. In contrast to our finding that teachers saw concern students as needing to be pushed, Power, like others, saw the teachers as giving the concern students easier tasks and trying to avoid overtaxing them.

Power also identified a group of what he called "success syndrome" students who look like the typical attachment group. These students were high in ability and achievement, had positive attitudes toward the class and high status among their peers, participated often and successfully in classroom interactions, interacted with the teachers often, and were willing to try to answer difficult questions and to volunteer for difficult assignments. In view of other failures to find teacher favoritism toward attachment students, it is interesting to note that Power did not report any teacher favoritism toward these students despite their positive qualities.

Taken together, the data reviewed in this chapter indicate that different types of students produce attitudes of attachment, indifference, concern, or rejection in their teachers, and that these teacher attitudes are associated with different patterns of teacher-student interaction.

4

Student Effects on Teachers

Although our attention was focused on teachers, even our earliest research on differential teacher behavior toward different students was providing information about student effects on teachers, not just teacher effects on students. We were aware of student effects, which is why we developed observational systems that would "hold students constant" and allow us to compare teachers in parallel situations. This also is why we used percentage scores like "percentage of correct answers followed by praise" instead of frequency scores like "times praised per hour." These methods make comparisons across teachers more valid by holding student differences constant, although student effects never can be held completely constant in a naturalistic study.

For example, the measure "praise following correct answers" allows comparison of teachers' behavior in specific situations: when they have asked questions and students have responded correctly. This is much more useful than comparisons based on simple praise rates which do not take into account the quality of student answers. On the other hand, all correct answers are not equally good or praiseworthy. Some are routine and expected, such as brief answers in drills on old material. Such answers are different from and less likely to be praised than detailed and insightful answers that exceed the teacher's expectations for the class in general or for the students who give them. Teachers are more likely to compliment students in these situations than when they answer easy questions. Thus, even percentage measures like "percentage of correct answers followed by praise" do not hold everything constant.

The ambiguities surrounding these and other aspects of our data, particularly the data on sex differences to be discussed below, gradually increased our interest in student effects on teachers. They also helped us remain aware of the fact that teacher-student interaction is a two-way process in which each party influences the other. It is not a one-sided relationship between an active, initiatory teacher and a passive, responsive student.

This emphasis emerging in our own work was part of a larger recognition of the fact that children and youths have important effects on adults that exist alongside the effects that adults have on them. This can be seen even in newborn infants. Those who are calm, responsive to cuddling, and free of feeding problems make it easier for adults to enjoy them and look forward to interacting with them. Those who are irritable, do not seem to want or enjoy cuddling, and are difficult to feed also are difficult to enjoy, even for their parents (Thomas,

Chess, and Birch, 1970). Bell (1968) reviewed numerous studies of child rearing and concluded that individual differences in children in their effects on parents had been largely ignored, and that certain commonly accepted findings in the child-rearing literature would be interpreted quite differently if child effects on parents were taken into account. The same is true for many of the findings in educational research.

Perhaps the most obvious example is indirect teaching. Indirect teachers use questioning and discussion much more than lecturing and demonstrating, praise often and criticize seldom, elicit student ideas often and reflect them to the class for reaction, and promote pupil-to-pupil interaction (Flanders, 1970). Numerous studies show that classrooms high in indirectness are high on measures such as achievement, attitudes, or classroom climate. These data have been taken as evidence that indirect teaching causes desirable outcomes.

However, classrooms high in indirectness almost invariably are high in student SES and IQ. This is not surprising. It is much easier (as well as probably more effective) to be indirect with advantaged or talented students than with less advantaged or talented ones.

Thus, the naturalistic data on indirect teaching can be interpreted very differently, depending on whether student effects on teachers are taken into account and how they are interpreted.

Because of factors like these, we have become impressed with the risks involved in taking classroom data at face value and also with the need for detailed analyses designed to explain what data mean (quite literally). In some cases, student differences are so extreme that most classroom measures, including most of those presumably dealing only with teacher behavior, probably reflect student effects on teachers.

Consider data from a large and unruly class of the lowest achieving eighth graders at a low SES school, compared to data from another eighth-grade class composed of the highest achieving students in a high SES school. There are such striking contrasts between these two settings that the classroom process data probably would not change much if the two teachers were to switch places. This does not mean that teacher effects are unimportant, even under such extreme circumstances. In fact, we believe that teachers are much more important and have greater effects than they are given credit for at times (Good, Biddle, and Brophy, 1975; Good, 1979; Brophy, 1979a). However, this example illustrates that student effects on teachers can be formidable, and that they set limits within which teacher effects can be observed. Certain classes will make fair progress even with inept teachers, while even the most dedicated and talented teachers can accomplish only so much with other classes.

SEX DIFFERENCES

Student sex differences in achievement and in patterns of interaction with teachers provide one of the most interesting illustrations of student effects on teachers. Questionnaire studies, particularly those involving preschool or elementary school teachers, regularly show that teachers perceive girls more favorably than boys, and have higher achievement expectations for girls (Stevenson, et al., 1976; Hartley, 1978; Clift and Sexton, 1979). These differences disappear or even become reversed by high school. Such data are usually interpreted with reference to teacher sex, student sex, and the nature of schooling, but not student effects on teachers.

Typically, girls are socialized to be better at and to enjoy more activities involving verbal skills. In contrast, boys typically favor activities involving mechanical or spatial skills. Also, girls are socialized to become interested in relatively quiet and verbal activities and to be conforming to adult authority figures, while boys are socialized to engage in noisier and more physical activities and are expected to be more independent and somewhat less conforming to authority (Maccoby and Jacklin, 1974). These differences in traditional childhood sex roles make school more enjoyable and easier to adjust to for young girls than for young boys. School rules and expectations are much easier for young girls to accept and follow.

The changes that occur over time also are explainable from comparisons of traditional sex roles with the student role. As they move into and through adolescence, girls begin to encounter peer pressures and general social expectations suggesting that they should not be too aggressive or even too intelligent. This leads many girls to achieve below their abilities or even to develop the idea that they cannot handle certain subjects even though they could if they approached them with more positive expectations.

While the situation of girls relative to schooling is deteriorating for these and other reasons, the situation of boys is improving. For one thing, many of those who dislike school drop out when they reach the legal age for doing so, and most of these dropouts are boys. This means that the boys remaining in school after this legal age is reached are a select sample, higher as a group in achievement and motivation than "the boys" would be if the dropouts were still in school.

Also, schooling gradually becomes more compatible with traditional male sex roles, and correspondingly less so with traditional female roles. One difference is the curriculum itself. By high school, there is less emphasis on language arts and more on activities of greater interest to males. Also, as males mature toward adulthood, they become more aware of the importance of education for the occupational and family breadwinner roles traditionally expected of them as adults. This causes them to take school more seriously, seeing it as something they need for their own purposes rather than as something imposed by outside authorities.

Teacher Sex Roles

We think that these role considerations explain most of the observed student sex differences related to schooling. However, there is another factor that has been stressed by some writers (Sexton, 1969; Austin, Clark, and Fitchett, 1971) but which we think is of little or no importance. This is the sex of the teacher. Many observers have noted that most teachers in preschools and elementary schools (until very recently) were female, but that many high school teachers were male. This has led to speculation about the possible effects of identification with the teacher and of teacher sexist bias.

The identification argument suggests that students are more likely to identify with a teacher of the same sex as themselves. This is a special case of a more general principle that people are likely to identify with models perceived as similar to themselves (Bandura, 1969). This probably is true as far as it goes, but it does not seem to be a very important factor, at least not for most students. Availability of a male teacher as a role model for a fatherless boy might be important, but there is little evidence that sex of the teacher makes much difference for typical students of either sex.

First, sex roles are learned from infancy in response to socialization from parents, siblings, peers, relatives, neighbors, books and games, and the media (especially television). Except in unusual cases, teachers will not have much influence on this process. In fact, a few studies in which teachers deliberately tried to counter traditional sex role stereotyping all showed no effects (Brophy and Laosa, 1971; Greenberg and Peck, 1973; Serbin and O'Leary, 1975). Students would go along with the teachers as long as they were actively pressured to engage in activities associated with the opposite sex, but they would revert to sex-typed behavior as soon as this pressure was removed. Thus, even though there may be a tendency for students to identify more easily with same-sexed teachers, teacher effects on sex roles seem to be minimal.

The most serious and at the same time least defensible claims relating to sex differences and education are claims of sexist bias and discrimination by teachers, particularly discrimination by female elementary school teachers against boys. Those who argue this claim can point to numerous questionnaire and interview studies that indicate that (primarily female) elementary teachers have more favorable attitudes toward and more positive expectations for girls. This sex difference appears so regularly that it can be considered an established fact, although interpreting what it means is difficult.

The fact that male teachers are more frequent in higher grades also supports the teacher bias point of view. Interestingly though, the same writers who portray female teachers as biased against males often portray male teachers as evenhanded and balanced in their treatment of students rather than as biased against females. In any case, based on questionnaire findings, it is possible to argue that some of the sex differences in school attitudes and achievement result from female teacher bias against male students (and possibly also from male teacher bias against female students).

The few studies that have shown female teachers to interact more favorably with girls than boys have been conducted in preschools (Fagot and Patterson, 1969; Biber, Miller, and Dyer, 1972). Even here, most studies suggest that teachers were merely reacting to existing sex differences in students' behavior, not just to their sex. The major exception was the Fagot and Patterson (1969) study, which showed that female preschool teachers were feminizing students of both sexes by rewarding feminine behavior and ignoring or punishing masculine behavior. However, the reinforcement that was received from peers counteracted this for boys, who reinforced one another for masculine behavior. In any case, there was no evidence that the boys had become less masculine or more feminine over the school year.

Many such studies have been reviewed in detail by Brophy and Good (1974), and they hang together nicely until one introduces the question of student behavioral differences and their effects on teachers. Then the data become ambiguous. For example, Martin (1972) found that boys tended to be both rated (on paper and pencil instruments) and treated (as inferred from classroom observations) in more extreme ways than girls. It was true that the students who were the objects of most negative teacher attitudes and who had the least desirable teacher-student interaction patterns tended to be boys. However, the students who were the objects of the most positive teacher attitudes and who had the most desirable teacher-student interaction patterns also tended to be boys.

Martin concluded that the boys were rated and treated more variably than the girls because they were more active. As a group, the boys had both more of the good and more of the bad. However, the boys were not an undifferentiated group. One subgroup of boys was rated very highly and had very desirable interaction patterns, while another subgroup was rated very unfavorably and had undesirable interaction patterns. There was no overlap between these groups. Martin argued that, in many ways, it makes more sense to deal with them separately than it does to speak of boys as if all boys were essentially the same.

Martin's findings have been replicated several times in our own studies (Brophy and Good, 1974). Such findings indicate that teachers respond to student personal characteristics and behavior, not to student sex as such. It is true that the sex differences in behavior are themselves sex typed. That is, the greater activity levels and salience of boys fit with generalized sex role expectation differences. Thus, children may act as they do in classrooms partly because of the sex role socialization to which they have been exposed. However, the data indicate that teachers do not respond to boys as boys or to girls as girls. Instead, they respond to students as students, based primarily upon student characteristics and behavior not directly related to sex.

This conclusion recognizes the importance of student sex role socialization, but it discounts the idea that teacher sexist bias is of any significance in explaining student sex differences. The sexism argument can be refuted more directly, however, with data comparing male versus female teachers. The few studies which have done this agree in finding no evidence at all to support the idea that teachers discriminate against students of the opposite sex. Good, Sikes, and Brophy (1973) found a significant relationship between teacher sex and student sex on only 1 of 62 possible measures (less than chance expectancy) in a study of teacher-student interaction in junior high school. This difference suggested that, if anything, female teachers were favoring male students rather than discriminating against them. Similar findings were reported by Lahaderne and Cohen (1972) and by Hillman and Davenport (1978).

More generally, studies comparing male and female teachers suggest a few sex differences in general teaching style, but not that teachers discriminate either in favor of or against students of the opposite sex. In summary, although student sex is of some importance in predicting differences in classroom behavior that will affect teachers, teacher sex appears to be of little or no importance as such (Good and Grouws, 1972). It seems clear that different teacher behavior toward male versus female students results from different student behavior, not teacher sexism. This observation naturally leads to questions about what kinds of student differences are affecting teachers.

One major difference is that boys are more active, and thus more salient, in the classroom (Brophy and Good, 1974; Serbin, et al., 1973; Hillman and Davenport, 1978; Martin, 1972). Some of this activity involves disruption or other problems for teachers, so that boys almost invariably have more frequent disciplinary contacts than girls (Brophy and Good, 1974; Serbin, et al., 1973; Hillman and Davenport, 1978; Martin, 1972; Good, Sikes, and Brophy, 1973; Leinhardt, Seewald, and Engel, 1979; Good, Cooper, and Blakey, 1980). However, boys also tend to call out answers and comments, and to volunteer often and respond vigorously to questions, so they are active in responding to academic input, as well (Brophy and Good, 1974).

Teachers typically initiate more contacts of all kinds with boys, not just disciplinary contacts (Brophy and Good, 1974; Hillman and Davenport, 1978), and may respond more intensely to boys, as well (Serbin, et al., 1973). So, except for private teacher-student contacts initiated by the students themselves (Good, Cooper, and Blakey, 1980), sex differences in frequencies of all kinds of teacher-student interaction tend to favor boys.

This "favoritism" of boys does not speak well for them, however. Disciplinary contacts are more frequent because boys tend to misbehave more often and more disruptively, and higher frequencies of teacher-initiated, private academic and procedural contacts indicate that teachers find it necessary to monitor boys more closely and intervene to provide direction more often. This is especially the case in the elementary grades, where boys are much more likely than girls to be hyperactive, to have limited attention spans, or to show various learning disabilities (Clarizio and McCoy, 1976; Rutter, 1975).

There are indications that this changes at higher grade levels, especially in subjects traditionally identified as masculine. Leinhardt, Seewald, and Engel (1979) found that boys had more contacts with teachers, including more cognitive time devoted to the subject matter, in math classes. The reverse was true in reading classes. This indicates that typical sex differences in classroom behavior may be exaggerated when the subject matter is associated with the female sex role, and reduced or even reversed when it is associated with the male sex role.

Becker (1979) found that boys had more public response opportunities than girls in high school geometry classes. In addition, ethnographic data indicated that teachers initiated more private contacts with the boys, and provided them with more encouragement and positive affect. In general, Becker felt that the teachers (male and female) were projecting mathematics as a masculine domain.

Back at the elementary level, though, there is little evidence of systematic teacher favoritism of either sex. Instead, teachers appear to be responding to students' behavior, not to their sex as such.

OTHER GROUP DIFFERENCES

The same appears to be true of race differences, ethnicity differences, and SES differences. First, contrary to popular belief, there are remarkably few studies that even suggest discriminatory teacher behavior against minority groups. In fact, the largest study of this kind yet done revealed no teacher tendency to favor white over black students (Hillman and Davenport, 1978). Second, even studies that do seem to imply such favoritism are ambiguous because they did not control for differences in student behavior. If taken at face value, they suggest that teachers systematically discriminate against certain groups by interacting with them less often or criticizing them more often (Jackson and Cosca, 1974) or by treating them less warmly (Friedman, 1976).

However, studies that include provisions for relating differential teacher treatment of students to differential student behavior routinely show that teachers respond to student personal characteristics and classroom behavior, not group membership. Where group differences are observed, it is because certain behavioral differences in students are systematically associated with group membership. However, individuals who are exceptions to group norms are treated differently. More generally, teachers usually deal with students individually and not as members of groups. Effective teachers adapt their techniques to their students (Brophy and Evertson, 1976). Sometimes, this means that different treatment of different students or even of different groups is desirable.

STUDIES OF STUDENT EFFECTS ON TEACHERS

In addition to these questions about the meanings of student sex difference data, interest in student effects on teachers was deepened by the findings of other studies relating to this topic. The earlier mentioned study by Yarrow, Waxler, and Scott (1971) is especially instructive. This study revealed that student individual differences affected the degree to which teachers implemented simple behavior modification strategies in a preschool. Two adult, female caretakers were trained to be either high or low in nurturance at varying times during the day. During high nurturance periods, they were supposed to be very warm and responsive with the children. During low nurturance periods, they were supposed to be brusque and impersonal (but not rejecting). These instructions seemed simple enough: be nurturant during high nurturance periods, be nonnurturant during low nurturance periods, and respond normally otherwise. If these instructions had been followed, the teachers would have been uniformly nurturant during high nurturance periods and uniformly nonnurturant during low nurturance periods.

This was not the case, however, and the investigators convincingly showed that differences among the students were the reason. Both teachers were much more nurturant during the high nurturance periods, but they sometimes failed to be nurturant when they were not supposed to be. Also, sometimes they were nurturant when they were supposed to be. These departures from their instructions were not random. Boys elicited much more nonnurturance than girls, and they were more salient and had stronger effects on the teachers. They were more likely to get nonnurturant or even rejecting treatment during supposedly high nurturance periods, and more likely to get negative teacher responses generally. They did this in particular by being persistent in seeking attention from the teachers and by making demands at times when the teachers were trying to do something else.

In addition to these sex differences, the investigators found individual student differences that are fascinating and instructive about student effects on teachers. Besides coding the frequencies of teacher-student interactions and the degree to which teachers were nurturant, they coded the degree to which students reinforced teachers by responding in a warm, friendly, or otherwise positive fashion, and the degree to which they punished teachers by being unresponsive or negativistic.

Analyses of these data in relationship to how long teachers waited before initiating another contact with the same student showed that teachers predictably returned sooner to students who responded positively. In short, even though the children were only preschoolers, they were conditioning the teachers by modifying their tendencies to seek them out to initiate contact versus avoid them. Understandably, teachers responded positively to students who rewarded them and negatively to students who punished them. These data are similar to those discussed in chapter 3 concerning teacher behavior toward various attitude groups, although they illustrate even more clearly that the findings result from student effects on teachers rather than vice versa.

Experimental studies in which student behavior was manipulated without the knowledge of the teachers (who were experimental subjects) have also shown predictable student effects on teachers. For example, Klein (1971) studied the behavior of 24 guest lecturers in classes where students behaved positively, neutrally, or negatively according to a prearranged schedule. Positive behaviors included attention, eye contact, and apparent interest. Neutral behaviors were normal, spontaneous reactions. Negative behaviors included inattention, looking out the window, and general restlessness. Unsurprisingly, the guest lecturers were more positive in their general behavior and more indirect in their teaching methods when students were positive than when they were negative.

Herrill (1971) showed student expectation effects on teacher behavior. The same man, unaware of the experiment, gave the same guest lecture in each of two college classes. One class had been told that he was warm and friendly, but the other class had been told that he was cold and indifferent. Observations revealed that he became increasingly warm while in the class that expected warmth, but became increasingly cold in the class where he was expected to be cold. Student ratings of the last segment of each class revealed that the class who expected him to be warm rated him as warmer, more relaxed, and more competent. Similar results have been obtained in research that induced student expectations by providing phony information presented as student evaluations from the previous semester.

Students' nonverbal responsiveness seems to be especially powerful in influencing teachers (Rankin, 1978). Feldman and Prohaska (1979) found that instructors felt happier with their performance and warmer toward the class when students (confederates of the experimenters) systematically responded with nonverbal signs of attention and interest than when they did not. Cantor and Gelfand (1977) found that responsiveness by (confederate) children increased responsiveness and helpfulness in adults, as well as their tendencies to rate the children as attractive, likeable, and competent. Bates (1976) reported similar findings. Thus, students who reward teachers with positive responsiveness tend to be both better perceived and better treated than other students.

Activity and initiative are also important, as noted earlier in discussing student sex differences. This also was seen in a study by Noble and Nolan (1976). They observed that students who volunteered more often got more response opportunities, and in general, that students conditioned teachers either to call on them (by attracting attention and projecting eagerness) or to pass them over (by remaining passive and avoiding eye contact). Taken together, the studies reviewed in this section show clearly that students can and do affect teachers' classroom behavior.

Attribution Studies

Another line of research illustrating some of the processes involved in student effects on teachers is research relating to attribution theory or causal attributions. In these studies, teachers (or experimental subjects who are acting or believe that they are acting as teachers) are led to experience relative success or failure (through information purporting to be feedback about their performance or about student learning). Following this, they are asked to assess the experience and offer explanations for it. In particular, they are asked to attribute causality for success or failure to themselves, to the students, or to other factors.

Many of these studies have focused on the question of whether or not teachers are defensive and blaming if they are led to believe that they have not succeeded. Studies using artificial situations that force subjects to rely completely on the information given to them typically find that teachers use this information, making them appear defensive. However, studies done under more naturalistic conditions typically find that teachers are not particularly defensive, and that they adjust their initial attitudes and expectations according to student behavior (Ames, 1975; Beckman, 1972; Brandt, Hayden, and Brophy, 1975). Like the studies designed to get teachers to develop unrealistic expectations by giving them phony information, these studies reveal that teachers typically change any misperceptions they may have once they encounter students and get opportunities to interact with them regularly.

Attribution theorists concern themselves not only with how teachers explain their own successes and failures to themselves, but also with how teachers explain student attributes. With regard to achievement, Weiner (1979) notes that teachers' attributions concerning degree of student effort determine their responses to student success and failure. Blame, rejection, and punishment are likely when teachers believe that students failed because they didn't try to succeed, but not when teachers believe that students failed because they lack ability or something else that effort could not overcome.

Cooper and Lowe (1977) theorize that teacher praise (for positive outcomes) and blame (for negative outcomes) should increase in proportion to the degree of responsibility for these outcomes that teachers attribute to students. Praise should be especially likely when students are perceived to have done well through their own efforts, and criticism when they are perceived to have failed for lack of trying or to have caused a problem through their own inappropriate behavior (which they could have inhibited but did not).

Medway (1979) found that teachers tended to attribute learning problems to limited ability, but behavior problems to other factors (note that the teachers did not mention their own behavior as an important cause of either type of problem). He found that criticism was frequent when problems were attributed to lack of effort. The teachers stated that they would use praise and contingent rewards to counter behavior problems, but not learning problems.

Brophy and Rohrkemper (1980), analyzing teachers' reports of how they would handle various learning and behavior problems, found major differences related both to the type of problem and to the teachers' attributions concerning the cause of the problem. Problems were classified by problem ownership (Gordon, 1974). Some, such as a student making paper airplanes instead of working or a student bullying a classmate, were owned primarily by the teacher. That is, the problem students here were not suffering any frustration of their own needs or desires, but they created problems for the teachers by threatening their authority, frustrating their attempts to teach, or causing disruption.

Other problems, such as a student being frozen out of the peer group or suffering severe self-concept devaluation, were owned primarily by the students themselves. The students' own needs and desires were being frustrated, but this did not directly cause a problem to the teacher. Still other problems, such as student hyperactivity leading to equipment breakage or loss of personal belongings by immature students who come to the teachers for help, are shared by the teachers and the students. The students have behavior problems in that their needs or desires are frustrated; but in their attempts to cope, they create problems for the teachers as well.

Brophy and Rohrkemper found that teachers attributed both controllability and intentionality to students when the problem was owned primarily by the teacher. That is, the students were seen as deliberately misbehaving in ways that they could eliminate if they tried. As a result, criticism and punishment were especially likely teacher responses to these teacher-owned problems. Other investigators also have reported that teachers react more strongly and negatively to aggressive or defiant behavior that threatens their security than they do to problems such as low achievement or social withdrawal (Clarizio and McCoy, 1976; Kedar-Voivodas and Tannenbaum, 1979).

Brophy and Rohrkemper report that teachers' attributions for student-owned problems contrasted with those for teacher-owned problems. Students with student-owned problems but not seen as in control of their behavior, or as acting intentionally. Consequently, they elicited a good deal of teacher concern and sympathy, as well as attempts to improve self-concept and adjustment through counseling, encouragement, and other mental hygiene approaches.

Finally, the students involved in teacher-student shared problems, even when seen as able to control their behavior, were not seen as acting intentionally. Their problems were seen as lapses, and attributed to immaturity, limited intelligence or memory, or a lack of sufficient self-control training. Consequently, blame or punishment were unlikely. Instead, teachers were more likely to prescribe contract systems or other behavior modification approaches. (Medway, 1979, also found this for minor behavior problems.)

Taken together, these studies done from an attribution theory perspective remind us that student effects on teachers are not determined by student behavior alone. Much depends on how teachers perceive that behavior and develop theories to explain it to themselves. Teachers' reactions are likely to be most extreme for achievement outcomes attributed to student effort (or a lack of it) and for behavior problems seen as involving deliberate, intentional misconduct.

In summary, we have become increasingly aware of the need to take into account student individual differences in personal characteristics and behavior in interpreting classroom process data. Without taking into account student characteristics and their effects on teachers, it is possible to interpret differential teacher behavior toward different groups incorrectly as evidence of effective or ineffective teaching or as evidence of teacher discrimination. When group differences in treatment by the teacher are investigated in connection with group differences in treatment of the teacher, many correlational findings are seen to reflect student effects on teachers, rather than vice versa.

Along with our continuing interest in understanding the causes and correlates of teacher expectations and attitudes, we have become interested in questions concerning what student characteristics and behaviors are important to teachers and how individual differences in them affect teachers. These are the core questions addressed in the Student Attribute Study.

Part 2

Presentation of Findings

5

The Student Attribute
Study: Rationale
and Methodology

RATIONALE FOR THE STUDENT ATTRIBUTE STUDY

Considerable information about teachers' beliefs, attitudes, and expectations and their relationships to teacher-student interaction has been reviewed. This is only a fraction of the information available, but it is enough to indicate the state of the field. Certain findings are generally well established, while other issues remain clouded as conflicting information continues to accumulate. One problem is the absence of clear theories to integrate and organize the data. Another is the great variety of methods used and questions asked. This makes it difficult to compare studies even when they purportedly address the same questions.

In our view, however, the biggest single source of confusion in this area is the fact that most studies have been small and isolated, so that conflicting interpretations of findings cannot be resolved by turning to related data. Relatively few studies have included both information about teacher perceptions of students and information about student characteristics or classroom behavior. Even when they have, there are questions about the degree to which the teacher perceptions were accurate and about what the behavioral data mean.

We have come to see that even the most reliable behavioral information cannot be taken at face value because it may not mean what we think it means. Praise is not necessarily reinforcing, and it does not necessarily indicate positive teacher attitudes toward a student. Criticism sometimes is a way to communicate positive expectations. Frequency of teacher-student interaction usually is associated with good teacher-student relationships, but teachers sometimes call on students to get their attention, and sometimes they have high frequencies of interaction with rejection students because they intervene to handle disciplinary problems often.

There are even more questions about self-report data from teachers. Taken at face value, they seem to add rich detail and elaboration to teacher expectation and attitude data. They help indicate other characteristics that teachers notice about students in particular expectation and attitude groups, as well as some of the reasons why teachers hold the expectations or attitudes that they hold. However, like any self-report data, teacher self-report data are distorted by halo effects, logical errors, and other sources of bias or inaccuracy.

The Willis and Brophy (1974) data on rejection students provide a good example. If you attend only to what the teachers had to say about these students, it is easy to see why the teachers rejected them, and also to see that teacher rejection was strong and unambiguous. However, when you inspect the objective test data from these students, you discover that teacher perceptions of their academic abilities were wrong. The teachers saw them as low ability students, but the test data showed that these students did not differ from their classmates in test scores. Thus, the teacher perceptions hang together nicely to make a consistent picture, but at least some of them were incorrect. This raises questions about the rest of them.

Concern about these and related questions led us to design the Student Attribute Study. We wanted to pursue the questions raised by the studies reviewed so far, but to try to answer them more definitively. One important aspect was to include a large sample of teachers and students. Studies involving small numbers of teachers are very sensitive to the unique attitudes and preferences of the teachers involved, so that their data may not be generalizable to other teachers. For example, we have seen that some teachers expect a sex difference in first-grade reading achievement and some do not, and that some teachers try to push concern students but other teachers try to minimize stress and move them along slowly through patience and encouragement.

These findings are not necessarily contradictory. They come from studies with small samples, and they might accurately reflect the attitudes and behaviors of the teachers involved. To try to avoid this problem, we wanted the Student Attribute Study to have a sample of teachers large enough to make it likely that such individual differences would cancel out. Thus, whatever findings emerged would be likely to generalize to most teachers.

We also wanted a broad and deep data bank, which included information thought to be objectively true and other data on teacher perceptions of unknown accuracy and teacher-student interactions of unknown meaning. By using the objective truth points as anchors, we could assess the accuracy of teacher perceptions and interpret the meaning of the teacher-student interactions.

Planning based on these considerations led to the longitudinal and complex study that we call the Student Attribute Study. The sample included 27 teachers and their students in four separate grades of elementary school. Data sets included teachers' expectations and attitudes; teachers' free response descriptions collected through interviews; and low inference coding of classroom behaviors and teacher-student interactions. By analyzing these data in relationship to one another simultaneously, we hoped to answer some of the questions raised or left unresolved by previous data. The data collection and analysis methods used in the Student Attribute Study will be described briefly in the following section, after which we will discuss the highlights of the findings.

METHODOLOGY

The Student Attribute Study was conducted in six elementary schools in an urban school district. Because of de facto segregation in housing and neighborhoods, most schools in the city were predominantly white Anglo, Chicano, or black. The schools involved in the study were overwhelmingly white Anglo in student population. There were a few black students, but not enough to analyze as a group. There also were a few students with Spanish surnames, but most of these lived in predominantly Anglo neighborhoods and spoke English as their primary or only language.

One school served a population which varied in SES from lower class to upper middle class. Its predominant orientation was upper middle class, however, because most of the students came from families connected with a nearby university. On the average, students at this school were brighter and more oriented toward education than students in the other schools, which were located in sections of town populated by working class Anglos. Few of these parents had college degrees, although most had finished high school and many had had vocational education. Most families were intact. The fathers typically worked at blue-collar jobs or low and middle level white-collar jobs. They were homogeneous in SES as well as in ethnicity. Most students came from homes that would be characterized as lower middle class or working class, with practically none from either clearly lower class or clearly upper middle class or upper class homes. Thus, the sample as a whole could be characterized as white middle class, and except for one predominantly upper middle class school, as lower middle class.

The teachers all were women varying in experience and age. Most were whites, although a few were blacks who had begun teaching in predominantly white schools several years previously as part of a "teacher crossover" plan to further desegregation. All teachers participated in the study voluntarily, although with varying degrees of enthusiasm. They were informed that the study concerned student attributes and how they affected teacher expectations, attitudes, and behavior, and they were briefed about the general design of the study and about what would be required of them. However, they never knew exactly what was being measured during classroom observations. Also, although they knew which students were being observed, they did not know the basis for student selection, and therefore could not have biased the results by systematically treating one group differently from another.

The observation phase conducted in the second year of the study involved 27 teachers, 6 in grade two, 5 in grade three, 10 in grade four, and 6 in grade five. The schools included the predominantly upper middle class school and three of the four working class schools included originally. A fifth school, very similar to the other working class Anglo schools, was included in the second year because the older students in one of the working class schools were transferred to a neighboring school to relieve overcrowding. Fortunately, most were transferred to the same school, so few students were lost for this reason.

All of the teachers except three in one school (who were team teaching) taught in self-contained classrooms. The teachers in the self-contained classrooms were asked to participate and all of them did, with teachers in grades one through four filling out ranking forms in the first year, and teachers in grades two through five doing it in the second year. The teachers were paid $25 for the time they spent filling out forms and being interviewed.

Rather than study whatever students happened to be enrolled in the classes of these teachers, we focused on target students who were *perceived consistently across almost two years and by two different teachers on one or more of 13 personal attributes*. Teacher self-report data were collected early, middle, and late in the first year of the study, and then again in the middle and at the end of the second year. The 13 scales measured student attributes that previous work had suggested as correlates of teacher expectations, attitudes, and behavior:

1. Calm versus restless
2. Careful versus careless
3. Happy versus unhappy
4. Probable high achiever versus probable low achiever
5. Mature versus immature
6. Cooperative versus not cooperative
7. Creative versus not creative
8. Attractive versus unattractive
9. Persistent versus gives up easily
10. Attachment (would like to keep in class again next year for the sheer joy of it) versus rejection (would like to have removed from class right now)
11. Concern (would like to have more time to spend with this student) versus low concern (does not feel that this student needs more time with teacher)
12. Noticeable versus not noticeable
13. Good eye contact versus avoids eye contact

By focusing our analyses on only those students who were perceived consistently across five sets of rankings by two different teachers on 1 or more of these 13 scales, we hoped to accomplish two things. First, the consistency across time and particularly across teachers increased the likelihood that the teachers' perceptions were accurate. Students perceived favorably by one teacher but unfavorably by another automatically were excluded, thus eliminating most instances of distorted teacher perceptions.

The second advantage of the consistency criterion was that the classroom behavior and general personal traits of the consistent students probably were stable in the past and likely to remain so in the future, compared to those of other students. This helped insure that the teachers' classifications were based on objective student characteristics. Our data (to be discussed) support the inference that the students actually were like the teachers said they were.

In the first year, the teachers were asked to rank all of their students on each of the 13 scales. To make sure that no one was left out, the teachers were provided with a complete class roster. The instructions and a sample scale are shown in Figures 5.1 and 5.2

The teachers found this procedure unduly cumbersome and time consuming. It was easy to rank students at the ends of the scales, but difficult to make meaningful rankings in the middles. We agreed with the teachers that attempts to make such fine distinctions were of questionable validity and thus not worth doing, so we simplified the procedure for the second year.

Instead of attempting to rank order their entire classes, teachers placed students into one of seven categories. In small classes, two were placed into each of the extreme categories (at the top and bottom of the page), three in each of the next most extreme categories, four in each of the next categories, and all of the rest in the middle category. In large classes, teachers placed three students in the extreme categories, four in the next, five in the next, and the rest in the middle (see Figures 5.3 and 5.4). In either case, the result was a seven-point, rank order scale that allowed the most extreme students to be given extreme scores but did not require the teachers to try to differentiate among those lumped together in the middle.

To get the data from the two years of study onto a common scale, rankings from the first year were converted into seven-point scales just like those from the second year. That is, the two students ranked highest on a scale were placed in the top category, then the next three, etc.

Identifying Target Students

Complete sets of four rankings were available on about 375 students. Of these, only 2 failed to meet our consistency criterion on any of the 13 scales. Thus, almost all students were consistent on at least one scale, and most were consistent on several (see Table 5.1). A few other students were dropped either because they moved out of the school when we were preparing to do classroom observa-

Figure 5.1. Instructions for Filling Out the Seven-Point Scales in Year 1.

For each scale, think of your whole class and rank all of your students from highest to lowest on each of the scales. If you feel that two or more students are about the same on a particular scale and you could not rank one higher than the other, just circle these names on the scale. Do not worry about making fine discrimination between students, but work through the scales fairly rapidly. Your first impressions are the ones that we want. .

Figure showing three handwritten ranking scales.

PROBABLE HIGHEST ACHIEVER   MATURE   COOPERATIVE, COMPLIANT

Mrs. M.   3rd grade

Andros, L.
Ballard, C.
Bonn, M.
Brodie, J.
Dempsey, J.
Christian, J.
Colter, C.
Crawford, W.
Durant, J.
Edgar, D.
Everts, C.
Garth, T.
Gonzales, L.
Heart, P.
Jackson, B.
Lindsey, T.
Miller, M.
Mitchell, A.
Neuman, G.
Nissen, R.
Ogden, J.
Rivers, D.
Sherman, G.
Sealer, H.
Temple, A.
Washington, W.
Weaver, S.

PROBABLE HIGHEST ACHIEVER	MATURE	COOPERATIVE, COMPLIANT
Edgar, D.	Miller, M.	Brodie, J.
Miller, M.	Christian, J.	Neuman, G.
Christian, J.	Neuman, G.	Miller, M.
Washington, W.	Edgar, D.	Edgar, D.
Neuman, G.	Lindsey, L.	Everts, C.
Ogden, J.	Washington, W.	Colter, C.
Everts, C.	Weaver, S.	Washington, W.
Temple, A.	Everts, C.	Christian, J.
Weaver, S.	Brodie, J.	Temple, A.
Brodie, J.	Temple, A.	Weaver, S.
Colter, C.	Nissen, R.	Crawford, W.
Gonzales, L.	Colter, C.	Sealer, H.
Crawford, W.	Gonzales, L.	Lindsey, L.
Sealer, H.	Andros, L.	Nissen, R.
Andros, L.	Crawford, W.	Durant, J.
Lindsey, T.	Sealer, H.	Rivers, D.
Nissen, R.	Ogden, J.	Dempsey, L.
Ballard, C.	Sherman, G.	Andros, L.
Bonn, M.	Ballard, C.	Gonzales, L.
Sherman, G.	Dempsey, L.	Heart, P.
Durant, J.	Heart, P.	Jackson, B.
Heart, P.	Jackson, B.	Ballard, C.
Dempsey, L.	Rivers, D.	Ogden, J.
Garth, T.	Durant, J.	Bonn, M.
Jackson, B.	Bonn, M.	Garth, T.
Mitchell, A.	Garth, T.	Sherman, G.
Rivers, D.	Mitchell, A.	Mitchell, A.

PROBABLE LOWEST ACHIEVER   IMMATURE   UNCOOPERATIVE, DEFIANT

Figure 5.2.   Sample Ranking Scales for Year 1.

60

Figure 5.3.   Instructions for Filling Out the Seven-Point Scales in Year 2.

For each scale, select your three highest and three lowest students and put their names in the highest and lowest sections of the scale. Then select your next four highest and lowest students and put their names in the next highest and lowest sections of the scale. Do the same thing for the next highest and lowest section. You may leave some blanks in this section if you feel that you do not have enough students whose names belong here. Put all the remaining students' names in the middle section. The students in each section of the scale will be considered to have the *same* ranking, so do not spend too much time making fine discriminations between students.

tions or because they had been assigned to a classroom where only two or three target students would be available. Given the large number of target students who were concentrated in greater numbers in other classrooms, it seemed inefficient to observe in classrooms where only a few target students were enrolled. Thus, we decided to concentrate on classrooms with larger clusters of target students (ranging from 7 to 14), thereby increasing the number of observations that could be made in each classroom.

Note that because most students were consistent (by our definition) on at least one scale, we ended up observing most students who had been present in their respective schools at the beginning of the first year and were still there in the middle of the second year. This came to 362 students in 27 classrooms, an average of more than 13 per class.

Classes averaged about 25 students each, so we observed about half of the students available. This and the sheer size of the sample leads us to believe that the students were representative of their respective schools. It is true that their residence had been stable for two years, and that most of those who were not included in the sample were from families who had moved into or out of the schools during the time span of the study. However, none of the neighborhoods was changing notably in SES or related indicators. The people moving in were similar to those who moved out.

All in all, the data seem generalizable to white working and middle class schools. It should be noted, however, that they might not generalize to upper middle or upper class schools or to schools populated primarily by nonwhite students or schools serving well-defined, white ethnic groups. This is particularly true of the data on sex differences, because these are known to vary by SES, race, and ethnicity. Finally, the data may not generalize directly to racially desegregated schools, where race might be an important factor.

Although target students were identified for observation in February, final classification was delayed until the fifth set of teacher rankings was collected in May. Recall that the scales were seven-point scales arranged so that few students

PROBABLE HIGHEST ACHIEVER | MATURE | COOPERATIVE, COMPLIANT

PROBABLE HIGHEST ACHIEVER

Edgar, D.
Miller, M.
Christian, J.
Washington, W.
Neuman, G.
Ogden, J.
Everts, C.
Temple, A.
Weaver, S.
Brodie, J.

Colter, C
Gonzales, L.
Crawford, W.
Sealer, H.
Andros, L
Lindsey, L.
Nissen, R.

Ballard, C
Bonn, M.
Sherman, G.

Durant, J.
Heart, P.
Dempsey, L.
Garth, T.
Jackson, B.
Mitchell, A.
Rivers, D.

PROBABLE LOWEST ACHIEVER

MATURE

Miller, M.
Christian, J.
Neuman, G.
Edgar, D.
Lindsey, T.
Washington, W.
Weaver, S.
Everts, C.
Brodie, J.

Temple, A.
Nissen, R.
Colter, C.
Gonzales, L.
Andros, L.
Crawford, W.
Sealer, H.

Ogden, J.
Sherman, G.
Ballard, C.
Dempsey, L.
Heart, P.
Jackson, B.
Rivers, D.
Durant, J.
Bonn, M.
Garth, T.
Mitchell, A.

IMMATURE

COOPERATIVE, COMPLIANT

Brodie, J.
Neuman, G.
Miller, M.
Edgar, D.
Everts, C.
Colter, C.
Washington, W.
Christian, J.
Temple, A.
Weaver, S.
Crawford, W.
Sealer, H.

Lindsey, L.
Nissen, R.
Durant, J.
Rivers, D.
Dempsey, L.
Andros, L.

Gonzales, L.
Heart, P.

Jackson, B.
Ballard, C.
Ogden, J.
Bonn, M.
Garth, T.
Sherman, G.
Mitchell, A.

UNCOOPERATIVE, DEFIANT

Mrs. M.   3rd grade

Andros, L.
Ballard, C.
Bonn, M.
Brodie, J.
Dempsey, L.
Christian, J.
Colter, C.
Crawford, W.
Durant, J.
Edgar, D.
Everts, C.
Garth, T.
Gonzales, L.
Heart, P.
Jackson, B.
Lindsey, T.
Miller, M.
Mitchell, A.
Neuman, G.
Nissen, R.
Ogden, J.
Rivers, D.
Sherman, G.
Sealer, H.
Temple, A.
Washington, W.
Weaver, S.

Figure 5.4.   Sample Ranking Scales for Year 2.

Table 5.1. Number of male and female students ranked consistently on one or more of the 13 scales for grades 2-5.

Number of consistent rankings	Grade 2 M	F	Grade 3 M	F	Grade 4 M	F	Grade 5 M	F	Total
13	0	0	0	0	1	1	0	0	2
12	0	3	1	3	2	3	0	3	15
11	4	3	3	1	6	7	3	4	31
10	1	4	4	2	10	18	4	6	49
9	6	8	7	11	11	16	4	2	65
8	5	4	5	4	17	7	3	2	47
7	10	5	8	3	10	6	3	3	48
6	3	3	10	10	8	7	3	1	45
5	2	5	1	5	2	3	2	3	23
4	1	1	3	1	2	2	2	2	14
3	1	1	4	1	5	2	1	0	15
2	1	0	0	1	2	1	0	3	8
1	0	0	0	0	0	0	0	0	0
	34	37	46	42	76	73	25	29	,362

were at the extremes and increasing numbers appeared as you moved toward the middle. A score of 1 was lowest and a score of 7 was highest. Three groups of consistently perceived students were identified. These were students whose rankings remained within the low, middle, or high ranges of the scales on all five of the teacher rankings for that scale. Students consistently ranked 1, 2, or 3 were classified as low for each scale; students consistently ranked 3, 4, or 5 were classified as middle for each scale; and students consistently ranked 5, 6, or 7 were classified as high for each scale.

The overlap between high and middle (at 5) and between middle and low (at 3) was allowed to reduce the shrinkage that occurred when the consistency criterion was applied across all five sets of rankings. The criterion for target student selection had to differentiate the low, middle, and high groups, but not be so strict as to exclude too many students. This method seemed to be a good solution to this problem.

An example of the data for a particular student is shown in Figure 5.5 (1, 2, 3 = L; 3, 4, 5 = M; 5, 6, 7 = H).

If students varied randomly from one ranking to the next, their chances of being classified in either the low or the high groups would be only 1 in 243 (one-third × one-third × one-third × one-third × one-third), or less than one-half of one percent. If this had been the case, we would have ended up classifying

Student #412	Rankings 1 2 3 4 5	Final classification
(female, 4th grade)		
Calm	7 6 7 7 6	Consistently high
Careful	4 2 3 6 5	Inconsistent
Happy	4 2 3 2 5	Inconsistent
Achieving	2 2 4 4 4	Inconsistent
Mature	3 3 5 4 6	Inconsistent
Cooperative	3 4 3 4 5	Consistently Middle
Creative	1 2 4 2 4	Inconsistent
Attractive	3 3 4 3 5	Consistently Middle
Persistent	6 6 7 6 7	Consistently High
Attachment	3 4 6 5 3	Inconsistent
Concern	6 5 3 4 5	Inconsistent
Noticeable	5 4 4 2 2	Inconsistent
Eye Contact	2 2 4 4 5	Inconsistent

Figure 5.5. Example showing how teachers' rankings of students on the 13 scales were classified as Consistent (High, Middle, or Low) or Inconsistent.

only about two students in each of the three "consistent" categories for each scale. However, as can be seen in Table 5.2, despite this fairly strict criterion for consistency, the numbers of students classified as consistent far exceeded chance in all three positions on each scale.

Most of the analyses discussed are based on data from these consistent students. Data from all target students were available on all measures, of course, but in considering a particular scale, we included only data from the consistent students for most analyses.

Students who did not meet the consistency criteria and thus were not classified as high, middle, or low on a given scale were classified into one of three other categories: upward movers, downward movers, or inconsistent. Upward movers were those who showed a continually upward movement in their rankings across the five sets, or who started low and then moved up to a plateau and stayed there. Downward movers showed the opposite pattern, starting high but dropping consistently across each set of rankings or reaching a low plateau and staying there. The remaining students were inconsistent. They moved around in the rankings sufficiently to exclude them from the three consistent groups, but their movement was not consistently upward or downward.

Some had score patterns like 3, 4, 2, 5, 6. In this case, the first three rankings from the year-one teacher indicated a low-to-middle view of the student on the

Table 5.2. Numbers of students ranked consistently high, middle and low for each of the 13 scales (Year 1 & 2 combined).

	Low	Medium	High	Total
Calm	56	112	69	237
Careful	58	110	77	245
Happy	37	101	51	189
Achieving	72	124	88	284
Mature	62	123	72	257
Cooperative	48	119	65	232
Creative	38	101	54	193
Attractive	47	104	52	203
Persistent	54	112	78	244
Attachment	39	95	67	201
Concern	63	99	45	207
Noticeable	40	93	57	190
Eye Contact	29	90	35	154

scale in question, while the rankings from the second-year teacher were higher. This type of inconsistency indicated a difference of opinion between the two teachers (perhaps based on change in the student from one year to the next).

Another kind of inconsistency is typified by a student with a score pattern such as 5, 2, 1, 5, 4. This pattern is inconsistent in the first year, dropping to a very low ranking after being medium to high. The drop was not maintained in the second year, however, so that the student was not classified as a downward mover but simply as inconsistent. Something presumably happened in the first year to cause the drop, but we seldom were in a position to find out what because we did not collect classroom observation data or detailed teacher interview data the first year. Thus, little will be said about these inconsistent students, except to note that they did occur with some regularity.

Classroom Observations

The classroom observation data were based on a coding system (Brophy et al., 1974) devised specifically for this study. We wanted to measure the classroom activity patterns and the quality of teacher-student relationships involving students rated consistently by their teachers on all 13 scales. The system allows for coding of the classroom activity of the target students in various contexts, and is addressed in particular to the affective aspects of teacher-student interaction. The system had three major divisions: public response opportunities, private interactions, and behavior-related interactions.

Public Response Opportunities.   These were academic interactions occurring in front of other students. We considered two situations in which such interactions occur: general class (the entire class is involved in a recitation or question-and-answer session) and small group (only a few students are involved in an academic activity with the teacher). This distinction seemed important because much teaching occurs in small group settings in the early grades, and we expected to see some differences in interaction patterns between the two settings. All of the categories discussed below were coded in either context.

1. *Method of selection.* We were interested in how students were chosen to answer questions in class. One of the following four categories was used to describe selection.

a. *Nonvolunteer.* The teacher called on a student to answer who had not raised a hand and had not called out the answer.

b. *Volunteer.* The teacher called on a student who had raised a hand to volunteer in a calm and patient manner.

c. *Wave.* The teacher called on a volunteer who had waved a hand enthusiastically, indicating eagerness to respond.

d. *Call out.* The teacher responded to a student who had called out the answer without being called on by the teacher first.

2. *Teacher feedback to answer.* We were interested in any evaluative response given by the teacher to students' answers.

    a. *Praise.* The teacher praised the answer.

    b. *Criticism.* The teacher criticized the answer. (Note that these categories referred only to teacher responses to the quality of the answer, not to the student's behavior. Praise or criticism of behavior is discussed in the section on behavior-related interactions.)

Private Interactions. These were contacts between the teacher and student that were essentially private, although other students might overhear them. Besides being interested in how many and what kind of contacts occurred, we wanted to know whether they were initiated by the teacher or the student. We also wanted to know how the noninitiator of the interaction reacted to the initiator.

With these needs in mind, we developed the following categories of private interactions. *Work-related contacts,* either teacher initiated or student initiated, were interactions involving discussion between the teacher and a single student about that student's work. *Housekeeping contacts,* either teacher initiated or student initiated, dealt with nonacademic jobs necessary for the class to run smoothly. For example, the teacher might ask a student, or a student might request to pass out books, carry a note to the office, or feed the fish in the aquarium. *Personal contacts,* either teacher initiated or student initiated, included nonacademic needs of one individual not relevant to the entire class. These might be sharpening a pencil, going to the bathroom or water fountain, locating a sweater, or cleaning up the area around one's desk. *Social contacts,* either teacher initiated or student initiated, involved interactions between the teacher and student that could be called social in nature since they did not concern any needs to be met. For example, there might be comments on new clothes, an upcoming trip or holiday, or a student's family.

In addition to these categories of contacts which could be initiated by either teacher or student, we recorded two other kinds of student initiations. *Approval seeking* was noted when a student approached the teacher with work, but obviously was not seeking help. Instead, he or she was expecting to show the teacher good work and receive praise for it. For example, the student might say, "Look how much I've done so far!" *Tattling* on another student was also noted.

Once an interaction was classified into one of these six categories, it was then further described in terms of who initiated it, whether the teacher or the student responded emotionally, how long it lasted, and other pertinent information, depending on the type of interaction. Below is an outline of the categories used to further describe each type of interaction.

    1. *Work-related Contacts.*

        a. *Teacher initiated.* The teacher approached the student to begin the interaction. Three types of information were recorded.

            (1). *Quality.* This was noted in order to describe the involvement or effort expended in the contact. The teacher could observe without saying anything, there could be a brief verbal interaction (only one to two sentences) or there could be a long verbal interaction.

(2). *Evaluation.* If the teacher praised or criticized a student's work after initiating this contact, it was noted.

(3). *Student emotional reaction.* If the student responded in either an extremely positive, happy manner or an extremely negative, unhappy manner, it was noted.

b. *Student initiated.* The student approached the teacher with a question about school work. (Note: This category does not include behaviors classified under approval seeking.) Two types of information were recorded.

(1). *Quality.* Again, this described the effort expended by the teacher in the contact. The teacher could refuse to listen to the student, have a brief contact, or a long contact.

(2). *Teacher emotional or evaluative reaction.* If the teacher offered praise or criticism of the work or seemed extremely impatient with the student, the response was noted.

2. *Housekeeping Contacts.*

a. *Teacher initiated.* The teacher approached a student and asked that student to perform some classroom errand. In addition to noting when this occurred, two other characteristics of the interaction were noted if relevant.

(1). *Thanks.* If the teacher thanked the student after the job was done, it was noted.

(2). *Reward.* If the teacher presented the request as a reward for good behavior, it was noted. For example, the teacher might say, "Because you have finished your work first, I'm going to let you take this note to the office."

b. *Student initiated.* The student approached the teacher and asked to do a job or run an errand. Three types of information were recorded about such interactions.

(1). *Refusal or approval.* It was noted whether the teacher allowed the student to perform the job or not.

(2). *Thanks.* If the teacher thanked the student after doing the job, this was noted.

(3). *Reward.* If the teacher gave permission to do the job and presented it as a reward for good behavior, this was noted.

3. *Personal Contacts.*

a. *Teacher initiated.* The teacher approached the student about fulfilling some personal responsibilities. In addition to noting that this occurred, the student's reaction was noted when it was either extremely positive and happy or negative and unhappy.

b. *Student initiated.* The student approached the teacher with a request concerning some personal need. Three types of information were recorded.

(1). *Refusal or approval.* It was noted whether or not the teacher let the student do what the student wanted.

(2). *Teacher emotional reaction.* When the teacher responded in an extremely positive, happy way or an extremely negative, unhappy way, this was noted accordingly.

(3). *Reward.* If the teacher approved the request and stated that it was due to the student's good behavior, this was noted.

4. *Social Contacts.*

a. *Teacher initiated.* The teacher approached the student and began a conversation about a social topic. Besides noting that this occurred, the student's emotional reaction was recorded if it was either extremely positive and happy or extremely negative and unhappy.

b. *Student initiated.* The student approached the teacher and brought up some social topic. The teacher's reaction was described as refusal (the teacher would not listen to the student), brief (the teacher gave some minimal attention and response to the student's initiation), or long (the teacher interacted with the student in a social contact with more than a brief comment).

5. *Approval seeking* (student initiated only). Two types of information were recorded.

a. *Refusal or feedback.* It was noted whether the teacher responded to the student with some feedback about the work or refused to listen to the approval seeking.

b. *Praise or criticism.* When the teacher praised or criticized the student's work, it was noted.

6. *Tattling* (student initiated only). When a student went to the teacher to tattle on a classmate, the teacher's response was noted: either listening to the student (approving), or rejecting his or her attempt to tattle.

Behavior-related Interactions. These formed the third major category of behaviors coded in the system. They were noted whenever a target student was approached by the teacher and contacted concerning the student's behavior. When this occurred, three types of information about the contact were noted: the student's behavior that caused the teacher to interact with him or her, the type of behavioral correction delivered by the teacher, and the student's emotional reaction to the correction.

1. *Student behaviors.* The type of misbehavior leading to the correction was noted. Student misbehaviors were classified into typical misbehaviors, both disruptive and nondisruptive, aggression directed toward the teacher, aggression directed toward peers, poor coping behavior, and noninteractive, antisocial behavior.

2. *Teacher responses to student behavior.* There were six possible ways in which the teacher could respond to the behavior. They are listed below in order of increasing severity.

a. *Praise* was recorded when the teacher liked the behavior and said so.

b. *Nonverbal intervention* was noted when the teacher gestured or used a facial expression to show displeasure.

c. *Management* was coded when the teacher gave a behavioral correction or direction in a noncritical, nonthreatening, calm manner.

    d. *Warnings* involved a more severe correction which implied a threat, although this was not stated. The teacher's voice had obvious irritation, although the teacher was not greatly angered.

    e. *Threats* were coded when the teacher specifically threatened punishment if the behavior did not stop or was not corrected.

    f. *Criticism* was the harshest level of teacher correction. It involved either extreme anger and/or punishment.

    3. *Student response to teacher correction.* Whenever the student responded in either an obviously cowed manner (acting humiliated and mortified) or a sullen and defiant manner, it was noted.

In addition to the three major parts of the coding system (response opportunities, private contacts, and behavior-related contacts), observers noted any adult critical incidents whenever they occurred. These included:

    1. Appointing a student as a monitor to take names while the teacher was out of the room

    2. Holding up a student as a good example in front of the entire class

    3. Holding up a student as a bad example in front of the entire class

    4. Flattery

    5. Physical affection

Preparation of Classroom Observation Data for Analyses

The coding system was used by 17 classroom observers who familiarized themselves with it and practiced using it until they were able to reach a criterion of 80 percent or better agreement with one or more partners in each of the major categories of the system. Practice coding was done in classrooms that were observed later, and it focused on target students who would be included in the study. Thus, the practice phase involved coding under realistic conditions. It accomplished the task of familiarizing the teachers and students to the presence of classroom observers at the same time the observers were familiarizing themselves with the system.

Observers could begin to accumulate data that would be used in later analyses as soon as they reached reliability criteria, although sometimes they continued to practice a little longer in certain classes because they had not yet memorized the code numbers of the target students. Each target student had a unique number, and all interactions involving this student were coded with this identification number so that they could be tabulated later. Raw codes were punched and tallied for each target student and each classroom, using a computerized tallying program developed specifically for this purpose (Crawford and Washington, 1974).

Each observer coded a given classroom five times. Observation periods included either an entire morning or an entire afternoon. Two separate observers were assigned to each classroom to minimize observer bias effects. This arrangement meant that each classroom was observed for a total of ten half days, or about 20 hours.

A total of 164 variables were derived from the raw coding through tabulation of frequency measures (such as "number of small group response opportunities") or computation of proportion measures (such as "percentage of teacher responses to misbehavior which were nonverbal interventions"). For analyses of differences by grade and sex of student, these raw scores were used.

Scores had to be standardized, however, for all analyses involving data on individual students. This was because different classrooms, grades, and even schools had different norms for many of the behaviors we measured. For example, small group instruction occurs for much of the day in the early grades because it is relied upon for teaching beginning reading. However, it begins to disappear around fourth grade, and is seldom seen thereafter.

The ideal way to adjust individual scores to take such group differences into account is to standardize scores separately for each classroom, so that each student's score on a variable reflects his or her status with respect to immediate classmates, not all other students in the study. However, standardization by individual classrooms was not feasible in this study, because the number of target students sometimes was too low. Therefore, we did the next best thing, standardizing scores within schools and grade levels. Thus, each student's score on each variable represents his or her status relative to other students in the same grade at that school.

This means that school averages and grade averages in the standardized scores are equal, and that many school and grade effects on individual scores have been eliminated. The standardized scores still were affected by individual teacher differences which were not controlled through the standardization process. The primary effect of any systematic teacher differences would be to increase the error variance in the student-level analyses, and thus reduce the number and strength of significant relationships. This probably happened, but not to any significant degree (i.e., there were many significant and near-significant relationships uncovered by the analyses).

Future research efforts could involve the use of the student as the unit of analysis in conjunction with the identification of teacher or class-related variance. This is possible through the use of deviation scores computed by subtracting each individual student's score from the mean of that individual's class. This process permits the study of within-class effects. Between-class effects could be examined (when the student is the unit of investigation) by assigning each student the class mean. The usefulness of these kinds of analyses in educational research has only recently become a topic of interest, and future research efforts might well benefit from them.

Selection of Data to Present in this Book

Analyses of variance of the scores of students ranked consistently high, middle, and low on each of the 13 ranking scales were computed for each of the 164 measures derived from the classroom coding system. Tables presenting these data are included in the technical report (Brophy et al., 1980). Only 73 of these measures are discussed in this book.

Measures were eliminated for a variety of reasons. Sixteen overlapped so closely with one or more other measures that they did not add any new information and were not worth retaining. Another 20 were dropped because they dealt with events that occurred too seldom to generate meaningful data.

The remaining 128 variables were reduced further by eliminating most of those that showed no significant relationships with consistent teacher rankings on the 13 scales, as well as those which showed only isolated and relatively weak relationships. In general, we retained only those measures that showed at least one relationship significant at the .01 (not just the .05) level of probability. Of the 128 measures considered, 60 met this criterion. This number was increased to 73 by adding selected measures chosen because they provided useful comparisons with variables that did meet the cut-off criterion or because they reflected teacher or student affect. For example, several measures of teacher praise that did not show any significant relationships were retained for discussion because of the general interest in praise, the belief that it reflects teacher affect or attempts to reinforce students, and the fact that several parallel measures of teacher criticism did meet the criterion.

Thus, the final set of variables discussed in this book include 60 that showed at least one relationship significant at the .01 level of probability, and another 13 added for comparison or interest value.

Teachers' Adjective Descriptions

During interviews conducted after classroom observations had been completed, the teachers were requested to supply three adjectives or brief phrases describing what they saw as the most salient or characteristic attribute of each target student.

Our main purpose in collecting these free response descriptions from the teachers was to discover student attributes that we had not included among the 13 scales. The free response format allowed the teachers to describe students in their own words, but it also meant that we had to develop a coding system to categorize synonymous or very similar descriptions together. This is a time-consuming process, even when relatively few adjectives are involved, so it was necessary to limit the number of responses made about each student. This limit also standardized the number of statements made, and thus made the students more directly comparable. The procedure was generally effective, although a few teachers gave more than three adjectives or gave two that later were coded as synonymous.

After an initial category system was developed, adjectives were scored separately by two independent raters, with differences resolved by discussion where possible. If adjectives could not be agreed upon as belonging in one of the categories they were placed into a residual category. A detailed account of the scoring system, including a complete list of all adjectives given and of how they were classified, is contained in Anderson et al. (1975).

The original responses were grouped and ultimately sorted into the categories shown in Table 5.3. Each category included several different adjectives and short descriptions, but for convenience of communication we have chosen a single adjective or phrase to characterize the category as a whole. Most of the terms are self-explanatory, although a few require comment.

Sociable (1) refers to friendliness and sociability in interaction, mostly with peers. Helpful (5) refers mostly to willingness or even eagerness to help the teacher by running errands or doing favors. However, it includes perceptions of general willingness to abide by teacher requests. Still, it has a more narrow and specific meaning than well behaved (6), which refers to students' general classroom conduct.

Motivated (8) refers to the degree to which the student appeared to be self-motivated in working on assignments and thus not in need of external pressure or reinforcement from the teacher. Good worker (11) refers to attentiveness, care, and persistence in working on seatwork assignments. Although there is a degree of correlation, for obvious reasons, good worker is independent from achieving (10), which refers to general student success in mastering the curriculum, independent of the work habits described under good worker.

Popular (12) refers to peer popularity, or the degree to which students were well liked by their peers. It differs somewhat from sociable (1) in that students classified as sociable were those who often initiated social interactions with peers. These highly sociable students were not necessarily popular with their peers, and not all students who were popular were particularly sociable. Both of these peer interaction categories also differ from social leader (24). Social leaders were students looked up to for leadership by the peer group. They were not necessarily highly sociable or even highly popular, although they usually were the latter.

Active (15) refers to sheer activity level, but aggressive (13) refers to hostile interactions with peers. Students classified as active were physically active but not necessarily aggressive. Those classified as aggressive were bullies or others who frequently got into disagreements or fights. Temperamental (18) refers to students who became upset easily, cried when frustrated, or were generally immature in emotional development. Temperamental does not have an aggressive connotation, however. In fact, the students classified as temperamental were in many ways the opposites of students classified as aggressive.

Humorous (21) included students described as having a good sense of humor, students described as being funny, and students described as being silly in their classroom antics. Likeable (25) refers to the degree to which students were perceived as likeable by the teacher. Students classified here were not necessarily well liked by their classmates. In contrast to likeable, which refers to students' general appeal to the teachers, attractive (26) is limited to perceptions of students' physical attractiveness. Students seen as attractive in a more personal sense were classified as likeable.

Students classified as dependent (27) were seen as particularly dependent on the teacher for continuous help, guidance, or reassurance.

Good home (28) refers to teacher statements that the student came from a

Table 5.3.   Adjective Description Variables Used Frequently by Teachers

		% of total adjectives used by teachers that were classified in each category.
1.	Sociable	4
2.	Mature	2
3.	Happy	3
4.	Quiet	6
5.	Helpful	5
6.	Well behaved	3
7.	Confident	3
8.	Motivated	5
9.	Intelligent	6
10.	Achieving	6
11.	Good Worker	9
12.	Popular	3
13.	Aggressive	1
14.	Responsible	1
15.	Active	2
16.	Considerate	2
17.	Inattentive	1
18.	Temperamental	1
19.	Unobtrusive	1
20.	Athletic	1
21.	Humorous	1
22.	Other Negative	2
23.	Other Positive	4
24.	Social Leader	1
25.	Likeable	3
26.	Attractive	3
27.	Dependent	1
28.	Good Home	7
29.	Creative	2
30.	Medical Problems	2

31.	Often Absent	1
32.	Sweet	1
33.	Underachiever	1
34.	Cries Easily	2
35.	Untrustworthy	1
36.	Broken Home	$\frac{2}{99\%}$

good home, that the student had been well prepared for school by the parents, that the parents were especially cooperative, and so on. Cries easily (34) is similar to temperamental (18), except that it refers specifically to students' tendency to cry when frustrated or to whine or pout when upset. These students also were included as a subset of the students classified as temperamental. However, many other students not so prone to cry also were included in the temperamental category.

Untrustworthy (35) students were those described as likely to lie, cheat, steal, copy, or be generally sneaky and untrustworthy in their behavior. These students had no credibility with the teachers because they had done such things frequently, so much so that the teachers mentioned them when asked to give their three most characteristic attributes.

Categories 1–21 and 24–36 occurred with sufficient frequency (at least 1 percent of the responses) to be useful for statistical analyses. In addition to these categories, there were many others with frequencies too low to be useful. However, most of the adjectives in them still could be classified as generally positive or generally negative in their implications about the students. Those that seemed to be clearly positive in their implications about the students (gentle, well rounded, dignified) were grouped into an "other positive" category (23). Similarly, leftover descriptions that seemed to be clearly negative in their connotations about the students (tattletale, clumsy, selfish) were grouped into an "other negative" category (22). A few descriptions that could not be classified either way (animal lover, low-key person) were not used at all.

Finally, a percent-positive score was computed for students by dividing the number of positive statements made about them by the total of positive and negative statements. As an example of the process, consider the adjectives given by the teacher describing Student # 412.

412 is quiet, well behaved, and gets along well with her friends. She was absent a great deal at the beginning of the year due to chronic tonsillitis, but is now better after having her tonsils and adenoids removed.

This information was scored as follows (category numbers refer to Table 5.3):

- "Quiet"—a positive score in category 4 (quiet)
- "Well behaved"—a positive score in category 6 (well behaved)

- "Gets along well with her friends"—a positive score in category 12 (popular)
- "Absent due to tonsillitis"—noted as present in categories 30 (medical problems) and 31 (often absent) [Percent positive equal 100: $(100 \times 3 \div 3$; all three adjectives given were positive in tone, and the medical information was nonevaluative]

Although we have used brief terms in Table 5.3 to facilitate communication, it should be kept in mind that many of the categories actually were bipolar categories that allowed for scoring students as low versus high on the variable. Other categories were unipolar ones on which students were scored 1 if the category was used in describing them and scored 0 if it was not.

Categories 1–12 and 24 were bipolar. Thus, sociable (1) really is "sociable versus unsociable." Students described as sociable were scored 2 on this variable, and students described as unsociable, shy, or socially withdrawn were scored 1. Similarly, the mature category (2) includes students described as immature, the happy category (3) includes students described as unhappy, and so on. In each case, the descriptor given in Table 5.3 indicates the characteristics of students scored high on the variable.

These variables were scored only for students mentioned as either high or low on the characteristic. All of them except for well behaved (6) and achieving (10) had two categories, high and low. The others had three categories. Students described as well behaved were scored 3, students described as having mild behavior problems were scored 2, and students described as having severe behavior problems were scored 1. Similarly, students described as high achievers were scored 3, students described as average achievers were scored 2, and students described as low achievers were scored 1.

Analyses involving these bipolar categories involved comparisons only among those students scored for the category. Thus, for these categories, the students scored low were compared with those scored high (for well behaved and achieving, three groups were compared). In contrast, all students were included in analyses involving unipolar scales. Students scored 1 for the variable were compared with all other students, who were scored 0.

Categories 13–27 and 29–36 were scored as unipolar categories because teachers mentioned students as social leaders, likeable, attractive, or teacher dependent, but they did not mention the opposites of these adjectives often enough to form bipolar categories. Ten of the categories based on teachers' adjective descriptions are synonymous in varying degrees with 10 of our 13 ranking scales: Calm (active), careful (good worker), achieving (achieving), mature (mature), cooperative (well behaved), attractive (attractive), persistent (motivated), happy (happy), creative (creative), and noticeable (unobtrusive).

Although the correspondence is less exact, the adjective description category likeable (25) is similar to the attachment scale. Thus, of the 13 scales, only 2 did not appear in some form in the adjective descriptions: concern and eye contact. The absence of eye contact is not surprising. First, most students apparently maintain eye contact regularly. Perhaps more importantly, those who do not probably were described with more general terms like shy or withdrawn than with specific descriptions of eye contact.

The remaining scale, concern, does not appear directly in any of the adjective descriptions, but it is easy to see that many of them would be related to teacher concern. It is reasonable to suppose, for example, that teachers would not be concerned about students described as happy, well behaved, or achieving, and that they would be concerned about students described as aggressive, temperamental, or underachieving.

The free response mode used in collecting adjective descriptions did succeed in supplementing our self-report data on students by introducing a variety of variables that do not appear on the 13 scales: sociability, quiet versus talkative, helpfulness toward the teacher, self-confidence, intelligence, popularity, aggression toward peers, responsibility, consideration for others, attentiveness, frustration tolerance, athletic ability, humorousness, social leadership, and the home backgrounds and general health of the students. This information proved helpful in determining some of the reasons why teachers ranked students as they did.

In general, the data in Table 5.3 suggest that the teachers perceived the students generally positively. If this is real, it may be another example of the familiarity effect noted in social psychology (Zajonc, 1968). Several studies have indicated that sheer familiarity breeds attraction. That is, individuals who share continuing and close relationships with one another for initially accidental reasons typically "grow on" and begin to like one another. Other experiments suggest that simple familiarity with a stimulus is likely to make it preferable to unfamiliar stimuli. Perhaps dynamics like these even affect perception, tending to make people see the positive and ignore or rationalize the negative in others with whom they are going to have to live together and get along.

6

Relationships among the Thirteen Scales

Perception is not automatic. We can see very different things in precisely the same situation depending upon our *perceptual set*. This term refers to a predisposition to notice, or even an active looking for, certain things rather than others. When we enter a situation with a clear perceptual set, we are set to perceive information relevant to our present concerns. This makes us especially likely to notice these things and not to notice others.

For example, suppose you are passing the display window of a department store. If you have made an appointment to meet a friend in front of the store, you will pay no attention to the display in the store window. Instead, you will concentrate on the people in an effort to pick out your friend. On the other hand, if you were window shopping without anticipating meeting a friend, you would notice the window display (and perhaps not notice a friend who happened to be passing by).

Perceptual sets structure what is noticed in the classroom, too. As with other institutions, schools have particular functions and well-established roles for those who populate them and fulfill their functions.

The teacher role includes organizing and running the classroom as an administrative unit, teaching the curriculum, and enforcing codes of conduct. These aspects of the teacher role tend to focus teachers' perceptions of students on student attributes most relevant to the role.

These attributes cluster together to form a student role which complements the teacher role. Students are expected to learn and follow codes of conduct at school and to master the curriculum, under the direction of the teacher. As a result of all of this, teachers do not perceive students simply as unique individuals perceiving other unique individuals. Because of a perceptual set focusing on these roles, teachers usually perceive students from the perspective of teachers and perceive the students in their roles as students. Student attributes most relevant to the everyday functioning of the classroom as a whole and to the academic progress of individual students are given primary attention, with correspondingly less attention to less relevant attributes. As a result, most teachers are much more aware of student attributes like classroom conduct, work habits, and achievement than they are of attributes like peer popularity or athletic skills.

Concentration on attributes of major concern can produce halo effects, or distortions of perception that occur because an observer develops a general impression of the person being observed, and this general impression influences perceptions of more specific attributes. Favorable impressions are likely to lead to favorable ratings on the specific attributes, and unfavorable impressions to lead to unfavorable ratings.

We expected halo effects in the teacher ratings, even though the teachers had had several months to observe and interact with their students, because teachers tend to be preoccupied with student attributes important to teacher and student roles. Specifically, we expected that students perceived favorably on achievement and/or conduct would also be perceived favorably on other attributes.

INTERCORRELATIONS OF THE THIRTEEN SCALES

Correlation coefficients indicating the degrees of relationship observed among the 13 scales are shown in Tables 6.1 and 6.2. The correlations in Table 6.1 are based on data from all target students on whom complete sets of ratings were available ($N = 360$), and were computed by calculating a mean rating on each scale for each student and then correlating these means. The correlations in Table 6.2 indicate the same relationships but were computed using only the data from students consistently perceived as high, medium, or low on the scales across the two years of investigation.

If each scale were utterly unrelated to all other scales, all correlations in Tables 6.1 and 6.2 would be zero. However, it is clear at a glance that the scales are highly intercorrelated. Eleven of the 13 correlated positively with one another in varying degrees, and all 11 of these correlated negatively with the concern scale, as expected. Only the noticeable scale did not consistently fit this pattern. In retrospect, we realized that this was because the noticeable scale only asked the teacher to state which students stood out; it did not mention the reasons why the students stood out. These and other data from the study indicate that some teachers listed students as noticeable because they stood out for positive reasons (good achievement, good conduct, etc.), while others chose students as noticeable for negative reasons (primarily misconduct).

Except for the noticeable scale, then, the intercorrelations shown in Tables 6.1 and 6.2 indicate that the scales were related, often quite strongly. In particular, there were high intercorrelations between calm, careful, achieving, mature, cooperative, and persistent, the scales that relate most directly to good work habits and successful school achievement. Also, these same six scales correlated strongly with the teacher attitudes of attachment and concern. Teachers tended to like students who were high on the scales and to be concerned about students who were low on them. The correlations for happy, creative, attractive, and eye contact followed this same general pattern, but much less strongly.

The fact that all 11 scales measuring attributes typically valued by teachers

Table 6.1. Intercorrelations of Mean Teacher Rankings of All Students.[1]

	Careful	Mature	Achieving	Creative	Persistent	Happy	Attractive	Noticeable	Eye Contact	Cooperative	Attachment	Concern
Calm	.54***	.52***	.35***	.13**	.49***	.29***	.19***	-.15**	.17***	.60***	.47***	-.35***
Careful		.61***	.63***	.31***	.73***	.33***	.33***	.14**	.33***	.55***	.51***	-.51***
Mature			.61***	.40***	.63***	.34***	.24***	.12*	.33***	.58***	.53***	-.48***
Achieving				.45***	.61***	.22***	.30***	.31***	.37***	.40***	.47***	-.56***
Creative					.33***	.19***	.31***	.30***	.30***	.19***	.30***	-.32***
Persistent						.43***	.33***	.18***	.35***	.58***	.60***	-.52***
Happy							.35***	.24***	.34***	.40***	.42***	-.30***
Attractive								.24***	.27***	.30***	.39***	-.24***
Noticeable									.30***	-.04	.13*	-.19***
Eye Contact										.22***	.39***	-.29***
Cooperative											.56***	-.46***
Attachment												-.42***

[1] These correlations are for all target students, not just those perceived consistently on each scale. Scales means were used when scores were missing. Many correlations were statistically significant because N was high (360).

*p < .05

**p < .01

***p < .001

Table 6.2. Intercorrelations among the 13 scales for students perceived as consistently high, middle, or low on each scale.

	Careful	Mature	Achieving	Creative	Persistent	Happy	Attractive	Noticeable	Eye Contact	Cooperative	Attachment	Concern
Calm	.76***	.69***	.46***	.23**	.71***	.50***	.33***	-.25**	.30**	.82***	.77***	-.53***
Careful		.75***	.79***	.48***	.90***	.54***	.55***	.25**	.57***	.76***	.77***	-.74***
Mature			.75***	.61***	.81***	.55***	.38***	.21*	.55***	.74***	.77***	-.74***
Achieving				.69***	.79***	.55***	.45***	.49***	.63***	.57***	.68***	-.77***
Creative					.52***	.40***	.54***	.52***	.64***	.33***	.52***	-.54***
Persistent						.70***	.53***	.32**	.64***	.78***	.82***	-.79***
Happy							.59***	.43***	.68***	.65***	.71***	-.54***
Attractive								.39***	.50***	.47***	.58***	-.41***
Noticeable									.72***	-.08	.25*	-.33***
Eye Contact										.44***	.68***	-.52***
Cooperative											.84***	-.70***
Attachment												-.69***

* p   .05

** p   .01

*** p   .001

81

(and by society generally) intercorrelated positively with one another, and also correlated negatively with the measure of teacher concern, indicates a degree of halo effect in the teacher ratings. That is, students viewed positively in any particular respect tended to be viewed positively in general, and students viewed negatively in any particular respect tended to be viewed negatively in general. Comparison of Table 6.1 with Table 6.2 indicates that this tendency was especially noticeable for the students who were perceived consistently on the scales (the correlations in Table 6.2 are consistently higher than the corresponding correlations in Table 6.1).

Cross-Tabulations

To illustrate the relationships among the rating scales more graphically, we have prepared the cross-tabulations shown in Table 6.3. This table indicates, for each pair of scales, the numbers of students that the teachers classified into each of the four possible combinations of high and low scores. To the extent that two scales are positively correlated, a student high on one scale is likely to be high on the other, and a student low on one scale is likely to be low on the other. In this case, scores will pile up in these two cells, and few students will be classified in the cells representing high scores on the first scale and low scores on the second, or in the cells representing low scores on the first scale and high scores on the second.

A contrasting situation that appears when two scales are unrelated is that roughly equal numbers of students appear in each of the four cells. As you can see in Table 6.3, this was not the case. Scores pile up in the high-high and low-low cells, except for the noticeable scale already discussed and the concern scale. Actually, the concern scale has the same kinds of strong relationships to the other scales as they do to one another. The difference is that the scores pile up in the opposite cells because this scale correlated negatively with other scales. Consequently, whereas a student ranked high in persistence would be expected to rank high in achievement or maturity as well, a low ranking would be expected on the concern scale. Similarly, most students ranked high in concern would be expected to rank low on the other scales.

Study the table to fully appreciate the magnitude of these relationships. Notice, for example, that the careful, achieving, and persistent scales did not contain a single exception to the prevailing pattern. A total of 36 children were listed as both highly persistent and high in achievement, and 52 children were listed as low in both. Not a single child of 360 was perceived as consistently high in achievement but low in persistence or (more probably) high in persistence but low in achievement.

In part, relationships like this occur for methodological reasons. We asked the teachers to rank the students on these scales separately, doing nothing to encourage them to think about the scales in combination. It is likely that teachers would have nominated certain students if we had asked something like, "Are there students in your class who will work long and hard at their assignments but still

		Care-ful		Mature		Achiev-ing		Cre-ative		Per-sistent		Happy		Attrac-tive		Notice-able		Eye Contact		Coop-erative		Attach-ment		Concern	
		L	H	L	H	L	H	L	H	L	H	L	H	L	H	L	H	L	H	L	H	L	H	L	H
Calm	Low	35	0	32	1	27	6	9	6	30	0	14	3	13	2	2	16	11	6	31	0	21	0	3	21
	High	0	34	1	37	5	33	2	15	1	34	2	23	5	15	12	10	3	13	0	40	0	34	25	3
Careful	Low			39	1	39	0	16	5	37	0	13	1	18	1	6	7	12	2	28	0	22	0	3	27
	High			1	45	0	52	1	25	0	60	1	26	1	21	3	21	1	20	1	41	1	41	38	0
Mature	Low					41	1	21	2	37	0	12	1	17	2	8	5	15	0	31	1	23	0	1	25
	High					1	49	1	25	1	48	0	27	5	18	7	18	2	17	1	42	2	44	35	1
Achieving	Low							26	2	36	0	9	0	21	1	15	3	17	0	21	1	21	2	2	30
	High							1	29	0	52	0	29	2	18	2	28	1	20	5	38	1	42	44	0
Creative	Low									16	1	5	0	15	0	11	1	7	0	8	2	13	2	3	12
	High									4	26	2	15	2	16	1	17	0	16	5	19	1	20	25	2
Persistent	Low											17	0	19	2	12	8	13	1	28	0	27	1	2	25
	High											1	31	1	20	3	21	1	20	1	44	1	46	39	0
Happy	Low													17	3	8	7	10	1	19	1	14	0	0	10
	High													0	18	2	24	0	16	1	23	0	28	22	2
Attractive	Low															12	5	11	1	20	0	22	2	3	13
	High															3	20	1	13	2	13	1	20	15	1
Noticeable	Low																	5	0	2	7	6	5	3	12
	High																	0	19	10	12	6	19	18	7
Eye Contact	Low																			10	0	14	0	1	13
	High																			2	10	1	18	14	3
Cooperative	Low																					24	0	1	30
	High																					0	38	22	0
Attachment	Low																							2	17
	High																							33	2

[1] Shown for each pair of scales are the numbers of students falling into each of four types: Those low on both scales; those low on the first scale and high on the second; those high on both scales; and those high on the first scale and low on the second.

do not achieve very highly compared to other students?" or, "Are there students in your class who are generally high achievers but who become frustrated and give up easily when they encounter difficult problems rather than persist in seeking solutions?"

Overwhelmingly lopsided relationships like these cannot be explained entirely on the basis of methodology, however. It becomes particularly obvious when you look at these cross-tabulations that halo effects were operating here. We had expected relationships among the scales similar to the ones we found, but we did not expect to see only a few exceptions, or even no exceptions at all, to the predominant patterns. Although most of these relationships probably are real (most high achievers are persistent, and vice versa), it seems obvious that there should be more exceptions than appear in these tables. Notice, for example, that, according to the teachers, no student who was cooperative was restless, no high achiever was careless, no low achiever was happy, no unattractive student was cooperative, and so on. Obviously, these perceptions are incorrect.

The cross-tabulation data remind us once again that things seldom are as simple or clear as they appear to be. Expectations, attitudes, and beliefs generally intercorrelate with each other quite nicely, but investigations that go beyond self-reports of perceptions in order to check out the accuracy of perceptions invariably indicate that these strong and clear patterns result more from cognitive consistency needs than from real relationships. Those whom we like rarely are as good as we think they are, and those whom we dislike rarely are as bad as we think they are.

Given that halo effects appear in the present data, the major question becomes "How much do these correlations indicate teachers' tendencies to perceive relationships that do not actually exist; and how much do they merely indicate tendencies to exaggerate relationships that do exist, but with less strength and clarity?" It is not possible to answer this question with numerical precision, but we can say that the data from the study as a whole indicate that any halo effects in these ratings represent exaggerations of real relationships among the attributes measured by the scales. As subsequent chapters will indicate, high correlations between scales tend to be accompanied by similarity in associated patterns of teacher adjective descriptions and teacher-student interactions. Even so, each scale had its own unique pattern.

GROUPING OF SCALES FOR DISCUSSION

To facilitate data presentation throughout the book, the 13 teacher ranking scales will be discussed in the order in which they are given in Tables 6.1, 6.2, and 6.3, divided into several clusters. The first cluster includes the calm, careful, and mature scales, grouped because they are all indications of student maturity and self-control. The second cluster includes achievement, creativity, and persistence, grouped because they are judged primarily according to students' performance on classroom assignments.

Actually, all of these first six variables intercorrelate positively and could have been grouped together. In addition, they could have been subdivided in different ways. For example, calm and mature could have been paired as indicators of general maturity and self-control; careful and persistent could have been paired as indicators of work habits; and achieving and creative could have been paired as indicators of accomplishment. The present groupings were used mostly because the careful scale showed many parallels and yet also many interesting contrasts with the correlations involving the calm scale, and these comparisons could be emphasized more easily by discussing the scales in consecutive order.

There are some interesting differences in the degrees to which these six scales correlate with one another and with other scales. For example, ratings on the calm scale show weaker relationships to achieving and creative than ratings on careful and mature do, but stronger relationships to cooperative and persistent. In general, high ratings on the calm scale seem to have implications similar to those for high ratings on the careful and mature scales, but low ratings on the calm scale have particularly negative implications about teacher-student relationships that exceed the negative implications of low ratings on the careful or mature scales. Compared to careless and immature students, restless students tend to be seen as not merely restless but also uncooperative.

Ratings on careful showed high relationships to achieving and mature, but especially to persistent. Within the domain of work habits, in fact, teachers perceived care and persistence as parts of the same essential dimension. Even so, the persistent ratings consistently showed higher correlations than the careful ratings with other scales, both in and out of this first set of six. High correlations with variables outside this set were also typical of the achieving scale.

The next five scales all deal with students' personal attributes. Happy and attractive are grouped as aspects of social attractiveness; noticeable and eye contact are grouped as aspects of students' salience to teachers; and cooperative indicates the students' relationships with the teachers, specifically their willingness to go along with the teachers' authority. The cooperative scale is discussed separately because it proved to be so fundamental and far-reaching in its implications for teacher-student interaction.

The five personal attribute variables tend to correlate positively with the first six variables described previously, although not as highly as these six variables correlate with one another. The major exception here is the noticeable scale, which produced low and somewhat mixed correlations because students could be rated as noticeable for either desirable or undesirable behavior. It is interesting to speculate about the students rated low on noticeable. The correlations suggest that the least noticeable students are calm and cooperative but not outstanding on any of the other characteristics included in the rankings. This suggests that these students are passive and compliant but not notably bright, high achieving, or possessed of other qualities that would call attention to themselves.

The data for eye contact indicate high correlations with happy, attachment, and noticeable. This pattern is interesting in view of both folk wisdom and psychological studies of body language (Efran, 1969) indicating that eye contact is associated both with self-esteem (which might explain the relationships with happy and noticeable) and mutual attraction (note the relationship to teacher attachment). Thus, eye contact apparently is a useful clue to student self-esteem and to the quality of the teacher-student relationship, at least within this sample.

The final cluster of rating scales includes the two measures of teacher attitude: attachment and concern. The correlations indicate especially strong relationships between these attitudes and ratings of cooperative and persistent, followed closely by careful, achieving, and mature. Thus, as we expected, teacher attitudes toward students were associated more strongly with teacher perceptions of students' performance of the student role than with their perceptions of students' more general, personal qualities such as happiness or physical attractiveness.

In summary, the 13 scales (with the partial exception of noticeable) showed such regularities of intercorrelation as to indicate a considerable degree of halo effect. This was especially noticeable in the data (Table 6.2) for the students perceived consistently as high, medium, or low on the scales across all five sets of ratings from two teachers. Even so, there were considerable differences between scales in the strength and patterning of relationships within this general picture, suggesting that most of the halo effect that may exist in any particular correlation represents teachers' exaggeration of the strength of a relationship that does actually exist in reality, and not perception of a relationship that really does not exist. This will become more clear in subsequent discussion of the relationships between teacher ratings on these 13 scales and other data from the study. As it happens, each scale produced its own unique pattern of relationships with teacher adjective descriptions and teacher-student interaction measures.

7

Grade Level

The main focus of the Student Attribute Study was on the contrasts in patterns of teacher description and teacher-student interaction between students ranked low and students ranked high on the 13 scales described in chapter 6. This material will be presented and discussed in subsequent chapters. First, however, we will discuss differences in patterns of teacher description and teacher-student interaction across the four grade levels included in the study (grades 2 through 5) and between the two sexes. This will help put the subsequent data into perspective by previewing the information they contain and the interpretations that might be placed on this information.

Until recently, educational researchers often generalized their findings from particular contexts without enough attention to the limits of these generalizations. Later research often revealed that findings developed in one context would not generalize to another, and sometimes findings from one context even were reversed in another. For example, Brophy and Evertson (1976) found that many teaching behaviors that apparently are effective at the higher grade levels are ineffective or irrelevant in the early grades. They also found that teaching behavior that is effective in the early grades with students from higher socioeconomic status families is not as effective with students from lower socioeconomic status families, and vice versa.

In particular, Brophy and Evertson found that the nature of the teaching-learning situation differed between the early grades, when teachers concentrate on teaching the fundamentals of the three Rs, and the higher grades, when students who have mastered these basics use them to learn other material. The students in the Student Attribute Study were in grades two through five when they were observed in the classroom. Within this range, grades two and three could be characterized as early elementary grades with the primary emphasis on learning the fundamentals. Among other things, this means heavy reliance on small group instruction, especially for reading, and emphasis on short seatwork assignments in language arts and mathematics. In contrast, grade four and especially grade five involve much less small group and more whole class instruction. Also, older students tend to learn more independently through extended seatwork assignments and special projects, which they are able to do because they have mastered the basics of the three Rs and are capable of independent learning.

These are generalizations, of course. Some students in grades two and three have mastered the basics and are capable of learning in ways that students typically learn at higher grades, and many students in grades four and five have not yet mastered the basics. These students cannot yet use tool skills successfully to work on longer and more complex assignments. In any case, grade level differences were analyzed to see whether findings would generalize across the grade levels studied or might instead be specific to certain grades.

For this purpose, the teacher adjective description data and classroom interaction data were subjected to two-way (sex by grade) analyses of variance to identify any main effects of sex or grade level and any interactions between them. Complete data are presented in technical reports (Baum et al., 1975; Brophy et al., 1980), and highlights are discussed in a journal article as well (Brophy et al., 1979). Consequently, only the major findings will be discussed here.

The data are summarized in Table 7.1 (Teacher Adjective Description Data) and Table 7.2 (Classroom Interaction Data). These tables contain not only the data for grade level but also the data for sex differences and for each of the 13 teacher ranking scales. We will refer to these tables frequently throughout the remainder of the book. The tables indicate the direction of significant relationships between the adjective description variables or classroom interaction variables and the grade level, sex, or rankings of the students on the 13 scales.

A plus sign indicates a positive relationship between the variables, a minus sign indicates a negative relationship, and a zero indicates no significant relationship one way or the other. Plus and minus signs that are accompanied by asterisks indicate relationships significant at the .01 level of probability. The other plus and minus signs indicate relationships that reached the .05 level of probability but were not strong enough to reach the .01 level.

In studying the tables, note that the signs indicate the direction of relationship between the variables as labeled. The grade level variable, for example, is labeled "Higher Grades" so that a plus sign indicates that the teacher description or classroom interaction variable was associated more with the higher grade levels (grades four and five) than with the lower grade levels (grades two and three). Thus, the plus sign at the intersection of the column labeled "Higher Grades" and the row labeled "36. Broken Home" in Table 7.1 indicates that teachers were more likely to refer to a broken home in talking about students in the higher grades than they were in talking about students in the lower grades. Conversely, the minus sign accompanied by an asterisk at the intersection of the column labeled "Higher Grades" and the row labeled "15. Active" in Table 7.1 indicates that teachers were more likely to describe students in the earlier grades as active than they were to describe students in the higher grades as active. Furthermore, the asterisk indicates that this difference reached the .01 level of statistical significance.

The data in the "Higher Grades" column in Tables 7.1 and 7.2 include plus or minus signs only when analyses of variance yielded a statistically significant main effect for grade level *and* the grade level means showed linear (or at least unidirectional) change across grades two through five. Thus, these signs indicate

Table 7.1. Relationships between the teachers' rankings of students on the 13 attribute scales and their free response descriptions of the same students (for students ranked consistently across all five sets of rankings).[1]

Adjective Description Variables	Higher Grades	Boys	Calm	Careful	Mature	Achieving	Creative	Persistent	Happy	Attractive	Noticeable	Eye Contact	Cooperative	Attachment	Concern
1. Sociable	0	0	0	0	0	0	0	0	0	0	+	ND	0	ND	0
2. Mature	0	0	ND	+*	+*	+*	ND	+*	ND	ND	ND	ND	ND	ND	ND
3. Happy	0	0	-*	0	0	0	0	0	ND	+	+	ND	0	0	ND
4. Quiet	0	0	+*	+	+*	0	0	0	ND	0	-*	ND	+*	+	0
5. Helpful	0	-*	+*	+*	+*	0	0	+*	+*	0	0	ND	+*	+*	0
6. Well Behaved	0	0	+*	ND	ND	0	0	ND	ND	ND	ND	ND	ND	+	ND
7. Confident	0	0	0	0	ND	0	ND	0	ND	0	0	ND	ND	ND	ND
8. Motivated	0	0	+*	+*	+*	+*	0	+*	+*	0	0	0	+*	+*	-*
9. Intelligent	0	-*	+*	+*	+*	+*	+*	+*	+*	+*	+*	+*	+*	+*	-*
10. Achieving	0	0	+*	+*	+*	+*	+*	+*	ND	+*	+*	ND	+*	+*	-*
11. Good Worker	0	0	+*	+*	+*	0	0	+*	+	0	0	0	+*	+*	-*
12. Popular	0	0	+*	0	0	0	ND	0	ND	ND	ND	ND	+*	ND	ND
13. Aggressive	0	+	-*	0	0	0	0	0	0	-	+	0	-*	0	0
14. Responsible	+	0	+*	+*	+*	+*	0	+*	+	0	0	0	+*	+*	0
15. Active	-*	+	-*	-*	-*	0	0	-*	0	0	+*	-	-*	-*	+*

89

	Higher Grades	Boys	Calm	Careful	Mature	Achieving	Creative	Persistent	Happy	Attractive	Noticeable	Eye Contact	Cooperative	Attachment	Concern
16. Considerate	0	0	0	+	0	0	0	0	0	0	0	0	0	0	0
17. Inattentive	0	+	0	-	0	-	0	-*	0	-	0	-	-	-*	+
18. Temperamental	0	0	-*	0	-	0	0	0	-	0	0	0	-	0	+
19. Unobtrusive	0	0	0	0	0	0	0	0	0	0	0	0	0	0	0
20. Athletic	0	0	0	0	0	+	+	0	0	+	0	0	0	0	0
21. Humorous	0	+*	0	0	0	0	0	0	0	0	+	0	0	0	0
22. Other Negative	0	0	0	0	0	0	-	0	0	-*	0	0	-	0	0
23. Other Positive	0	0	0	0	0	0	+	0	+	0	+	0	0	0	0
24. Social Leader	0	0	0	0	0	0	+	0	0	0	+	+*	0	0	0
25. Likeable	0	0	0	0	0	0	0	0	0	0	0	0	0	0	0
26. Attractive	0	0	0	0	0	0	0	0	0	+*	0	0	0	0	0
27. Dependent	0	0	-*	0	-	0	0	0	0	0	0	0	0	0	0
28. Good Home	0	0	0	+	+*	+*	0	+*	+*	0	0	+*	+*	+*	-*
29. Creative	0	0	0	0	+	+*	+*	0	0	0	+	+	0	0	0
30. Medical Problems	0	0	0	0	-	0	0	0	0	-	0	0	-	0	+*

	Higher Grades	Boys	Calm	Careful	Mature	Achieving	Creative	Persistent	Happy	Attractive	Noticeable	Eye Contact	Cooperative	Attachment	Concern
31. Often Absent	0	0	0	0	0	-*	0	-	-*	-	-*	-*	0	0	0
32. Sweet	0	-*	+*	0	0	0	0	0	0	0	0	0	+*	0	0
33. Underachiever	0	0	-	-	0	0	0	0	0	0	0	0	-*	-	0
34. Cries Easily	0	0	0	0	0	0	0	0	0	0	0	C	0	0	0
35. Untrustworthy	0	0	-	-	0	-	0	0	0	0	0	-	-*	-*	0
36. Broken Home	+	0	0	0	0	0	0	0	0	0	0	0	0	0	0
37. % Positive	0	-*	+*	+*	+*	+*	+*	+*	+*	+*	+	+*	+*	+*	-*

[1] Plus signs (+) indicate positive relationships between the variables as labeled; minus signs (-) indicate negative relationships; zeroes (0) indicate lack of any significant relationship; and "ND" indicates "no data," or insufficient data to allow statistical analysis. Relationships marked with an asterisk are significant at the .01 level; the others are significant only at the .05 level.

Table 7.2. Relationships between student grade level, student sex, and teachers' rankings of students on the 13 attribute scales and 73 measures of classroom interaction (for students ranked consistently across all five sets of rankings).[1]

(for students ranked consistently across all five sets of rankings)[1]

Classroom Interaction Variables

A. Types of Contact

	Higher Grades	Boys	Calm	Careful	Mature	Achieving	Creative	Persistent	Happy	Attractive	Noticeable	Eye Contact	Cooperative	Attachment	Concern
1. Rate: All dyadic contacts combined	0	+*	-*	-*	-*	-*	0	-*	0	0	+*	0	-*	-*	0
2. Rate: All public response opportunities combined	+*	0	0	0	0	0	+*	0	+	+	+*	+*	0	0	0
3. % of total contacts that were public response opportunities	+*	0	+*	+*	+*	+*	+*	+*	+*	0	0	+*	+*	+*	-*
4. Rate: Total public response opportunities that occurred in general class (not small group)	+*	0	0	0	0	+*	+*	0	+*	0	+*	+*	0	+	-*
5. % of public response opportunities that occurred in general class (not small group)	+*	0	0	0	+	+	+	+	+	0	+	+*	0	0	0
6. % of total contacts (excluding behavior contacts) that were private, nonacademic	-*	-	-*	-	-	-*	0	-	0	0	0	0	-	-*	0
7. % of total contacts that were student initiated	+*	-*	0	0	0	0	0	0	+	0	0	0	+	0	-
8. % of total contacts that were behavioral	-*	+*	-*	-*	-*	-*	0	-*	-*	0	+*	0	-*	-*	+*

. Public Response Opportunities

	Higher Grades	Boys	Calm	Careful	Mature	Achieving	Creative	Persistent	Happy	Attractive	Noticeable	Eye Contact	Cooperative	Attachment	Concern
9. % of small group responses given as a nonvolunteer	0	0	0	0	-	0	-*	0	0	-	-	0	-*	-	+*
10. % of small group responses given as a volunteer	0	-*	+*	+*	+	0	0	+	+*	0	0	+	+*	+*	-*
11. % of small group responses given after hand waving	0	0	-	-*	0	0	-	-*	-	0	0	0	0	0	0
12. % of small group responses called out	0	0	0	0	0	0	0	0	0	0	0	0	0	0	0
13. % of general class responses given as a non-volunteer	0	0	0	0	0	-*	-*	0	0	0	-*	-*	0	-	+*
14. % of general class responses given as a volunteer	0	0	+	0	+	+	0	+*	+*	0	0	+	+	+*	-*
15. % of general class responses given after hand waving	0	-*	0	0	0	0	0	0	0	0	0	0	0	0	0
16. % of general class responses called out	+*	+*	-*	0	0	0	+	0	-	0	+*	0	-*	0	0
. Teacher Initiated Contacts															
17. Rate: All teacher initiated contacts combined	0	+*	-*	-*	-*	-*	-	-*	-	0	-	-	-	-*	+
18. Rate: Teacher initiated academic contacts	0	+	-*	-*	-*	-*	-	-*	-	-	0	0	-*	-*	+

93

Classroom Interaction Variables:	Higher Grades	Boys	Calm	Careful	Mature	Achieving	Creative	Persistent	Happy	Attractive	Noticeable	Eye Contact	Cooperative	Attachment	Concern
19. Rate: Teacher initiated housekeeping contacts	-*	0	0	+*	0	0	0	0	0	0	+*	0	0	0	0
20. Rate: Teacher initiated personal contacts	0	+	-*	-*	-*	-*	-	-	0	-	0	0	0	-*	0
21. Rate: Teacher initiated social contacts	0	0	0	0	-	-*	0	-*	0	0	0	0	0	0	0
22. % of total contacts that were teacher initiated	0	0	0	0	0	0	-*	0	0	0	-*	-*	0	0	0
23. % of teacher initiated contacts that were academic	+*	0	0	-*	0	0	0	0	0	0	0	0	0	0	0
24. % of teacher initiated academic contacts that involved observation only	0	0	+*	0	0	0	0	0	+	0	0	+	0	0	0
25. % of teacher initiated contacts that were housekeeping	-*	0	+	+*	+*	+*	+	+*	+	+*	0	0	+*	+*	0
26. % of teacher initiated contacts that were personal	0	0	-	0	0	0	0	0	0	0	0	0	0	0	0
27. % of teacher initiated contacts that were social	0	0	0	0	0	0	0	0	0	0	0	0	0	0	0

Classroom Interaction Variables	Higher Grades	Boys	Calm	Careful	Mature	Achieving	Creative	Persistent	Happy	Attractive	Noticeable	Eye Contact	Cooperative	Attachment	Concern
D. Student Initiated Contacts and Behavior Contacts															
28. Rate: All student initiated contacts combined	0	-*	-*	-*	0	0	0	0	0	0	+*	0	0	0	0
29. Rate: Student initiated academic contacts	+*	0	0	-*	0	0	0	0	0	0	0	0	0	0	0
30. Rate: Student initiated approval seeking contacts	-*	-*	-	0	0	0	0	0	0	0	+*	0	0	0	0
31. Rate: Student initiated housekeeping contacts	0	-	0	0	0	0	0	0	+*	0	0	0	0	0	0
32. Rate: Student initiated personal contacts	-*	0	-	0	0	0	0	0	0	0	0	0	-	0	0
33. % of student initiated contacts that were tattling	-*	0	-*	-*	-*	0	0	-*	0	0	+	0	-*	0	0
34. % of student initiated contacts that were social	+*	0	0	0	0	0	0	0	0	0	+	0	0	0	0
35. % of behavioral contacts that involved misbehavior	0	+	-	-*	-*	-	0	-	-	0	0	0	-*	-	+

Classroom Interaction Variables	Higher Grades	Boys	Calm	Careful	Mature	Achieving	Creative	Persistent	Happy	Attractive	Noticeable	Eye Contact	Cooperative	Attachment	Concern
36. % of typical misbehavior that were disruptive	0	+	-*	0	-	0	0	0	0	0	0	0	-*	-	0
37. % of behavior contacts involving griping, sassing, or defying	0	0	-	-*	0	0	0	-	-	0	0	0	-	-	0
38. % of behavior contacts involving non-interactive behavior (cheating, sleeping)	0	0	0	0	0	-	0	0	0	0	0	-*	0	-	0
E. Student Affective Reactions to Teachers															
39. % of teacher initiated academic contacts that included positive student affect	0	0	0	0	0	0	0	0	0	0	0	0	0	0	0
40. % of teacher initiated social contacts that included positive student affect	0	0	0	0	0	0	0	0	0	0	+	ND	0	0	0
41. % of teacher initiated academic contacts that included negative student affect	0	0	0	0	0	0	0	0	0	0	0	-	0	-	0

Classroom Interaction Variables	Higher Grades	Boys	Calm	Careful	Mature	Achieving	Creative	Persistent	Happy	Attractive	Noticeable	Eye Contact	Cooperative	Attachment	Concern
42. % of teacher initiated personal contacts that included negative student affect	0	0	0	0	0	0	0	0	0	0	0	0	0	-*	0
43. % of teacher initiated social contacts that included negative student affect	0	0	0	0	+	0	0	0	0	0	0	ND	-*	0	0
44. % of behavioral contacts in which student was coded as sullen	0	0	-*	-*	-*	-	0	-	-*	0	+	0	-*	-*	+
F. Teacher Praise and Criticism															
45. Rate: Praise during teacher initiated academic contacts	0	0	0	0	-	0	0	0	0	0	0	0	0	0	0
46. % of teacher initiated academic contacts that included praise	0	0	0	0	0	0	0	0	0	0	0	0	0	0	0
47. % of volunteer and call out responses followed by praise	0	0	0	0	0	0	0	0	0	0	-*	0	0	0	0
48. % of student initiated academic or approval seeking contacts that included praise	0	0	0	0	0	0	0	-*	0	0	0	0	0	0	+

Classroom Interaction Variables	Higher Grades	Boys	Calm	Careful	Mature	Achieving	Creative	Persistent	Happy	Attractive	Noticeable	Eye Contact	Cooperative	Attachment	Concern
49. % of total academic contacts (public plus private) that included praise	0	0	0	0	0	0	0	0	-	0	-	-	0	0	0
50. Rate: Criticism during teacher initiated academic contacts	0	+*	-*	-	-*	0	-	-*	0	0	+	0	-*	-*	0
51. % of teacher initiated academic contacts that included criticism	0	+*	-*	-*	-*	0	-*	-*	-*	0	0	-*	-*	-*	0
52. % of volunteer and call out responses followed by criticism	0	0	0	0	0	0	0	0	+	+	+	0	0	0	0
53. % of student initiated academic or approval seeking contacts that included criticism	0	0	0	0	0	0	0	0	+	0	0	0	0	0	0
54. % of total academic contacts (public plus private) that included criticism	0	C	-*	-	-*	0	-	0	-	0	0	-*	-*	-*	0

Classroom Interaction Variables

G. Teacher Critical Behaviors and Affective Reactions to Students.

Positive

Classroom Interaction Variables	Higher Grades	Boys	Calm	Careful	Mature	Achieving	Creative	Persistent	Happy	Attractive	Noticeable	Eye Contact	Cooperative	Attachment	Concern
55. Rate: Teacher appoints student as monitor	0	0	0	0	0	0	0	0	0	0	0	0	0	+	0
56. Rate: Teacher holds up student as good example to class	+*	0	0	0	0	0	0	0	0	0	0	0	0	0	0
57. Rate: Teacher flatters student	0	0	0	0	0	0	0	0	0	0	0	+*	0	0	0
58. Rate: Teacher displays physical affection toward student	0	0	0	-*	-	-	0	-	0	0	0	0	0	0	0
59. Rate: Teacher rewards student with special privilege	-	+	0	0	0	0	0	0	0	0	0	0	0	0	0
60. % of total contacts that included positive teacher affect	0	0	+*	0	0	0	0	0	0	0	-*	0	0	0	0
61. % of behavioral contacts that included praise of good behavior	-*	0	+*	+	+*	0	0	0	+	0	+	0	+	0	0

Classroom Interaction Variables	Higher Grades	Boys	Calm	Careful	Mature	Achieving	Creative	Persistent	Happy	Attractive	Noticeable	Eye Contact	Cooperative	Attachment	Concern
62. % of behavioral contacts plus teacher critical behaviors that included positive teacher affect or reinforcement	0	0	+*	0	0	0	0	0	+	0	0	0	+*	0	0
Negative															
63. Rate: Teacher holds up student as bad example to class	0	0	-	-*	0	0	0	-	0	0	0	0	0	:	+*
64. % of student academic initiations that included teacher impatience	0	0	0	0	-	0	0	-	0	0	0	0	0	-*	-
65. % of student academic initiations refused by teacher	-*	0	-*	0	-*	-	0	0	0	0	0	0	0	-*	0
66. % of student housekeeping initiations refused by teacher	0	+*	-	0	-*	0	0	0	0	0	0	0	-*	-*	0
67. % of student personal initiations refused by teacher	0	+	0	0	0	0	0	0	0	0	+	0	-	-	0
68. % of student tattling initiations rejected by teacher	0	+*	-	0	0	0	0	0	0	0	+*	0	-	0	0

Classroom Interaction Variables	Higher Grades	Boys	Calm	Careful	Mature	Achieving	Creative	Persistent	Happy	Attractive	Noticeable	Eye Contact	Cooperative	Attachment	Concern
69. % of student social initiations refused by teacher	-*	0	0	0	0	0	0	0·	0	0	+	+	0	0	0
70. % of total contacts that included negative teacher affect	0	+*	-*	0	-	0	0	-*	0	0	0	0	-*	-*	0
71. % of misbehaviors responded to with warnings	0	0	-*	0	0	0	0	-	-*	-	0	0	0	-*	+
72. % of misbehaviors responded to with threats	0	0	-	0	0	0	0	0	-	0	+	0	-*	0	0
73. % of misbehaviors responded to with criticism or punishment	0	0	-*	-	-	0	0	-	0	0	0	0	-*	-	+

[1] Plus signs (+) indicate positive relationships between the variables as labeled; minus signs (-) indicate negative relationships; zeroes indicate lack of any significant relationship; and "ND" indicates "no data," or insufficient data to allow statistical analysis. Relationships marked with an asterisk are significant at the .01 level; the others are significant only at the .05 level.

that the teacher description or classroom observation variable became either systematically more frequent or systematically less frequent across the four grade levels studied. Statistically significant main effects for grade were also observed for a number of other variables, but inspection of the means indicated nonlinear relationships. For example, some teacher descriptions or classroom interaction variables were infrequent at second grade, frequent at third and fourth grade, but then infrequent again at fifth grade. Others had the opposite pattern. These kinds of findings are difficult to interpret and tangential to the focus of this book, so they will not be presented here. Discussion of grade level differences is confined to those variables that either increased or decreased between grades two and five.

Adjective Description Data

Significant and linear grade level effects were seen for only 3 of the 37 teacher description variables summarized in Table 7.1. Two of these were already used above as examples: teachers in the higher grades were more likely to mention broken homes, but less likely to describe students as active. In addition, they were more likely to describe students as responsible. None of these differences were specifically expected, but none are surprising.

It is commonly observed that children become less physically active and more able to sustain long periods of quiet concentration and work as they progress through childhood. Furthermore, hyperactivity gradually reduces in intensity as children get older. Thus, physical activity and especially hyperactivity are more likely to occur in the early grades, and thus more likely to be mentioned by teachers.

The more frequent mention of broken homes in the later grades makes sense as well, not because of direct effects of the students themselves, but simply because the older students came from families where the parents were older and had been married longer (on the average), so that a greater percentage of them would have become broken by separation or divorce.

Finally, the greater mention of responsible in the higher grades probably reflects the fact that older children generally are more responsible, at least in the sense that they can handle more of their everyday affairs on their own and require less adult supervision. These differences in adjective descriptions, then, probably are based on real differences in students across the grade levels studied.

Classroom Observation Data

Significant relationships were observed for 21 of the 73 variables in Table 7.2, 20 of these at the .01 level of significance. Most of these reflect the developmental trends discussed by Brophy and Evertson (1976, 1978). Because of the length of Table 7.2, each of the 73 classroom observation variables will be identified by number when mentioned in the text.

There were no grade level trends for the sum of all dyadic contacts in which teachers interacted with individual students (1), but there were contrasting patterns in the types of contact that made up this total. Classroom activities became much more focused on academics as the students got older. There were more public response opportunities (2, 3) because there was increasing emphasis on recitation and discussion, in which teachers call on students to respond to questions. Furthermore, increasing percentages of these public response opportunities came in whole class settings rather than in small groups (4, 5), as teachers phased out the reading groups and other types of small group instruction that dominate the early grades and turned more to whole class instruction in the higher grades.

Socialization of students gradually becomes more thorough and successful across these grade levels, as indicated by reductions in the frequency of behavior contacts (8), which usually occur because a student has misbehaved, and in the frequency of nonacademic private contacts (6). These contacts focus not on work assignments but on social interaction, daily housekeeping tasks, tattling, getting permission to meet personal needs (student-initiated personal contacts), or reminders to put away materials, straighten up, or fulfill other personal responsibilities (teacher-initiated personal contacts).

The percentage of total contacts that were initiated by the students rather than the teacher also increased (7). This suggests that older students were more likely than younger students to initiate interactions with the teachers, and also that the teachers felt less need to monitor students as closely and initiate interactions with them as frequently as in the early grades.

The data on types of public response opportunities (9–16) revealed only one significant relationship: students in the higher grades were more likely to call out responses to teacher questions in the general class setting, and to have these responses acknowledged by the teachers (16). This is part of a general pattern of greater initiation by the older students, but it probably also represents an increase in the sophistication and appropriateness of the call outs that occurred. In order to be credited with a called out response opportunity, students had to not only call out an answer but succeed in getting the teacher to attend to and accept that answer (rather than ignoring the answer or merely cautioning the student to stop calling out but not dealing with the answer itself). Data from this and previous studies indicate that the frequency of call outs depends at least as much on teachers' willingness to accept them as on students' tendency to call out.

In the early grades, in fact, teachers usually have to suppress call outs consistently in order to train students to respect one another's turns and keep the more assertive ones from dominating group activities (Brophy and Evertson, 1976; Anderson, Evertson, and Brophy, 1979). Furthermore, most group activities involve small groups in which the teacher systematically tries to see that each student gets a turn to respond. By the middle grades, however, most activities occur in the whole class setting, and teachers are more oriented toward moving the group along at a good pace than toward seeing that every individual student gets a turn. Consequently, call outs are more welcome in this setting and, given the ages of the students, more likely to be relevant and useful contributions to the discussion. Thus, there are several reasons for teachers in the middle grades to be more accepting of call outs than teachers in the early grades are.

The increased concentration on academics across these grade levels is also seen in the teacher- and student-initiated contacts (17–35). These were private contacts between the teachers and individual students. Across the four grade levels studied, teachers in the higher grades initiated more academic contacts (23) involving checking on or helping students with their work, and fewer housekeeping contacts (19, 25) in which they requested students to perform errands or housekeeping chores. For their part, students also initiated more academic contacts with teachers (29) in order to discuss or get help with their work, but they came to the teachers less often to seek approval for completed work (30), to request permission or help in meeting personal needs (32), or to tattle on their classmates (33).

All of these trends indicate the increasing maturity of the students as well as their gradual socialization into the student role. They became less dependent on teachers to provide reminders or help in keeping track of their possessions, dealing with supplies and equipment, and meeting other personal needs. As they became more socially mature and peer oriented, and less adult dependent, they were less likely to come to the teachers to tattle or to seek praise or approval. In general, they became less dependent on the teacher for either emotional support or direct help.

They did, however, begin to initiate more social contacts with teachers (32), especially the girls. Thus, as students moved away from childish patterns of interaction with their teachers, they did not become alienated from them but instead moved into more mature patterns, marked mostly by concentration on academic matters but also featuring social conversation. All of this is part of the same developmental pattern that can be observed in the interactions of children of these ages with adults in any settings, not just in school.

Data on behavior contacts indicate that misbehavior is less frequent in the higher grades (8), but that the types of misbehavior that do occur are neither more nor less likely to involve disruption (36), hostility directed at the teacher (37), or noninteractive problems such as cheating, lying, or sleeping (38). Thus, the general mixture of behavior problems confronting the teacher remains similar, but the frequency of such problems is reduced.

Student affective reactions to teachers (39–44) showed no significant trends one way or the other. Thus, noteworthy positive and negative affect directed at teachers was neither more nor less frequent in the higher grades than the lower grades. The same was true of teacher praise and criticism of students, and of most indicators of teacher affect directed toward the students (45–73), with the exceptions noted below.

Teachers were more likely to hold up students as good examples to the rest of the class (56) in the higher grades but less likely to reward them with special privileges (59) or to praise their good conduct (61). This suggests an (appropriate) reduction in attempts to shape student behavior through verbal praise and other aspects of behavior modification ("I like the way that Mary is sitting up straight and listening"). These techniques can be effective with younger, adult-oriented students, but they are likely to be ineffective and may even backfire by causing peer problems with older students. In any case, the data indicate that the frequency of this approach decreased sharply after second grade. This may represent a recognition by the teachers that students change in their orientation toward authority figures versus the peer group as they mature.

The increase in the frequency of holding up students as good examples to the rest of the class was unexpected, and the reasons for it are unknown. To the extent that this is restricted to students' creations and accomplishments it might be effective, but to the extent that it involves calling attention to good conduct it probably is not effective. Such teacher behavior is more likely to irritate than to motivate fifth graders, and may cause them problems with peers if they become labeled as teacher's pet.

There were no grade level changes in direct expressions of teacher affect, but there were reductions in the frequency with which teachers refused students' academic (65) and social (69) initiations. We interpret these data not so much as indicators of teachers' feelings about students, but as indications of the sophistication of students in recognizing appropriate times and reasons for initiating private contacts with teachers. Younger students often come to teachers at bad times (especially when they are busy trying to teach reading groups), seek the teacher's help with work they could do themselves if they tried, seek to socialize when the teacher wants them to concentrate on their work, or otherwise initiate interactions that teachers see as inappropriate in some way. Thus, teachers in the early grades often have to refuse these student initiations and redirect the students. As students learn from these experiences, and as they mature generally, they become less likely to initiate in ways that teachers see as inappropriate, and thus less likely to be refused.

Taken together, the data on grade level trends contain few surprises. They are about what would be expected given that the students are making a transition from being preoperational thinkers who are mostly oriented toward adults as authority figures to individuals functioning at Piaget's stage of concrete operations who are more and more oriented toward their peers. They also are making the transition from learning the tool skills as ends in their own right to mastering these skills and being able to use them as means for learning other things. As these changes occur, schooling makes the transition from heavy emphasis on individualized and small group instruction and practice of tool skills to reliance on these skills for coping with increasingly lengthy and sophisticated reading assignments and individualized projects, and especially to more frequent whole class recitation and discussion. Concentration on socializing students to the student role is reduced, and greater percentages of classroom interaction focus on academic activities (Brophy and Evertson, 1978).

These trends should be kept in mind in interpreting the data to be discussed in subsequent chapters. For example, relationships involving tattling were based mostly on events occurring in the early grades, and relationships involving social interactions between teachers and students were determined mostly by interactions observed in the higher grades.

It also should be kept in mind that the group differences described in this chapter and in the rest of the book are relative, not absolute. Each difference discussed was at least large enough to reach the .05 level of significance in an analysis of variance, but most such differences involve relatively minor variations on major themes established by the overall base rates of occurrence and ranges of variation observed in the measures.

For example, we have reported that teachers were more likely to hold up students as good examples to the rest of the class in the higher grades than in the lower grades. This does not mean, however, that the teachers in higher grades held up students as good examples to the rest of the class regularly or often. In fact, none of the teachers did this very frequently. This can be seen in the data in Tables 7.3 and 7.4

Table 7.3 shows the means and standard deviations for the rates of occurrence of the various classroom events coded in our observation system. Each mean expresses the average number of times that an individual student would be coded for the behavior variable during our ten classroom visits (or 20 hours of classroom observation). The table indicates that students averaged about 64 individual contacts with their teachers during these 20 hours of observation, and that most of these were public response opportunities or private, academic-related contacts. That is, on the average, the majority of teacher-student interactions were devoted directly to the business of teaching and learning. Behavior contacts and the various forms of nonacademic contacts (housekeeping, approval seeking, personal, social, tattling) occurred much less frequently.

Also, most classroom interaction was businesslike, without strong emotional involvement. Teachers did not often praise or (especially) criticize students, and there were very low frequencies for critical behaviors and affective reactions such as appointing students as monitors, holding them up as good or bad examples to the class, flattering them, or displaying physical affection. Even in dealing with student misbehavior, teachers were likely to respond with simple management directives, and did not usually include stronger or more emotional responses such as warnings, threats, criticism, or punishment.

Table 7.4 gives percentages showing the relative frequencies with which various classroom events actually occurred in the contexts in which they could have occurred 100 percent of the time. Again, it is clear that the rates of occurrence for certain events are very low, especially those involving strong emotional response by either the teachers or the students. This was true even for behavior contacts, where the most intense exchanges are normally observed. Note that only a small proportion of the behavior contacts observed involved intense or disruptive misbehavior, and that students seldom responded sullenly or griped, sassed, or defied the teacher in even these negatively toned interactions. Similarly, teachers seldom lost their tempers with students who misbehaved, seldom showed impatience in dealing with students who came to them for help

Table 7.3. Means and Standard Deviations for the classroom interaction variables observed in the Study Attribute Study (per individual student for 20 hours of observation).

Variable	Mean	SD
Total: All dyadic contacts combined	64.05	32.54
Total public response opportunities	14.07	11.92
General class response opportunities	8.50	9.15
Small group response opportunities	5.57	9.11
Total behavioral contacts	13.36	15.40
Nonvolunteer response opportunities, small group	2.08	3.36
Volunteer response opportunities, small group	1.56	3.74
Hand waving response opportunities, small group	0.08	0.39
Call out response opportunities, small group	1.38	3.60
Nonvolunteer response opportunities, general class	2.27	2.85
Volunteer response opportunities, general class	3.56	4.75
Hand waving response opportunities, general class	0.21	0.69
Call out response opportunties, general class	1.61	3.55
Total teacher initiated contacts	13.05	7.87
Teacher initiated academic contacts	7.85	6.49
Teacher initiated housekeeping contacts	2.69	2.84
Teacher initiated personal contacts	1.26	1.78
Teacher initiated social contacts	0.16	0.49
Teacher initiated academic contacts, observation only	1.02	1.83
Total student initiated contacts	23.75	15.49
Student initiated academic contacts	13.12	9.04
Student initiated approval seeking contacts	1.79	3.04
Student initiated housekeeping contacts	1.12	1.77

Variables	Mean	SD
Student initiated personal contacts	3.06	3.89
Behavioral contacts involving disruptive behavior	1.11	2.41
Total teacher praise for good answers or good work	2.62	2.99
Total teacher criticism for poor answers or poor work	0.64	1.22
Teacher appoints student as monitor	0.17	0.69
Teacher holds up student as good example to class	0.17	0.74
Teacher flatters student	0.02	0.14
Teacher rewards student with special privilege	0.15	0.56
Total contacts that included teacher positive affect	0.41	1.00
Teacher expresses physical affection toward student	0.96	2.04
Teacher praises student's good conduct	0.44	1.18
Teacher holds up student as bad example to class	0.01	0.11
Teacher refusals of student initiated work contacts	0.39	0.84
Teacher refusals of student initiated housekeeping requests	0.25	0.78
Teacher refusals of student initiated personal requests	0.68	1.58
Teacher refusals of student initiated attempts to tattle	0.50	1.25
Teacher refusals of student initiated social contacts	0.16	0.60
Total contacts that included teacher negative affect	0.24	1.08
Teacher responds to misbehavior with warning	2.50	4.35
Teacher responds to misbehavior with threat	0.16	0.59
Teacher responds to misbehavior with criticism or.punishment	0.76	1.92

Table 7.4.   Relative frequency data indicating the actual incidence of various classroom events as percentages of the contexts in which they have occurred.

Variables	Percentage
Percent of total dyadic contacts which were public response opportunities	24
Percent of public response opportunties which occurred in general class	67
Percent of total contacts (excluding behavior contacts) which were private, nonacademic contacts	50
Percent of total contacts which were student initiated	36
Percent of total contacts which were behavioral	15
Percent of small group responses given to non-volunteers	44
Percent of small group responses given to volunteers	31
Percent of small group responses given after hand waving	2
Percent of small group responses called out	24
Percent of general class responses given to non-volunteers	36
Percent of general class responses given to volunteers	46
Percent of general class responses given after hand waving	2
Percent of general class responses called out	15
Percent of total contacts which were teacher initiated	22
Percent of teacher initiated contacts which were academic	57
Percent of teacher initiated contacts which were housekeeping	25
Percent of teacher initiated contacts which were personal	12
Percent of teacher initiated contacts which were social	2
Percent of student initiated contacts which were academic	62

Variables	Percentage
Percent of student initiated contacts which were approval seeking	5
Percent of student initiated contacts which were housekeeping	5
Percent of student initiated contacts which were personal	14
Percent of student initiated contacts which were tattling	4
Percent of student initiated contacts which were social	10
Percent of behavioral contacts which involved misbehavior	90
Percent of typical misbehaviors which were disruptive	10
Percent of behavioral contacts involving griping, sassing, or defying	2
Percent of behavioral contacts involving noninteractive behavior (lying, cheating, sleeping)	2
Percent of teacher initiated academic contacts which included positive student affect	3
Percent of teacher initiated social contacts which included positive student affect	35
Percent of teacher initiated academic contacts which included negative student affect	3
Percent of teacher initiated personal contacts which included negative student affect	5
Percent of teacher initiated social contacts which included negative student affect	2
Percent of behavioral contacts in which student was coded as sullen	1
Percent of teacher initiated academic contacts which included praise	6

Variables	Percentage
Percent of volunteer and call out responses followed by praise	6
Percent of student initiated academic or approval seeking contacts which included praise	7
Percent of total academic contacts (public plus private) which included praise	8
Percent of teacher initiated academic contacts which included criticism	4
Percent of volunteer and call out responses followed by criticism	0.3
Percent of student initiated academic or approval seeking contacts which included criticism	I
Percent of total academic contacts (public plus private) which included criticism	2
Percent of total contacts which included positive teacher affect	5
Percent of behavioral contacts which included praise of good behavior	5
Percentage of behavioral contacts plus teacher critical behaviors that included positive teacher affect or reinforcement	18
Percent of student initiated academic contacts which included teacher impatience	I
Percent of student initiated academic contacts refused by teacher	3
Percent of student initiated housekeeping contacts refused by teacher	20
Percent of student initiated personal contacts refused by teacher	23
Percent of student initiated·tattling contacts refused by teacher	44
Percent of student initiated social contacts refused by teacher	8
Percent of total contacts which included negative teacher affect	I
Percent of misbehaviors responded to with warnings	19
Percent of misbehaviors responded to with threats	I
Percent of misbehaviors responded to with criticism or punishment	5

with their work, and seldom refused student initiatives (except for tattling, which was frequently refused but which also was an infrequent event in the first place).

The data in Tables 7.3 and 7.4 outline the major trends of classroom interaction within which group differences must be understood. This is especially important with measures of teacher and student emotional responsiveness in the classroom. These measures tap events which are salient, intense, and likely to be especially diagnostic with respect to the quality of teacher-student relationships. Such events are infrequent, however. For example, if we translate the data into real-time school days, we find that even the students who most often respond sullenly to their teachers or gripe, sass, or defy them do so at rates averaging less than once or twice per week. Most students do so not merely less often, but not at all.

Group differences on these low frequency variables can be both statistically significant and diagnostically meaningful. Even so, they must be interpreted within the base rates of occurrence observed. Thus, it would be inappropriate to conclude from such a difference that the group who responded sullenly to the teacher more often did so frequently or regularly in any absolute sense. The same is true of teacher treatment of different groups on low frequency variables. For example, we have noted that teachers rarely respond to student misconduct with strong personal criticism or punishment. A significant group difference on this variable might be obtained if Group A students were criticized or punished following 10 percent of their misbehaviors, but Group B students were criticized or punished following only 1 percent of theirs. This indicates a reliable teacher tendency to respond more sharply to the misbehavior of students in Group A. However, Group A students may (and probably do) misbehave both more often and more disruptively than Group B students. Thus, it would be inappropriate to conclude from the group difference data that teachers were hypercritical of Group A students or that they criticized them frequently in an absolute sense.

These considerations should be kept in mind when reading the findings throughout the rest of the book. We have been careful to phrase our descriptions of group differences in relative terms, except for a few places where absolute terms are justified. Even so, the very fact that we will be constantly emphasizing the contrasts between groups will tend to magnify their apparent differences. Actually, most such differences will involve relatively minor variations on the major themes indicated in Tables 7.3 and 7.4.

8

Student Sex Differences

As described in chapter 4, elementary teachers usually favor girls over boys in questionnaire responses, but there are a number of reasons to believe that this is due to differences in student characteristics rather than to female teacher bias in favor of female students or against male students (Brophy and Good, 1974). First, studies of male teachers indicate that they have the same kinds of attitudes toward and interactions with their students as female teachers do, at least as far as student sex is concerned (Good, Sikes, and Brophy, 1973; Lahaderne and Cohen, 1972). Also, analysis of traditional sex role socialization indicates that, during the elementary years, the female sex role is very compatible with the student role, but the male sex role is not (Bank, Biddle, and Good, 1980). The traditional socialization of girls toward verbal activities and responsibility, and of boys toward physical activities and competition, make it likely that girls will do better in their studies and conform more closely to classroom rules throughout most of childhood.

These considerations explain not only much of the teacher questionnaire data, but also certain replicated findings from classroom observational research, such as the finding that males usually get more criticism for misbehavior than females. Observational research that has linked teacher behavior to student behavior classified by sex of student has indicated that student behavior and not student sex is the primary determinant of teacher behaviors such as praise, criticism, reward, or punishment.

The large sample of teachers and students included in this study, combined with its rich and varied body of data, made it ideal for assessing these interpretations of the relationships among student sex, teacher attitudes, and teacher-student interactions. Data from the teacher adjective descriptions and the classroom observations are given in Tables 7.1 and 7.2, and in addition, there were sex differences in the teacher rankings on the 13 scales.

TEACHER RANKINGS

Significant differences appeared on 11 of these 13 scales, all of which favored the girls. Teachers saw the girls as calmer, more careful, more mature, higher achieving, more persistent, happier, more attractive, more likely to maintain eye contact, and more cooperative. They also were more likely to mention girls as objects of attachment and less likely to mention them as objects of concern. Girls were ranked higher on creativity, as well, but the sex difference was not significant. Boys were ranked higher on noticeable, but again not significantly.

The large number of students included in these analyses made it possible for relatively small sex differences to reach statistical significance, but even so, the data provide an overwhelmingly consistent picture of sex differences in teacher attitudes. The difference favored the girls on all 12 of the scales that can be characterized as reflecting favorable versus unfavorable perceptions, and 11 of these differences were significant.

The higher ranking of boys on noticeable does not indicate favorable perceptions, because students can be noticeable for undesirable as well as desirable behaviors. If anything, a bigger difference than what was obtained was expected here, given that boys generally are more physically active and present more frequent behavior problems in the classroom. Perhaps the explanation is methodological: we provided the teachers with class rosters to refer to when making their rankings, and this may have reduced any tendency to rank boys as more noticeable. If we had simply asked the teachers to name their students from memory, as Jackson, Silberman, and Wolfson (1969) did, a significant difference might have appeared. In any case, the teacher ranking data bear out many previous findings indicating that elementary teachers perceive girls more favorably than boys.

ADJECTIVE DESCRIPTION DATA

Teachers also favored girls in their adjective descriptions. About two-thirds of their comments about girls were positive, but only about half of their comments about boys were. Even so, sex differences reached statistical significance for only 8 of the 37 variables summarized in Table 7.1.

Girls were more likely to be described as helpful, motivated, or sweet, and boys more likely to be described as aggressive, active, or inattentive. These perceptions fit stereotypes picturing girls as sweet and cooperative and boys as inattentive, misbehaving, and poorly motivated. In view of these data, and the data from teacher rankings discussed above, it is surprising that significant differences did not appear for other adjective description variables like work habits, achievement, or likeable.

Boys also were more likely to be described as humorous. On balance, this probably is positive, because most of the adjectives in this category suggested a good sense of humor or being funny. However, the category did include being silly, so that even this difference is not clearly favorable to boys. Taken together, the adjective description data and the rankings data indicate a clear pattern of more favorable teacher perceptions of girls than of boys. These consistent differences were not particularly strong, however, and should not be overemphasized. It is worth mentioning that no significant differences appeared for adjective description variables such as mature, quiet, well behaved, intelligent, good worker, responsi-

ble, considerate, likeable, or untrustworthy. Thus, most of the perceived differences between boys and girls are related to the differences in fit between sex roles
and the student role, and they do not indicate generalized teacher dislike of boys or
beliefs that boys have serious personal or moral defects.

CLASSROOM OBSERVATION DATA

Significant sex differences appeared for 22 of the 73 variables in Table 7.2, 14 of
these at the .01 level of significance. Differences were stronger and more
numerous for variables indicating frequencies and types of contact than for
variables indicating teacher or student affect.

Boys had higher rates of total contact with the teachers than girls (1), partly
because teachers initiated more contacts with them (17), but mostly because they
had more behavioral contacts (8). Girls had higher percentages of contacts that
were private and nonacademic (6), indicating that the bulk of the boys' contacts
with teachers were related either to their academic work or their misbehavior.

Boys were more likely than girls to call out answers in general class settings
(16), but girls were more likely to raise their hands and wait to be called on as
volunteers (10, 15). In the general class setting, however, girls were more likely
to be called on after having waved their hands to gain attention rather than after
merely raising their hands quietly (15). These data indicate that students of both
sexes were willing to contribute to lessons and discussions, but that they used
contrasting styles of gaining response opportunities. The girls stifled their eagerness enough to conform to teacher expectations that they raise their hands and
wait to be recognized, but boys frequently would blurt out answers without
waiting for recognition. This is part of a general pattern of sex differences in
activity level and degree of conformity to classroom rules.

Turning from public response opportunity situations to private teacher-student
interactions, the data indicate that girls initiated more private contacts with the
teachers than boys did (7, 28), especially approval-seeking and housekeeping
contacts (30, 31). Approval-seeking contacts occurred when students who had
completed an activity or assignment brought their work up to the teacher to show
off. They were not seeking help or direction, but instead were showing completed work in the expectation of getting praise, approval, or other positive
teacher response. The sex difference on this variable indicates that girls were
more teacher-oriented than boys and more interested in pleasing the teachers.

Data on student-initiated housekeeping contacts indicate that girls were more
likely than boys to request permission to run errands or perform housekeeping
chores. This also suggests that girls were more interested than boys in pleasing
the teachers, although it could mean only that girls had a greater desire to keep
busy, and to do so in ways that were allowable in the classroom.

Even though girls frequently initiated contacts with the teachers, the teachers
did not reciprocate in this regard. In fact, teachers initiated more private contacts
with boys (17), especially academic and personal contacts (18, 20). The

academic contacts occurred during times when teachers were circulating around the room monitoring seatwork progress, and their higher rates of initiation with boys suggest that the boys were not working as consistently or successfully on their assignments as the girls were. In any case, teachers felt it necessary to intervene and provide direction more frequently with the boys.

Teacher-initiated personal contacts occurred when teachers asked students to clean up their desks or areas, take off or put away clothing, or attend to other personal tasks or responsibilities. The sex difference here indicates that teachers felt it necessary to remind boys to do things that girls tended to do on their own without having to be told. Again, this indicates that girls are better socialized to the student role at these grade levels.

Data on behavior contacts indicate that boys misbehaved not only more often (8, 35), but more disruptively (36). Yet, they were no more likely than girls to express hostility (37) or respond sullenly (44) to the teachers, even during behavior contacts. Nor were there any sex differences in other measures of student affect expressed toward teachers (39–43). These classroom observation data support the teacher adjective description data in suggesting that even though the boys' difficulties in conforming to the student role required teachers to direct or discipline them more frequently, this did not lead to alienation or strong negative affect.

Measures of teacher praise and criticism showed no sex differences for praise but a greater frequency of criticism during teacher-initiated academic contacts with boys (50, 51). Thus, teachers not only felt it necessary to initiate academic contacts with boys more often, but they were more likely to criticize the boys during such contacts. This again suggests that the boys were not working as carefully or efficiently as the girls (because most teacher criticism during academic contacts is for failure to work at all or failure to work carefully, and not just for failure to produce correct answers or high quality work).

This pattern of findings for teacher praise and criticism will be repeated frequently for several of the types of students defined by the 13 teacher ranking scales. That is, measures of teacher praise rarely showed significant group differences, but measures of teacher criticism frequently did. Part of the reason for this is that praise was much less frequent than criticism, except for brief praise of good answers during public recitations. Also, though, most teachers try to praise even their lowest achieving and most troublesome students when they get opportunities to do so, and try to avoid overtly favoring or overpraising successful and well-liked students. These factors reduce group differences on praise. Criticism usually works differently, however. Teachers seldom criticize successful and well-liked students, not only because of their good relations with these students, but also because the students rarely do things that would justify such criticism. Even when they do behave inappropriately, they are likely to respond to a brief corrective message that stops short of personal criticism. On the other hand, teachers often become very frustrated with the repeated problems presented by certain kinds of students (most of whom are boys), and end up criticizing them on occasion, even when they may be trying to avoid doing so. In any case, the data on teacher praise and criticism as they relate to sex of student are typical of the pattern seen for students rated high versus low on the 13 scales.

The last 19 variables in Table 7.2 concern teacher affective reactions to students or critical behaviors that suggest systematic differential treatment of students. The measures of positive teacher behaviors (55–62) yielded only one significant difference: teachers were more likely to reward boys than girls with special privileges (59). This finding does not so much suggest favoritism of boys as teacher attempts to use behavior modification principles with them. That is, more boys than girls failed to respond satisfactorily to teachers' ordinary socialization methods (basically, expounding rules, instructing students in what to do and how to do it, and praising them for doing so), so teachers sometimes would turn to extraordinary measures geared to gain their cooperation (and to avoid having to rely on punishment). Some teachers respond to problem students by spending a lot of extra time with them and developing close relationships with them. Others take a less personalized approach and begin to offer incentives for students who do not respond to ordinary instruction and encouragement. Thus, the fact that teachers did this more frequently with boys than girls is not so much a tendency to be more positive in dealing with boys. as a tendency to perceive boys (correctly) as requiring these kinds of extra incentives more often than girls do.

It should be noted that there were no sex differences on measures more directly related to positive affect by the teachers. Boys were no more likely than girls to be appointed as monitors, held up as good examples to the class, or flattered, and were no more likely to receive physical affection or other indications of positive teacher affect.

Similarly, there were no significant sex differences on indicators of negative teacher affect such as holding up the student as a bad example to the class, showing impatience during academic interactions, or responding punitively to misbehaviors. However, nonsignificant sex differences on these and other specific measures of negative teacher affect showed higher scores for boys, so that the percentage of total teacher-student contacts that included negative teacher affect did show a significant difference (70). Across all contacts combined, teachers were more likely to show negative affect to boys than to girls, although as noted above, the general pattern of data suggests that this difference reflects frustration with misconduct rather than more generalized alienation or rejection.

There also were several significant differences in teachers' responses to student initiations. Specifically, teachers were more likely to refuse boys than girls when they requested permission to perform errands or housekeeping chores (66), sought permission to meet personal needs or desires (67), or attempted to tattle on their classmates (68). The general pattern of data on these "teacher refusal of student initiation" variables suggests that group differences are not determined so much by teacher feelings (such as attempts to spite students who are disliked or who have misbehaved) as differences in student behavior. Students were likely to be refused or rebuffed if they came to the teachers at inappropriate times or made requests that teachers felt justified in refusing. The latter included such things as repeated requests to get a drink or go to the washroom by students who seemed to be trying to avoid work or requests to run errands by students whom the teachers believed (justifiably) might not be able to perform them successfully, might take advantage by dawdling or misbehaving, or simply had more important things to do first. Teachers were simply much more likely to respond favorably to the requests of students who were more mature, well behaved, and caught up on their work than students who were not.

Taken together, the teacher rankings, the adjective descriptions, and the classroom observation data reveal a widespread pattern indicating that girls were more successfully adjusted to the student role than boys were, and therefore were perceived more favorably by the teachers. Girls also were oriented more positively toward the teachers, initiating contacts with them more frequently, showing off their work to seek their approval, and offering to run errands or perform housekeeping chores for them. Girls also conformed more completely to classroom rules and apparently worked on their assignments more efficiently and successfully.

Boys misbehaved much more often and more disruptively, but were no more likely than girls to be alienated from the teachers or to express negative affect toward them. Nor were teachers alienated from them, although they were slightly more likely to express negative affect in interactions with boys than in interactions with girls. All in all, the sex difference data reviewed here reinforce and extend the patterns observed in earlier research: teachers perceive girls more positively than boys and share more positive patterns of interaction with them, but most if not all of these differences are attributable to differences in the behavior of the students themselves and not to significant teacher favoritism of girls or rejection of boys.

9

Student Maturity and Self-control

In this chapter, and in the rest of the book, we will present data on the relative differences between students rated consistently high and students rated consistently low by the teachers, in their scores on teacher adjective description measures and teacher-student interaction measures. Data presentation in this and the other chapters in Part 2 will involve describing the meanings of the statistically significant results presented in Tables 7.1 and 7.2. Later, the material will be integrated and discussed from a broader perspective in Part 3.

In this chapter we will contrast the calm students with the restless students, the careful students with the careless students, and the mature with the immature students. Recall that, along with the achieving, creative, and persistent scales, these three scales form part of a complex of teacher ratings dealing with the degree to which students conform to the idealized student role.

CALM

The calm versus restless scale correlated highly not only with various ratings indicating success at school tasks (mature, achieving, persistent), but also with cooperation and teacher attachment. These correlations with indications of teacher affect and the quality of the teacher-student relationship were due especially to negative teacher reactions to restless students.

Adjective Description Data

Teacher rankings on the calm versus restless scale showed significant relationships with 18 of the 37 adjective description variables. The descriptions of the calm students constitute a stereotype of the ideal student: quiet, helpful, well behaved, motivated, intelligent, achieving, good worker, and responsible. In addition, the teachers also described calm students as popular, sweet, and unlikely to be particularly happy, temperamental, or dependent. The general pattern for calm students suggests intelligence, self-control, and generally positive attributes, although these do not include notable happiness.

Restless students, in contrast, were seen to have the opposite of these qualities, and in addition, as likely to be aggressive, highly active, underachieving, and untrustworthy. Thus, in teachers' minds, hyperactivity is associated with undesirable personal attributes. (See Table 7.1.)

Classroom Observation Data

Consistent teacher rankings on the calm versus restless scale showed significant relationships with 36 of 73 variables in Table 7.2 (25 of these were below the .01 level). None of the other 12 scales had more than 32 significant relationships.

Calm students were below average in their total contacts with teachers (1), especially nonacademic contacts (6) and behavioral contacts (8). This supports the teachers' perceptions of them as not merely calm but well behaved and work oriented. Because they were below average in nonacademic and behavioral contacts, their average levels of public response opportunities (2) constituted a high percentage of their total contacts with the teacher, compared to those of restless students.

Restless students had the opposite pattern: high contact rates caused in particular by high rates of nonacademic and behavioral contacts. Teachers often had to intervene with restless students.

Restless students created many of their response opportunities by waving their hands to get the teacher's attention (11) or by calling out answers (16). Calm students did this much less often and got the bulk of their response opportunities by quietly raising their hands and waiting to be called on as volunteers (10, 14).

Calm students were below average for teacher-initiated contacts (17), especially academic (18) and personal (20) contacts. Restless students were above average on the same measures. When making rounds, teachers often merely observed the calm students working, without interrupting them to say anything to them (24). This indicated that calm students were seen as progressing well in their seatwork, so that no teacher intervention was required.

With restless students, however, teachers initiated interaction much more frequently, both in regard to academic work (18, 20) and in regard to personal matters (20, 26). Teacher-initiated personal contacts usually involved telling students to straighten their desks, put things away, or perform other tasks that should have been done on their own initiative.

Teacher-initiated housekeeping contacts (19) were no more frequent for calm than for restless students, but a greater percentage of the contacts that teachers initiated with calm students were housekeeping contacts (25).

This kind of significant group difference on a proportion measure, in the absence of a parallel difference in the corresponding rate measure, occurs because of differences on other variables. In this case, high percentages of teacher initiations with restless students were for academic and personal contacts, so their housekeeping contacts constituted a lower percentage, even though they were as frequent in absolute terms as housekeeping contacts with calm students were. In this case, then, the data on housekeeping contacts as a percentage of total teacher initiations (25) have little significance.

Data on student initiations complement the pattern seen in the data on teacher initiations. Compared to calm students, restless students were much more likely to initiate contact with the teacher (28). They were not more likely to come to the teacher for help with their work (29), but they were more likely to bring up completed work and seek the teacher's approval (30), to request permission to fulfill some personal desire (32), or to tattle (33). They also were more likely to misbehave (8), and to do so in a way that disrupted the class (36) or that involved griping, sassing, or defying the teacher (37). In addition, the restless students were more likely to be coded as sullen when corrected for their misbehavior.

These behavioral data provide some support for the adjective description data that indicate that teachers attribute a variety of positive qualities to calm students and negative qualities to restless students that go beyond their differences in activity level. The students consistently rated as calm seemed to be unusually well behaved and adjusted to the student role, and the students consistently rated as restless frequently misbehaved disruptively and responded to teachers with hostility. Yet, they also came to the teachers more often to tattle on their peers or to seek approval for their completed work. The data on teacher praise and criticism and on teacher affect provide clues as to why this was so.

None of the measures of academic praise were related to the calm versus restless rankings, but the criticism data indicate that restless students were much more likely than calm students to be criticized for not working or for doing poor work (50, 51, 54). Teachers were likely to express positive affect (60, 62) toward calm students and to praise them for good classroom conduct (61), and unlikely to do this with restless students. In contrast, the teachers were especially likely to express negative affect (70) toward the restless students, to respond with rejection or punishment to their misbehavior (71, 72, 73), to hold them up as bad examples to the rest of the class (63), and to refuse their requests for help (65) or permission (66) and their attempts to tattle (68).

Taken together, these data indicate teacher liking for the calm students, and especially, dislike of the restless students. To some extent, of course, the teachers' high rates of criticism of restless students can be explained by the frustration involved in coping with their continuing hyperactivity and misconduct, and their refusals of restless students' initiatives and requests can be explained by the presumably greater tendency of these students (relative to calm students) to come at inappropriate times or with inappropriate requests. Even so, the pattern of teacher response to these students is unremittingly negative, compared to other types of students that the teachers rated unfavorably (to be discussed). There is no indication that the teachers systematically tried to reinforce the positive behavior of these restless students or to compensate for their rejecting and punitive treatment by awarding special privileges or trying to be pleasant at other times. Apparently, either the stress that these students created for the teachers became overwhelming, or there was something about their personal qualities that alienated the teachers (students consistently rated as restless were also likely to be listed on the low end of the attachment scale among those the teacher would like to be rid of).

In view of this negative teacher response, and also the defiance and sullen reactions to the teacher that the restless students presented, the tendency of these students to come to the teacher to tattle or seek approval is surprising. It suggests that the students may have been aware of the teachers' feelings and attempted to counter them somewhat by currying favor with them when opportunities arose. This was generally ineffective, however, because their requests for help or permission were likely to be refused and their attempts to tattle rejected. This was true even though the teachers often characterized the restless students as dependent on them in their adjective descriptions. Apparently, the frustration and irritation produced by the intense, disruptive misbehavior and the hostile attitude of these students were more than the teachers were willing to take.

CAREFUL

The data for the careful versus careless scale are similar in many ways to those for the calm versus restless scale. However, there are fewer significant effects, and as expected, these focus more on work habits than on general activity levels. Students seen as careless are not viewed as negatively as students seen as restless.

Adjective Description Data

Significant differences between groups of students ranked consistently on the careful versus careless scale were observed for 15 of the 37 adjective description variables. As with the calm students, many of these relationships pictured the careful students as ideal: quiet, helpful, motivated, intelligent, achieving, responsible good workers. Careful students were also described as mature, considerate, and likely to come from good homes, and careless students were described as active, inattentive, and likely to be underachievers or untrustworthy. These differences all favor the careful over the careless students. Comparisons with the pattern for the calm versus restless scale suggest that teachers' positive feelings toward the careful students were not as strong or widespread as their positive feelings toward the calm students, and that their negative reactions to the careless students were not as intense or widespread as their negative reactions to the restless students (see Table 7.1).

Classroom Observation Data

The same is true for the classroom observation data, where 25 of the 73 variables in Table 7.2 showed significant relationships (20 of these at the .01 level). Most of these concern interactions during private contacts and behavior contacts rather than public response opportunities. ·

Like restless students, careless students had high rates of contact with their teachers because they had frequent nonacademic or behavioral contacts (1, 6, 8). As a result, they had low percentages of public response opportunities relative to total contacts (3). Careful students had high percentages of public response opportunities, because they had relatively few nonacademic contacts with teachers.

Group differences in activity levels show up in patterns of response opportunity during small group interactions (10, 11). Careful students got most of their response opportunities after being called on as volunteers, but careless students often were called on after waving their hands to get the teachers' attention. However, they were no more likely than other students to call out answers, suggesting that they were somewhat more controlled than the restless students.

Teachers initiated private academic interactions with careful students at below average rates (18, 23), indicating that they felt less need to check up on these students systematically. In contrast, they often initiated private contacts with careless students (17) both to check up on their work (18, 23) and to remind them of their personal responsibilities (20).

Teachers were more likely to invite careful students to perform housekeeping tasks, and less likely to do so with careless students (19, 25). Taken together, these data on teacher initiations indicate that the teachers were acting systematically upon their perceptions of careful students as responsible, good workers and careless students as requiring continuous monitoring.

Careless students initiated more private contacts with the teachers than careful students did (28), especially to seek help with their work (29) or to attempt to tattle on their peers (33). Yet, the careless students also misbehaved more often (35), were more likely to gripe, sass, or defy the teacher when doing so (37), and were more likely to be sullen when corrected (44).

These data parallel those for restless students in suggesting that the careless students combined a certain dependency on the teacher with tendencies to misbehave frequently and treat the teacher with hositlity. However, unlike restless students, careless students were not especially likely to be disruptive when they misbehaved, and their initiatives with the teachers were more likely to involve seeking help with their work than to involve attempts to get teacher approval or permission to meet their personal needs. This made the careless students both less threatening and less demanding to the teachers than the restless students were, which may explain why they were not perceived as negatively or described as dependent, and why their initiatives met with a better teacher response, on the average.

Teachers did not differentiate between careful and careless students in their praise, but they criticized careless students more often (54), particularly during teacher-initiated academic contacts (50, 51). Teacher reactions during nonacademic contacts showed even more differentiation. Careful students were especially likely to be praised for good conduct (61) and unlikely to be criticized or punished for misbehavior (73). The opposite was true of careless students, who also were likely to be held up as bad examples to the class (63).

However, there is one remarkable exception to this pattern of favoritism of careful over careless students: teachers were especially likely to show physical affection toward the careless students (58). This, along with the fact that teachers were not especially likely to refuse the initiatives of the careless students (as they were with the restless students), indicates that the teachers did not respond with rejection or other intense emotional reactions to the pressures that the careless students presented, and that they even were able to reach out toward these students during nonstressful interactions. It may be that the physical affection was directed primarily toward the careless students who were least sullen and defiant, but in any case it is clear that the troublesome behavior of the careless students as a group did not affect the teachers nearly so negatively as the troublesome behavior of the restless students.

Similarly, teachers' positive behavior toward careful students was less widespread and intense than it was toward calm students. They did praise the careful students more often for exhibiting desirable classroom conduct, but they did not praise their academic work more often nor favor them with positive affect or special privileges. Their interactions with the careful students were mostly positive but impersonal, centered around behaviors built into the teacher and student roles.

MATURE

As would be expected from the correlations presented in Tables 6.4 and 6.5, the data involving teacher rankings of mature are similar to those for rankings of calm and careful. Significant relationships are less numerous and extreme than for the calm scale, but more numerous than for the careful scale.

Adjective Description Data

Significant effects appeared for 15 of the 37 adjective description variables. Many of these relationships define the same "ideal student" pattern seen earlier for calm and careful students. Mature students were described as quiet, helpful, motivated, intelligent, achieving, and responsible, good workers. They also were seen as more creative and more likely to come from good homes than were immature students, who were described as likely to be hyperactive, temperamental, dependent on the teacher, or above average in frequency of medical problems (see Table 7.1).

All of these perceived differences favor the mature over the immature students. However, the undesirable characteristics attributed to the immature students are less negative than those attributed to careless and especially to restless students. The immature students were not any more likely than other students to be described as unhappy, aggressive, inconsiderate, inattentive, underachieving, or untrustworthy. This pattern of descriptions indicates that the immature students were not seen as being at fault or blameworthy for the problems they presented.

Classroom Observation Data

Significant relationships were observed for 29 of the 73 variables in Table 7.2, 16 at the .01 level. There are many similarities to the data from the calm and careful scales, but also two general differences. First, the teachers seemed more genuinely fond of the students they described as mature, and they had clearly positive patterns of interactions with them. This contrasts with the more neutral patterns observed for calm and careful students. Also, although the immature students presented problems that the teachers had to deal with, teachers generally responded to them much more positively than they did to the careless students and especially the restless students.

Data on types of contact with teachers indicate the same general patterns seen on the previous scales: immature students had higher than average rates of contact because they had high rates of nonacademic and behavioral contacts (1, 6, 8). As a result, relatively low percentages of their contacts involved public response opportunities (3). In addition, the public response opportunities that immature students did receive were more likely to come during small group activities than in the general class setting.

The immature students had high rates of teacher-initiated contacts (17), mostly because teachers felt it necessary to come to them frequently to check on their work (18), or to remind them about their personal responsibilities (20). However, teachers also initiated social contacts frequently with these students, suggesting attempts to get to know them and build good relationships with them (21). Because teachers initiated so many academic and personal contacts with immature students, their proportion of teacher-initiated housekeeping contacts (25) was low.

Mature and immature students did not differ significantly in student-initiated contacts except for tattling, which was much more frequent among the immature students, as expected (33). Immature students also were much more likely to misbehave (8, 35), often disruptively (36). They also were likely to respond sullenly when disciplined (44).

On the whole, however, the immature students apparently had neutral to positive contacts with the teachers. They were no more likely than other students to gripe, sass, or defy (37), or to show negative affect during teacher-initiated academic or personal contacts (41, 42). Furthermore, they were actually less likely to express negative affect toward teachers during teacher-initiated social contacts (43). Perhaps this has something to do with why the teachers were more likely to initiate such social contacts with the immature students than they were with the mature students.

Even though the teachers felt it necessary to monitor the immature students closely and frequently initiated academic contacts with them, they were likely to praise these students during such contacts (45). The immature students were the only group of all those studied for whom this was true, suggesting that teachers were making special efforts to encourage their progress. Less surprisingly, teachers also were likely to criticize the work of the immature students when they initiated academic contacts with them (50, 51, 54).

Teachers also were likely to display physical affection toward the immature students (58). Other data suggest that this probably occurred during teacher-initiated academic or social contacts, where praise and positive affect were often observed. Unfortunately, this positive pattern did not extend to student initiated contacts and behavior contacts, where the teachers were much less positive in their responses to immature students.

Teachers often refused the academic initiations of the immature students (65), and often showed impatience during the contacts that they did allow (64). They also were likely to refuse housekeeping initiations by these students (66), and to respond to their misbehaviors with criticism or punishment (73). Consequently, a relatively high percentage of the interactions involving immature students included negative affect on the part of the teachers (70).

Teachers' interactions with the mature students were generally neutral and businesslike, concentrated on academics rather than social, personal, or behavioral matters. Teachers were especially likely, however, to single out the mature students for praise of their good classroom conduct (61).

Taken together, the data indicate that teachers were friendly and encouraging when they could interact with immature students on their own terms, particularly during teacher-initiated academic and social contacts. They were often unreceptive when the immature students came to initiate contacts with them, however, and easily angered when they misbehaved. Apparently the teachers were frustrated with the hyperactivity, dependency, and other problematic behaviors that these students presented. In any case, the data indicate notable teacher impatience and negative affect directed toward the immature students, even though these students did not seem to be generally alienated from the teachers and did not rebel against them in active, hostile ways.

10

Student Achievement, Creativity, and Persistence

The achievement, creativity, and persistence ratings discussed in this chapter all deal with the nature and outcomes of students' work on classroom assignments. Achievement and creativity tend to be judged by the quality of the finished products the students turn in, and seem to reflect teachers' perceptions of the students' native abilities, at least in part. Persistence, like careful, refers to students' work habits while they are in the process of completing their assignments.

In general, the three scales discussed in this chapter produced fewer significant relationships than the three discussed previously. Furthermore, the significant effects that did appear for these scales are mostly related clearly to the specific student attributes involved, and are less generalized to other measures, as was the case with the scales discussed in the previous chapter.

ACHIEVEMENT

Achievement ratings showed strong positive correlations with careful, mature, and persistent, and negative correlations with concern. Notable positive correlations were also seen for creative and attachment. In general, then, teachers were fond of high achievers and tended to attribute their success at least in part to good work habits and persistence, and they were concerned about and somewhat rejecting of low achievers. Taken alone, these patterns suggest that teachers were taking student effort (as they perceived it) into account in making the achievement ratings, so that those ranked at the bottom of the scale were seen as underachievers who were not making full use of their abilities rather than merely as low achievers who had limited abilities. The adjective description data dispute this conclusion, however.

Adjective Description Data

Significant relationships were seen for 12 of the 37 adjective description variables (see Table 7.1). Relative to low achievers, high achievers were seen as more mature, motivated, intelligent, achieving, responsible, attentive, athletic, creative, and likely to come from a good home, and as less likely to be absent. Low achievers were seen to have the opposite traits, and in addition were seen as more likely to be untrustworthy.

On the whole, this pattern is not what was expected on the basis of the intercorrelations among the 13 scales because it suggests that teachers were looking more at ability than at motivation in ranking the students on achievement. The strongest relationships were for the descriptions mature, intelligent, achieving, and coming from a good home. It is true that high achievers were likely to be described as highly motivated and low achievers as poorly motivated, and a similar difference in attentiveness was seen as well. However, there were no significant relationships for such descriptions as good worker or underachiever. In general, then, it appears that teachers' perceptions of students ranked consistently on the achieving scale were determined primarily by student ability, and not by effort or classroom conduct.

The relationship between the achievement rankings and the teachers' perceptions of students as athletic, although not specifically expected, was not surprising. Studies of pupil characteristics consistently show small but statistically significant positive relationships between achievement as measured by standardized tests and measures of physical maturity, height and weight, and athletic ability. Thus, the link between athletic ability and achievement perceived by the teachers probably is objectively accurate.

Classroom Observation Data

Significant relationships were observed for 18 of the 73 variables in Table 7.2, 11 of these at the .01 level. As expected, most of these relationships come from measures of academic interactions rather than nonacademic or behavioral contacts.

Compared to low achievers, high achievers had fewer interactions with teachers (1), particularly nonacademic (6) or behavioral (8) contacts. Partly because of this, high percentages of the contacts that they did have came as public response opportunities (3, 4), especially in general class settings (4, 5). Furthermore, most of these response opportunities occurred after the high-achieving students raised their hands and were called on by the teacher (13, 14).

Low achievers, in contrast, had fewer public response opportunities and more private contacts with teachers. They did not raise their hands and volunteer frequently in public response opportunity situations (14), so the teachers had to call on them as nonvolunteers more frequently (13).

Group differences in private contacts were due to teacher rather than to student behavior. The low- and high-achieving students did not differ in rates of initiation of private contacts with the teacher or in types of contacts initiated. However, teachers initiated private contacts with low achievers very frequently (6, 17). This included both academic contacts (18) and personal (20) and social (21) contacts. As a result of these higher rates of other types of teacher initiations, the low achievers had a relatively low percentage of teacher initiations that involved housekeeping requests (25).

Information on student-initiated contacts revealed no significant differences: low-achieving students were just as likely to initiate interaction with the teacher as high achievers were. In general, then, the data presented so far suggest good relationships between the teachers and the low achievers, who were not avoiding the teachers even though they did not tend to volunteer for public response opportunities very often. Teachers responded to their needs by initiating academic interactions allowing them to monitor and check their work more often, and although they did find it necessary to remind them to fulfill their personal responsibilities more often, they also initiated social interactions with them more often.

This positive picture might seem to be contradicted by the negative relationships for behavior-related contacts (8, 35), but the group means indicated that these relationships were due to unusually low rates of misbehavior by high achievers rather than to high rates of misbehavior by low achievers. The same is true for sullen reactions to teacher interventions (44). Here again, the relationship appeared because this type of reaction was extremely infrequent for high achievers, and not because it was frequent for low achievers. Furthermore, the misbehaviors of the low achievers were likely to involve nonthreatening, noninteractive behaviors such as copying answers or sleeping (38). Low achievers were not especially likely to be disruptive or defiant.

Teachers were more likely to refuse the academic initiations of the low achievers (65), although the general pattern of results here suggests that this was because low achievers often came at inappropriate times rather than because the teachers were avoiding these students in any general sense. The overall picture is that these students needed a lot of monitoring and assistance with their work, and that the teachers tried to provide this.

Finally, the teachers were more likely to display physical affection toward low achievers than high achievers (58). All in all, the data for this scale indicate that teachers had very positive but not especially affective relationships with the high achievers, who were very successful in meeting classroom demands. The low achievers had limited abilities and thus were much less successful. They were especially unlikely to be called on as volunteers during public discussions, and teachers sometimes refused them or delayed them when they came seeking help with their work. Otherwise, however, their relationships with teachers were neutral to positive. They initiated interaction with teachers just as often as high achievers did, and showed no evidence of general alienation toward the teacher or the classroom. Teachers came to them frequently to help with work, to remind them of their duties, or simply to socialize, and they were more likely to display physical affection toward them than they were toward the high achievers. Thus, the teachers were reaching out toward the low achievers and attempting to meet their needs.

Some of the nonsignificant findings helped fill out this picture. Despite large differences in classroom success, teachers were no more likely to praise the high achievers or criticize the low achievers. Nor were there differences on such variables as holding up the student as a good or bad example, treating the student with impatience, flattering the student, or providing special privileges. In general, to the extent that the classroom behavior and teacher-student interactions of consistently high-achieving or low-achieving students differed from average, they did so in ways directly related to these achievement patterns and did not tend to generalize to the more personal or affective aspects of the teacher-student relationship.

CREATIVITY

Creativity rankings were most closely associated with achievement rankings, although they did not correlate strongly with any of the other 12 scales. In general, the data indicate that these teachers had difficulty differentiating creativity from intelligence.

Adjective Description Data

Significant relationships appeared for only 7 of the 37 adjective description variables (see Table 7.1). Relative to students low in creativity, those high in creativity were seen as more intelligent, achieving, athletic, creative, and likely to be social leaders. This pattern makes sense, given that students who are creative as well as bright are likely to be social leaders, and given the remarks noted earlier about the relationship between athletic ability and achievement.

Teachers had more miscellaneous negative comments about students ranked low in creativity, and a high percentage of their comments about students they saw as creative were positive comments. Thus, we did not find the pattern reported by Getzels and Jackson (1962) indicating that teachers are likely to have negative perceptions of highly creative students. In their study, however, student creativity was measured with tests of divergent thinking abilities, whereas in the present study it was implicitly defined individually by teachers as they made their rankings. Perhaps the teachers ranked highly only those students whose unusual statements or behavior were not only creative but also socially acceptable. In any case, all of the group differences here reflected positively on the highly creative students when compared with the less creative students.

Classroom Observation Data

Significant relationships appeared for only 16 of the 73 variables in Table 7.2, 7 of these at the .01 level. As far as it goes, the pattern here resembles that for the achievement scale.

Compared to students rated low in creativity, those rated as creative had many more public response opportunities (2, 3) especially in the general class setting (4, 5). In part, this is because they frequently called out answers (16). Students rated low in creativity seemed generally passive in the general class setting. They seldom called out answers (16), and they often had to be called on as nonvolunteers (13). Their behavior in the small group setting was somewhat different, however. They still had to be called on more frequently as nonvolunteers (9), but they also received a greater portion of their responses after waving their hands to get the attention of the teacher (11). The last finding suggests that these students may have been somewhat immature, not merely low in creativity.

Students rated low in creativity had low percentages of teacher initiations involving requests for housekeeping assistance or errands (25), because the teachers were much more likely to initiate both academic (18) and nonacademic (17, 20, 22) contacts with these students than with those seen as more creative. This suggests that students low in creativity were generally low in ability. In any case, the pattern is much like it was with the low achievement students: the teachers apparently felt the need to monitor and initiate interactions with these students regularly, but there is no indication that these students were alienated from the teachers or that they tended to misbehave more often or more intensively.

The only other variables showing significant relationships concerned criticism during teacher-initiated academic contacts (50, 51, 54). Students rated low in creativity got more such criticism than students rated high. It is of interest that these relationships were not seen for students high versus low in achievement, again suggesting that students rated low in creativity might have been somewhat more passive and immature than other low-achieving students.

None of the indications of teacher or student affect showed significant relationships. Apparently, the less creative students got along well enough with the teachers despite low achievement and passivity, and the highly creative students did not get along with the teachers any better than other students. This indicates that teacher rankings of creativity, even more so than rankings of achievement, were mostly based on teachers' perceptions of students' abilities, and were essentially unrelated to personality variables.

PERSISTENCE

Teacher rankings on persistence correlated highly with calm, careful, happy, achievement, mature, cooperative, attachment, and concern (negatively). Thus, the persistence rankings were linked more closely to rankings on the other scales than the achievement and creativity rankings were. This would be expected from attribution theory (Weiner, 1979), because the ratings of achievement and creativity were based mostly on assessments of intelligence, but ratings of persistence get more directly at effort, which is more clearly under the control of the student. Thus, students can be expected to be held praiseworthy or blameworthy for their persistence, in ways that do not apply to their achievement or creativity.

Adjective Description Data

Significant relationships were observed for 12 of the 37 adjective description variables. Persistent students were seen as mature, helpful, motivated, intelligent, achieving, and responsible good workers who also were likely to come from good homes. Students ranked low in persistence were seen as having the opposite traits, and also as likely to be active or inattentive. This is a broader pattern than was observed for the achievement and creativity scales, and yet it is concentrated mostly on variables having to do with school achievement and performance in the student role; more general student personality characteristics are absent (see Table 7.1).

Classroom Observation Data

Significant relationships were observed for 27 of the 73 variables on Table 7.2, 14 of these at the .01 level. This is more than for the achievement and creativity scales. The differences are due to more frequent significant relationships for behavioral interactions, indicating that students who give up easily on assignments not only lack persistence but apparently misbehave when they are not working on their assignments.

Compared to those rated low, students rated high in persistence had fewer overall contacts with teachers (1), largely because they had fewer nonacademic (6) and behavioral (8) contacts. Also, greater proportions of the contacts that they did have were public response opportunities (3), especially in the general class setting (5). All of this indicates that these students were generally higher achievers and better students than those ranked low in persistence.

The persistent students received most of their response opportunities as volunteers (10, 14), and they seldom waved their hands at the teacher in an attempt to get called on (11). The students ranked low in persistence had the opposite pattern, and also were more likely to be involved in nonacademic and behavioral contacts with the teachers (6, 8).

The data on teacher initiations show the same pattern as seen for low achievers. The percentage of teacher initiations with students ranked low in persistence that involved housekeeping requests (25) was low because teachers initiated more of the other types of private contacts with these students. Many of these were academic contacts in which they monitored the students' work or provided help (18), but many also were personal or social contacts (20, 21). In general, teachers felt it necessary to monitor and initiate interactions with the low persistence students much more often than with the high persistence students.

Data on student initiations and affect indicate that the teachers had problems with the students they rated low in persistence. These students were more likely to come to them to tattle (33), more likely to sass, defy, or gripe during teacher interventions (37), more likely to express negative affect toward the teacher (41), and more likely to be coded as sullen (44). Students seen as high in persistence had the opposite pattern.

Teacher reactions to students seen as low in persistence were mixed rather than totally negative, however. Teachers were likely to criticize them during teacher-initiated academic contacts (50, 51), presumably because they were not working, but they also were more likely to praise these students when they came to them for help or to seek approval for completed work. Thus, the data suggest that teachers were trying to use their praise and criticism of these students as behavior modification techniques in ways that were not seen with other types of students described so far.

The data on teacher critical behaviors and affective reactions to the students also indicate a mixed picture. Teachers were likely to hold up as bad examples to the class the students who were low in persistence (63), and to express impatience during academic interactions with them (64). They also were more likely to express negative affect generally (70), and to respond to their misbehaviors with warnings (71), criticism, or punishment (73). This indicates that they frequently found these students very frustrating and showed it. On the other hand, they also were more likely to display physical affection toward these students than they were toward the persistent students (58).

Taken together, the data indicate that teachers frequently found themselves criticizing or even punishing the low persistence students because they were not on task, and yet they seemed to be making systematic efforts to try to change these students by praising or rewarding them when they did well. Even though these students sometimes were sullen or negativistic, teacher response to the problems they presented could be characterized more as frustration than rejection. Thus, in contrast to the data for restless students, for example, the classroom observation data for students low in persistence reveal teacher attempts to work on the problem and reinforce appropriate behavior in addition to criticizing or punishing inappropriate behavior. Teachers apparently were aware of their difficulties with these students and tried to do something about them by initiating social contacts with them, showing physical affection, and praising when they had the opportunity to do so.

11

Student Attractiveness

In this chapter, we will consider two student attributes that contribute to general social attractiveness: happiness and physical attractiveness. Students consistently perceived as happy usually are well liked and enjoyed by teachers, because they have cheerful dispositions and friendly, optimistic approaches to classroom living. People with such traits usually are popular in any context. In contrast, consistently unhappy people are less likely to be well liked by others. If the reasons for their unhappiness are known and understandable, they may be pitied rather than disliked. However, their own unhappiness may make others around them uncomfortable, so that they are unlikely to be very popular and may even be social isolates.

Physical attractiveness is a personal attribute that has no logical linkage to school achievement or teacher-student interaction, but was included in the study because previous research had shown that attractive individuals were perceived more favorably than less attractive individuals (Dion, Berscheid, and Walster, 1972; Berscheid and Walster, 1972). Furthermore, some studies suggested that physical attractiveness might make a difference in teacher perceptions and treatment of students.

For example, in one study (Clifford and Walster, 1971), fifth-grade teachers were asked to make predictions about educational success and other matters, based on student report cards. Report cards for comparison students were identical, except that some were accompanied by a picture of a student judged to be physically attractive, and others were accompanied by a picture of a student judged to be physically unattractive. Even though the reports were identical except for the photos, more promising predictions were made about the attractive students.

Relationships between attractiveness and other variables are not completely illogical, although they are stronger than they deserve to be. In part, their reasonableness depends on what kinds of things are taken into account when teachers (or anyone else) rate attractiveness. If ratings are based on purely physical features, there should be few relationships to anything else. However, if differences in attractiveness are affected by differences in nutrition and general health care, which in turn are related to differences in socioeconomic status, some genuine relationships might be expected. Even stronger relationships would be expected where ratings of attractiveness took into account not only purely physical characteristics but also manners, social sophistication, clothing, grooming, and other attributes reflective of general socioeconomic status and even of family values.

We asked teachers to restrict themselves to purely physical features in rating attractiveness, but this is difficult to do. It seems likely that certain students' ratings were enhanced or reduced by cleanliness, grooming, quality of clothing, and other factors related to the socioeconomic status and general lifestyles of their families. Consequently, we did expect some positive relationships between physical attractiveness and the other student attributes examined in the study, although we expected that attractiveness would be one of the weaker variables. Furthermore, we expected that attractiveness would correlate more consistently in the perception data than in the observational data, because the correlates of attractiveness that we expected to influence perceptions were not expected to influence classroom interaction much, if at all.

In summary, our main interest in examining the data for happy versus unhappy was to see if students consistently perceived as happy showed generally positive dispositions and popularity with teachers and peers. Our major interest in studying unhappy students was to see the degree to which they elicited pity versus rejection from teachers and peers. In examining attractive versus unattractive students, we wanted to see if physical attractiveness did affect perceptions to any significant degree, and also if students' physical attractiveness related to their classroom behavior or their interactions with teachers.

HAPPY

The correlations in Tables 6.1 and 6.2 indicate that consistent rankings on the happy versus unhappy scale were associated with consistent rankings on cooperation, attractiveness, persistence, and attachment. Thus, as expected, ratings of happiness were based mostly on the students' personal attributes, and not their general intelligence or achievement. The happy students were seen as cooperative and persistent, but relationships with calm, careful, achieving, and creative were notably weaker.

Adjective Description Data

Significant relationships were observed for 10 of the 37 adjective description variables. Happy students were seen as helpful, motivated, intelligent, and responsible good workers likely to come from good homes, and the opposite was true of unhappy students. This pattern is similar to but not as strong or widespread as the patterns seen for the calm, careful, mature, and persistent scales (see Table 7.1).

Happy students also were seen as likely to be social leaders and as unlikely to be temperamental or frequently absent. The opposite was true of unhappy students. These differences make sense as far as they go, but it is interesting that significant relationships were not seen for other variables that might have been included here: sociable, humorous, likeable, or cries easily. In addition, there were not enough data in certain adjective description categories to allow tests of relationships for certain relevant descriptors such as happy and popular. In general, the pattern of relationships suggests that teachers were rating happiness versus unhappiness as an individual trait manifested mostly when the students were alone or interacting with the teachers rather than as a social trait reflecting interaction with peers. They did see happy students as likely to be social leaders, but other descriptors indicating social traits either did not show significant relationships or were not mentioned often enough to analyze for such relationships.

Classroom Observation Data

Significant relationships were observed for 27 of the 73 variables in Table 7.2, but only 9 of these reached the .01 level. Most of these relationships were due more to undesirable patterns involving the unhappy students than to distinctively desirable patterns for the happy students.

Happy and unhappy students did not differ in their rates of total contact with teachers (1), but there were several differences in types of contact. Happy students had more public response opportunities (2, 3), especially in the general class setting (4, 5). They also initiated more contacts with the teachers (7). Unhappy students, on the other hand, misbehaved more frequently and thus were involved in more frequent behavioral interactions (8, 35).

Even though happy students had good relationships with teachers and often initiated interactions with them, they were unlikely to wave their hands seeking to be called on in the small group (11) or to call out answers in the general class setting (16). Instead, they would raise their hands and wait to be called on as volunteers (10, 14). Unhappy students were more likely to do the opposite.

Bearing out their perceptions of differences in work habits, the teachers clearly felt it necessary to monitor the unhappy students closely and initiate interactions frequently to check, and perhaps help them with, their work (17, 18). They were much less likely to do this with happy students, and in fact frequently confined themselves to merely observing these students at work without intervening to speak to them (24). Because teachers initiated so many academic contacts with unhappy students, their percentage of teacher initiations related to housekeeping requests or errands was low (25). There were no differences in patterns of teacher-initiated social or personal contacts, however.

The only significant relationship among the student-initiated contacts also involved housekeeping contacts: happy students were much more likely than unhappy students to request permission to run errands or perform housekeeping chores (31). The happy versus unhappy scale was the only one to show a significant relationship on this variable. Apparently, the happy students enjoyed doing such tasks and sought opportunities to do so even beyond the (average number of) opportunities given them at the teachers' initiation. Unhappy students, on the other hand, were less likely to approach the teachers with requests to do such chores.

Unhappy students were much more likely than happy students to misbehave (8, 35), and also more likely to gripe, sass, or defy the teacher (37) or to be coded as acting sullenly (44) during such contacts. Given that they also seldom volunteered answers and generally avoided the teachers, it is clear that they presented the teachers with many problems. However, they were no more likely than other students to behave disruptively (36) or to express negative affect toward the teacher (41, 42, 43). Apparently, their negative reactions were confined to times that the teachers criticized their behavior.

Perhaps this relative absence of disruptive misbehavior, coupled with the fact that unhappy students apparently were in fact troubled and were perceived by the teachers as unhappy, explains the "kid gloves" approach that the teachers took toward them. Unhappy students were especially likely to be praised for good answers or good work (49), and unlikely to be criticized for poor answers or poor work, when they initiated academic or approval-seeking contacts with the teachers (53). They also were called on frequently in small groups after waving their hands (11), and were allowed to call out answers unusually often in the general class setting (16). Furthermore, they were less likely to be criticized for such calling out (52). All of this indicates that teachers were aware of the tendency of unhappy students to withdraw from themselves (the teachers) and from academic activities, and that they were systematically trying to change this behavior by going out of their way to accept the initiatives of these students and to reinforce their successes. However, this pattern of response in academic situations was not generalized to include behavioral interactions: the teachers were notably unlikely to praise the unhappy students for good classroom conduct (61, 62). They frequently responded to their misbehaviors with warnings or threats (71, 72), although they were not especially likely to respond with criticism or punishment (73). Thus, even in behavior contacts, the teachers tempered their reactions to these unhappy students.

Returning to academic contacts, we find that the data for teacher-initiated contacts are much less positive than the data for student-initiated contacts and public response opportunities. Despite the unusual degree of academic encouragement that the teachers provided to the unhappy students, they also delivered a lot of criticism when they initiated academic contacts with them (51, 54). Thus, even though teachers avoided expressing negative affect toward these students or holding them up as bad examples to the class, they nevertheless pressured them consistently to do their work and criticized them when they failed to do so.

In general, the data indicate that happy students were generally good students who worked carefully and obeyed the teachers but also had unusually cheerful dispositions and social leadership qualities. They had good relationships with the teachers, and in particular frequently ran errands or performed housekeeping chores, both at the teachers' and their own initiative. They were more likely than unhappy students to be praised for good behavior, but otherwise there was little evidence of teacher favoritism of the happy students.

Unhappy students appeared alienated from teachers and school work. They generally avoided the teachers and often misbehaved, sometimes even defying the teachers. Teachers responded by monitoring these students closely, frequently criticizing them for not working or warning them about inappropriate conduct. They usually stopped short of rejection or punishment, however, and showed little evidence of strong negative affect toward these students despite the problems they presented. Furthermore, they tried to encourage and reinforce these students when opportunities arose, especially when the students showed some interest in contributing to class discussions or came up to the teachers to show their work. Thus, in contrast to their reactions to other kinds of troublesome students, teachers seemed willing to make allowances for the students they perceived as troubled and unhappy.

ATTRACTIVE

Correlations between the attractive scale and the other 12 ranking scales were generally low, as expected. The correlations in Tables 6.1 and 6.2 indicate that teachers saw attractive students as careful, happy, and persistent, and as objects of teacher attachment. This is a generally positive pattern as far as it goes, but it is notably weaker than those for most other scales. Thus, teachers' perceptions of physical attractiveness, while relevant, are not associated with strong biases or personal reactions to students.

Adjective Description Data

Significant relationships were seen for 11 of the 37 adjective description variables. Attractive students were seen as likely to be intelligent and achieving, but there were no significant relationships with descriptors such as motivated or good worker. Thus, teachers associated attractiveness with intelligence, but not necessarily with achievement motivation (see Table 7.1).

Attractive students also were described as happy, athletic, and attractive, and unattractive students as likely to be aggressive, inattentive, often absent, or having medical problems. Miscellaneous additional negative descriptions were applied to unattractive students, as well. These descriptors suggest that the attractiveness ratings were affected by perceptions of physical health as well as physical attractiveness. There is also the suggestion that attractive students were happier and generally better adjusted than unattractive students.

Classroom Observation Data

Significant relationships were observed for only 7 of the 73 variables in Table 7.2, and only one of these reached the .01 level of significance. These figures are only slightly above chance, indicating that teacher perceptions of attractiveness have very little effect on the quantity or quality of teacher-student interaction, even though they do affect teacher perceptions. This was the only one of the 13 scales that did not yield classroom-observation data that suggested reliable differential patterns for students perceived low versus high on the scale.

The effects that did appear are consistent with the notion that the students seen as attractive by the teachers were somewhat more intelligent and better adjusted than the students seen as unattractive. The attractive students had more public response opportunities (2), and the unattractive students were more likely to be called on as nonvolunteers (9) and more likely to have teacher-initiated academic contacts (18) and personal contacts (20). This suggests that the unattractive students were somewhat passive or inattentive in lessons, and the teachers felt it necessary to monitor them closely during seatwork times.

Attractive students had a higher percentage of housekeeping contacts (25) among their teacher initiations, because the teachers initiated so many more academic and personal contacts with unattractive students. Unattractive students were more likely to be warned for misbehavior (71), but less likely to be criticized for calling out (52). None of the measures of teacher or student affect or critical incidents showed significant relationships.

In general, the data indicate that students seen as attractive were bright and successful in the classroom, and that students seen as unattractive were less so. As a result, the teachers monitored the less attractive students more closely, attempting to encourage their participation in lessons, to see that they stayed on task when doing seatwork, and to remind them of their personal responsibilities when necessary. These differences in physical attractiveness and intelligence did not extend to personality: there were no significant relationships involving teacher or student affect.

12

Noticeable Students

In this chapter we will discuss relationships for the noticeable and eye contact scales. Both scales involve salience, or the degree to which students stand out from the crowd, relative to their classmates.

Among students ranked consistently as highly noticeable, some were outstanding students but others came to the teachers' attention because of high rates of activity and misbehavior. Thus, high rankings on noticeable are ambiguous and will not be stressed here. Low rankings are interesting and meaningful, however, because they indicate that teachers agree that certain students have attributes that make them fade into the background. In general, these "invisible" students seem similar to those seen as objects of teacher indifference in other studies.

Eye contact also proved to be an interesting scale. It had little variance and a skewed distribution of scores compared to other scales because most students maintained good eye contact with the teachers. Therefore, most relationships involving this scale were due to the minority of students who shied away from such eye contact. The relationships are very interesting in their implications about such students, however.

NOTICEABLE

This scale had a mixed and mostly weak pattern of correlations with the other 12 scales. The correlations in Tables 6.1 and 6.2 reveal that the noticeable scale was associated positively with happy, achieving, creative, attractive, and persistent; and negatively with calm and cooperative. This mixed pattern illustrates the point made above that some students were noticeable for positive attributes, while others were noticeable for more negative attributes.

Adjective Description Data

Significant relationships appeared for 13 of the 37 adjective description variables (see Table 7.1). Compared to the invisible students, noticeable students were likely to be described by teachers as sociable, happy, intelligent, achieving, aggressive, active, humorous, creative, and as social leaders. Invisible students were more likely to be described as quiet and as being absent often. Taken together, the correlations with the other 12 scales and with the adjective description variables suggest that the invisible students were quiet and did not stand out in any way, positively or negatively.

Classroom Observation Data

Significant relationships appeared for 26 of the 73 variables in Table 7.2, 13 of these at the .01 level. Invisible students had low rates of contact with teachers (1), especially behavior contacts (8), and public response opportunities (2). They were especially passive in general class activities, so that most of the response opportunities they did have came in small group settings (4, 5). They rarely called out responses (16), and were so passive that teachers often had to call on them as nonvolunteers (13), even in the small group setting (9).

This pattern of passivity in public response opportunity situations is also seen in private contacts. Invisible students seldom initiated interactions with teachers (28), particularly not approval-seeking (30), tattling (33), or social (34) contacts. In general, they avoided teachers except when they had to come to them for help with their work.

As a result of this avoidance, teacher-initiated contacts constituted a high percentage of the total contacts that the invisible students shared with teachers (22). However, this is due to their low rates of initiation with teachers rather than to high rates of teacher initiations with them. Teachers were no more likely to initiate interactions with the invisible students than with the more noticeable students, and even were less likely to invite the invisible students to perform housekeeping chores (19). Thus, teachers did not compensate for the avoidance of the invisible students by initiating high rates of interactions with these students, except to call on them as nonvolunteers when they did not contribute to class discussions. This suggests that the invisible students were completing their seatwork assignments acceptably, and that teachers did not feel the need to monitor them closely.

Even though the invisible students seldom initiated contact with the teachers, their behavior seems to indicate only passivity, and not alienation or negative affect. They misbehaved less often than other students, and were less likely to react sullenly when corrected by the teacher (44). On the other hand, they also were less likely to express positive affect to teachers (40). Thus, they not only minimized their interactions with teachers, but also minimized their affective responses to teachers when such contacts did occur.

Teachers responded to this by trying to win them over, although apparently without much success. The invisible students were more likely to be praised following their volunteered or called out responses (47) and received high rates of praise across academic contacts as a whole (49). They also received less criticism following volunteered and called out responses (52) and less criticism across teacher-initiated academic contacts as a whole (50). Yet, there is little evidence that this increased praise and decreased criticism was effective in getting these invisible students to participate more actively in classroom activities or initiate more interactions with teachers (although it also is possible that the participation rates of these students might have been even lower than they were if teachers had not treated them as they did).

Other data also indicate that teachers were going out of their way to treat the invisible students positively. Teachers were especially unlikely to refuse these students' personal (67) or social (69) initiations, or to reject their attempts to tattle (68). They also were unlikely to threaten them when they misbehaved (72), and they provided them with high rates of positive affect across all contacts together (60). The only exception to this trend is the finding that teachers were less likely to praise the invisible students for good classroom conduct than they were to praise the more noticeable students for such conduct (61). This is quite understandable, though, partly because the invisible students rarely did things that stood out and warranted such praise, and partly because they apparently did not need much such praise because they already were behaving acceptably (in the sense that they were not breaking classroom rules).

In summary, passivity was the primary defining attribute of the invisible students. They avoided the teachers except when they needed help, and they did not volunteer to answer questions or call out answers. Teachers tried to reach them by initiating more interactions with them, praising them more often, and criticizing them less often. Apparently, the invisible students were unlikely to respond favorably to these teacher overtures, although they also were unlikely to respond negatively. They were detached and inactive in their behavior, and unemotional in their responses to teachers.

These invisible students make interesting contrasts with other groups, especially those classified as unhappy or immature. The data on the latter groups indicated that they were having a difficult time, either in school or in their lives generally. In contrast, the invisible students appeared inactive and passive, but not necessarily poorly adjusted or otherwise worse off than their classmates. Their passivity may simply have been a matter of personal style, without any implications about mental health or adjustment.

EYE CONTACT

Teachers found it difficult to discriminate among students who typically showed eye contact, so that this scale essentially reflects a division between students who avoided eye contact and all other students, rather than a continuum from very low to very high eye contact. The correlations with other scales indicated that the teachers perceived students who avoided eye contact as unhappy, and that they did not like these students (see Tables 6.1 and 6.2).

Adjective Description Data

Significant relationships appeared for only 9 of the 37 adjective description variables. Compared to those who avoided eye contact, teachers were likely to describe students who maintained eye contact as intelligent, social leaders, creative, and likely to come from good homes. Those who avoided eye contact were more likely to be described as active, inattentive, frequently absent, or untrustworthy. The latter is particularly interesting in view of the cultural association between these attributes (shifty eyed, etc.). In any case, the general pattern here indicates that teachers associated poor eye contact with undesirable personality traits and not merely with shyness or inhibition (see Table 7.1).

Classroom Observation Data

Significant relationships were observed for 17 of the 73 variables in Table 7.2, 10 of these at the .01 level. Students who avoided eye contact had low rates of public response opportunities (2, 3), especially in the general class setting (4, 5). They did not differ from other students in rates of nonacademic and behavioral contacts, however. Thus, although they did not volunteer often to participate in class discussions, neither did they show the generalized pattern of passivity seen in invisible students.

Because they seldom volunteered (10, 14), teachers were forced to call on them frequently as nonvolunteers (13), at least in the general class setting. Teachers also initiated higher than average rates of interaction with these students (17, 22), and when they were supervising seatwork, teachers were more likely to initiate interaction with these students than to merely observe them (24). These relationships indicate some but not much extra effort by teachers to maintain contact with these students and involve them in classroom activities.

The students who avoided eye contact did not respond well to teacher overtures, however. They were more likely than other students to respond with negative affect when teachers initiated interactions with them (41). They were not particularly likely to respond sullenly or with hostility, however (44, 37). Nor were they especially likely to behave disruptively (36), although they were more likely to be coded for noninteractive behaviors such as cheating or lying (38). This provides some support for the teachers' perceptions of them as untrustworthy.

Teachers often praised these students for good answers or good work (49), but they also frequently criticized them for poor answers or poor work (54), especially in teacher-initiated contacts (51). This suggests that these students frequently were not doing their work, or were doing it carelessly. The only other significant findings indicate that teachers were particularly unlikely to flatter these students (57), but also unlikely to refuse their social initiations (69).

Taken together, the data indicate that students who avoided eye contact were well enough behaved in the sense that they did not violate classroom rules, but they also did not participate actively in academic activities and often had to be prodded to get them to resume working or to work more carefully on seatwork assignments. In contrast to the invisible students, with whom teachers made strenuous efforts to win over and put at ease, there was little evidence of teachers reaching out toward students who avoided eye contact. Furthermore, the few measures that did suggest such efforts were merely verbal—directing questions at them when they did not volunteer and praising them when they did good work. No measure of teacher positive affect favored these students.

Perhaps the avoiding manner and negative affect projected by these students made the teachers ill at ease. In any case, there was no evidence of increased social contact, positive affect, or other indications of teacher efforts to win them over. Instead, these students apparently conditioned the teachers to keep their interactions impersonal and focused on academics.

13

Classroom Conduct

Previous research led us to expect that cooperation, along with persistence and achievement, would form the core of student attributes determining teacher attitudes and expectations. Our results support these expectations. Relationships involving the cooperation scale were both numerous and indicative of strong teacher reactions to the students ranked at the extremes.

The correlations in Tables 6.1 and 6.2 indicate strong relationships between the cooperation scale and rankings on calm, careful, mature, persistent, and attachment, as well as moderate positive relationships with happy and achieving and a moderate negative relationship with concern. Thus, cooperative students were seen as mature, high in self-control and compliance, and likeable. Uncooperative students had the opposite pattern. Correlations of cooperation with achieving and creative were lower than those with calm, careful, and persistent, indicating that cooperation ratings were based more on students' conduct than their achievement.

Adjective Description Data

Significant relationships were found for 19 of the 37 adjective description variables. Compared to uncooperative students, cooperative students were described as quiet, helpful, motivated, intelligent, achieving, and responsible good workers. They also were more likely to be described as popular, sweet, and coming from good homes. Uncooperative students were more likely to be described as aggressive, active, inattentive, temperamental, having medical problems, or being underachievers or untrustworthy (see Table 7.1).

This list implies a great deal of difference between cooperative and the uncooperative students, and the observation data bear out this expectation.

Classroom Observation Data

Significant relationships were observed for 31 of the 73 variables in Table 7.2, 22 of these at the .01 level. Many of these reflect the frequent misbehavior of the uncooperative students and the teachers' efforts to cope with it.

Uncooperative students had high rates of interaction with teachers (1), because they had high rates of nonacademic contacts (6) and especially behavior contacts (8, 35). Low percentages of their total contacts with teachers were student initiated (7), partly because they had so many behavior contacts but partly because they avoided the teachers as well. They also had low percentages of public response opportunities (3), in contrast to the cooperative students who had high percentages.

Uncooperative students often called out answers without permission (16), and yet teachers often had to call on them as nonvolunteers (9), because they seldom raised their hands and waited to be recognized (10, 14). In addition, teachers probably called on them as nonvolunteers at times because they were not paying attention and this was a way to refocus them on the activity. In any case, it is clear that the uncooperative students frequently misbehaved during lessons and activities, even though they tended to call out answers during times when they were paying attention.

Compared to cooperative students, uncooperative students had high rates of teacher-initiated private interactions (17), due to high rates of teacher-initiated academic contacts (18). Teachers felt it necessary to monitor these students closely and intervene frequently with them because they were not doing their work or were not doing it carefully or correctly.

Unlike other types of problem students, the uncooperative students did not have particularly high rates of teacher-initiated personal or social contacts (20, 21). This elaborates the picture of uncooperative students as locked in conflict with the teachers, and not as merely immature, hyperactive, or forgetful. Teachers were not especially likely to try to win these students over by socializing with them, probably because they were uncomfortable with them. Finally, their percentage of teacher initiations involving housekeeping requests (25) was low, because the teachers initiated so many private academic interactions with them.

Despite their problems with teachers, the uncooperative students did seek contact with them, at least in nonacademic situations. Like the restless students, they were particularly likely to initiate contacts with teachers in attempts to get their personal needs met (32) or to tattle on their peers (33). They were not particularly likely to come to the teacher to seek approval for completed work, however (30).

The misbehavior of the uncooperative students was intense and overt. Most of their behavior contacts were for misbehavior (35), and they were especially likely to be disruptive (36), to gripe, sass, or defy the teacher (37), and to respond sullenly when corrected (44). Cooperative students, on the other hand, not only were well behaved but had good relationships with the teachers, and were particularly unlikely to express negative affect toward the teachers (43).

Teachers did not differentiate between cooperative and uncooperative students in praising good academic answers or work, but they often criticized the uncooperative students for not working or for working poorly (50, 51, 54). They were likely to praise the cooperative but not the uncooperative students for good conduct (61, 62) and likely to respond to the misbehavior of uncooperative students with threats or punishment (72, 73).

Despite the teachers' concern about poor work by the uncooperative students, the teachers were especially likely to refuse their student-initiated academic interactions (65). They also were more likely to refuse their student-initiated housekeeping requests, personal requests, or tattling (66, 67, 68). Finally, teachers were much more likely to express negative affect toward the uncooperative students than the cooperative students (70).

To a degree, the pattern here is completely negative: uncooperative students presented frequent and severe problems of misbehavior to the teachers, and in addition they tended to be poor students who needed close monitoring even when they were not overtly misbehaving. Teachers often found it necessary to correct them, and this often included personal criticism. For their part, uncooperative students often responded to this treatment with negative affect.

Despite all this, however, the data do not indicate complete alienation of the uncooperative students from the teachers. The students themselves did not avoid the teachers, and in fact frequently came to them to initiate various types of nonacademic interactions. The teachers often refused these initiatives, but this apparently did not discourage the uncooperative students from returning frequently. Thus, lines of communication were maintained despite strain in the relationship. Furthermore, although the teachers often found it necessary to criticize or punish the uncooperative students, evidence of really intense negative affect or rejection is lacking. The teachers were not especially likely to hold up these students as bad examples to the class or to show impatience with them. In contrast to the patterns for students ranked low on the attachment scale, for example, which indicate mutual teacher-student rejection, the patterns for uncooperative students suggest only mutual frustration (the students themselves being frustrated with teacher attempts to make them conform, and the teachers being frustrated with the continuing and disruptive misbehavior of these students).

14

Teacher Attachment
and Concern

The 11 scales discussed so far all have dealt with student attributes and behavior as they affect teachers. We now turn to the two scales that measured teacher attitudes directly. These included the attachment scale which measured general attitudes of like versus dislike of students, and the concern scale, which measured the degree to which teachers were concerned about students to the point that they felt the need to spend more time with them.

ATTACHMENT

The students ranked consistently high and low on this scale were the ones most intensely liked or disliked by the teachers. Those ranked highly (whom we will call *preferred* students) were mentioned as students that the teachers would like to be able to retain in their classes for an extra year just for the sheer joy of teaching them. Those ranked low (whom we will call *rejected* students) were students whom the teachers would like to remove from their class rosters were they able to do so.

The correlations in Tables 6.1 and 6.2 indicate that attachment rankings were related most strongly to rankings on the persistence and cooperation scales, although there also were significant correlations with all of the other scales. This suggests that teacher attitudes toward students were most strongly affected by the degree to which students conformed to the ideal student role, although the personal attributes of the students played a role as well.

Adjective Description Data

Significant relationships were observed for 14 of the 37 adjective description variables. Preferred students were likely, and rejected students unlikely, to be described as well behaved, intelligent, achieving, or good workers. Preferred students also were likely to be described as quiet, helpful, motivated, responsible, and coming from good homes. Rejected students were likely and preferred students unlikely to be described as inattentive or underachieving. In addition, rejected students also were likely to be described as active or untrustworthy. As expected from the correlations of the attachment scale with other scales, these adjective descriptions include a mix of behaviors relevant to the student role and more personal attributes. All differences clearly favor the preferred students over the rejected students (see Table 7.1).

Classroom Observation Data

Significant relationships were seen for 32 of the 73 variables in Table 7.2, 20 of these at the .01 level. This is second only to the calm versus restless scale in sheer number of significant relationships, and the differences between the preferred and the rejected students typically were among the largest observed in the study. This is especially the case for measures of teacher emotional response to students and student emotional response to teachers.

Rejected students had high rates of contact with the teachers (1), due to frequent nonacademic (6) and especially behavioral (8) contacts. Preferred students had relatively more public response opportunities (3), especially in the general class setting (4). They also were more likely to be called on as volunteers (10, 14), compared to the rejected students who were more likely to be called on as nonvolunteers (9, 13). Thus, the preferred students conformed to classroom rules and participated actively in academic activities, but the rejected students often misbehaved and seldom volunteered during academic activities. In order to get them to participate, and perhaps also in order to keep them attentive, teachers frequently called on them as nonvolunteers.

There were no differences in rates of student initiation of private contacts with teachers, but there were the expected differences in teacher initiation. The percentage of teacher initiations with rejected students that involved housekeeping requests (25) was low, but the teachers did often initiate contact with rejected students (17). Most of the time, this was to monitor their seatwork (18) or to remind them of their personal responsibilities (20). This pattern indicates that the preferred students consistently were doing what they were supposed to be doing without need for special teacher intervention, but that the rejected students needed close monitoring and frequent intervention.

Rejected students not only misbehaved more often (8, 35), but more disruptively (36). They also were more likely to lie or cheat (38), gripe, sass, or defy the teacher (37), and respond sullenly (44) or with other negative affect toward the teacher (41, 42). This is the most negative pattern observed for any of the groups studied, and it indicates a pattern of mutual rejection between these students and the teachers.

Even the uncooperative students, who reacted negatively when teachers disciplined them (44) or initiated social contacts (43), did not have a general pattern of negative affect toward the teachers running throughout all of their various contacts with them (46). Furthermore, their behavior problems were marked more by high frequency and disruptiveness than by direct hostility toward the teacher. Their conflicts with teachers came about as by-products of their disruption of classroom activities. In contrast, the misbehavior of the rejected students was more likely to involve direct defiance of teachers or hostility toward them.

This pattern of negative affect is seen in the teachers, too. Teachers were especially likely to criticize the rejected students for poor answers or poor work (54), especially in teacher-initiated academic contacts (50, 51). Preferred students were especially unlikely to get such criticism. They also were more likely to be appointed as classroom monitors (55), although the remaining indicators of teacher affect do not suggest special positive treatment of this preferred group.

The indicators of negative teacher affect showed a stronger and more consistent pattern of relationships with the attachment scale than any of the others. The teachers were unlikely to refuse academic, housekeeping, or personal initiations by the preferred students (65, 66, 67), but likely to refuse such initiations by rejected students. In addition, they were likely to hold up the rejected students as bad examples to the class (63), and to show impatience during academic interactions with these students (64). They also were more likely to warn the rejected students when they misbehaved (71), as well as to follow through with criticism or punishment (73). Across all types of contacts combined, they were much more likely to express negative affect toward these students than toward the preferred students (70).

In general, the teachers saw the preferred students as conforming to the idealized student role, and the rejected students not only as often misbehaving but as underachieving and untrustworthy. The observation data supported these perceptions in that the rejected students misbehaved much more often and more intensively than average, and apparently needed a tighter rein kept on them to make sure that they were doing their work. They misbehaved more often and more intensely than students in general, and reacted negatively to teachers, who reacted mostly negatively to them.

In contrast to teacher behavior toward students seen as restless, uncooperative, or otherwise undesirable, the data reveal no indications of teacher efforts to reach out toward the rejected students by improving the teacher-student relationship or by motivating these students to improve their behavior. No measures of praise or reinforcement revealed significant relationships here, and several measures revealed that teachers were likely to rebuff rejected students when they came to initiate interaction. Apparently, the frequent misbehavior and especially the defiance and hostility presented by these students were more than the teachers were willing to take, so they responded negatively.

Several indications of teacher favoritism toward preferred students were observed. They had higher percentages of their housekeeping and personal requests approved, and they volunteered for and received more public response opportunities (although this may merely reflect their high achievement and compliant behavior rather than any direct teacher favoritism). Preferred students also were more likely to be appointed as monitors (the attachment scale was the only one to show a significant relationship with this variable). This indicates particular teacher liking and trust for these preferred students, although it can cause problems with peers, especially if the student is expected to monitor the class in the teacher's absence and to report on classmates who misbehave.

Despite the teachers' expressions of attachment toward the preferred students, and despite the indications of favoritism described above, there were no significant relationships involving either student or teacher positive affect. The absence of findings in these areas replicates previous work reporting no obvious, strong positive emotional reactions on the part of either these students or the teachers. Apparently, attachment shows itself in frequent public response opportunities and in the absence of negative teacher behavior, but not through direct expression of positive affect. Attachment is shown not through overt affection but through subtle favoritism involving treating preferred students pleasantly and interacting with them in ways that suggest recognition of their maturity and responsibility. In particular, preferred students are treated with respect, even when they misbehave (which is less often than average).

CONCERN

The concern scale measured the degree to which teachers were concerned about students to the point that they felt the need to spend more time with them. Students ranked highly on this scale were having a difficult time coping with school demands, and the teachers were concerned about helping them to be able to cope. This concern did not necessarily indicate attachment or empathy, however.

Students consistently ranked low on the concern scale were not necessarily disliked or even viewed neutrally by the teachers. The wording of the scale was such that low ranking on the scale meant only that the teacher did not see a need to spend extra time with these students. Ordinarily, this meant only that teachers recognized that such students were doing well and did not need special attention, rather than any desire to avoid them. Thus, being ranked consistently low on the concern scale was part of a generally positive pattern for most students, and being ranked high on the scale was part of a generally negative pattern.

Intercorrelations of the teacher rankings indicated negative relationships for concern with achievement and cooperation. The relationship with achievement was expected on the basis of earlier data indicating that poor achievement is the primary reason for teacher concern. The relationship with cooperation indicated that classroom conduct was related to teacher concern ratings, as well. In addition, concern showed low to moderate correlations with the other ten scales (see Tables 6.1 and 6.2).

Adjective Description Data

Significant relationships appeared for only 10 of the 37 adjective description variables. Compared to students ranked high on this scale (concern students), students ranked low were seen as more highly motivated, more intelligent, higher achieving, better workers, and more likely to come from good homes. Concern students were more often described as active, inattentive, temperamental, or having medical problems. In general, this pattern is more similar to the pattern seen for students described as immature or low in achievement than for students described as uncooperative or rejected. That is, the data indicate that teacher concern was based mostly on immaturity and limited intellectual ability than on negative personal qualities or a troubled teacher-student relationship (see Table 7.1).

Classroom Observation Data

Significant relationships were seen for 16 of the 73 variables in Table 7.2, 8 of these at the .01 level. This is fewer than we had expected on the basis of earlier research, probably because so many of the classroom observation measures in this study concerned not merely quantity but quality of teacher-student interaction, and especially indications of affect. Both earlier data and data from the present study indicate that teacher concern reflects itself most directly in the quantity rather than the quality of teacher-student interactions.

Surprisingly, the concern students did not have significantly higher than average rates of total contact with teachers (1), although they did have high rates of behavior contacts (8). Furthermore, they were below average in rate of initiation of contact with teachers (7), and in frequency of public response opportunities (3), especially in general class settings (4). The latter findings apparently were due to the failure of the concern students to volunteer frequently (10, 14), so that teachers often had to call on them as nonvolunteers (9, 13).

As expected, teachers initiated interaction with the concern students frequently (17), particularly to check on their work (18). The group differences here were not extreme, however, and were not accompanied by other significant differences on variables indicating teacher initiations. Thus, the data support the expectation that the concern students would be low achievers who required frequent monitoring by the teacher, but there is no evidence of the extremely high rates of interaction with these students seen in some previous studies.

The concern students frequently misbehaved (8, 35), but most of this involved social chatting or other typical off-task behaviors that did not disrupt the class or involve open defiance or hostility toward the teacher. Concern students were more likely than students rated low on the concern scale to be coded as sullen in interactions with teachers (44), but this was not a strong difference and was not accompanied by other indications of negative affect toward teachers. Thus, the concern students apparently got along well enough with teachers except at times when teachers were reprimanding them for inappropriate behavior.

When concern students approached the teachers to show off completed work or to get help with an ongoing assignment, they were especially likely to be praised for what they had accomplished (48). In addition, even though teachers often initiated interactions with them to check their work or monitor their progress, they were not especially likely to criticize these students (50, 51).

Thus, even though these students were making poor progress, and even though this was due in part to poor motivation, teacher concern showed itself in attempts to encourage these students and in a minimizing of criticism. This treatment contrasts with the treatment of students that the teachers rejected or saw as careless or uncooperative. Apparently, the teachers attributed the problems of the concern students to limited ability or background, and thus did not blame them for the problems they presented (which were not very threatening to the teachers, in any case).

This "kid gloves" treatment is also seen in data indicating that teachers were especially unlikely to become impatient in dealing with concern students when they came for help with their work (64). Thus, academic interactions with concern students were marked by teacher patience and encouragement, although not by notably strong affect on the part of either the teachers or the students.

Data on behavioral interactions did indicate a tendency for concern students to be coded as sullen when teachers disciplined them (44), but otherwise the pattern of kid gloves treatment by teachers continued. Significant relationships involving the concern scale were seen only for teacher tendencies to hold up the student as a bad example to the class (63) and to respond to misbehavior with warnings (71) or criticism or punishment (73). In each case, the significant relationship appeared because teachers were especially unlikely to do these things with the students ranked low on the concern scale. They were not especially likely to hold up the concern students as bad examples or to respond punitively when they misbehaved.

In summary, the teachers saw concern students as having difficulty meeting school demands and as presenting frequent behavior problems. Also, they were likely to describe these students as inattentive, immature, and unable to cope successfully with stress or frustration.

Observation data indicated that concern students seldom volunteered to respond publicly and thus often had to be called on as nonvolunteers. Concern students also initiated fewer private interactions with teachers, but when they did come to show their work or get help, teachers were especially patient and encouraging with them and likely to praise them when they attained some success. The teachers compensated for the avoidance of the concern students by calling on them as nonvolunteers in public situations and by initiating many private interactions with them, especially to check their work. Again, they revealed noteworthy patience and encouragement during such interactions.

Concern students misbehaved often but not intensively or disruptively. They were more likely than average to be coded as sullen when teachers disciplined them, but otherwise did not display notable negative affect toward the teachers. For their part, the teachers seemed to hold back criticism or punishment of these students even when they misbehaved, and in general were more patient and encouraging with them than they were with other types of problem students.

Part 3

Summary and Discussion of Findings

15

Student Success in Meeting Role Demands

We will review the findings in this and subsequent chapters, beginning here with the findings relating to teacher rankings on calm, careful, mature, achieving, creative, and persistent. These scales all reflect degree of student success in conforming to the demands of the ideal student role: attending and contributing to lessons and working carefully and successfully on assignments.

Regardless of other personal attributes, student status on these variables is likely to affect the quantity and quality of teacher-student interaction because of the very nature of schooling and the roles that it assigns to teachers and students. Teachers are not merely authority figures but instructional leaders charged with seeing that their students master basic knowledge and skills. This task will be easier and more pleasant to the extent that students are interested in learning what is taught, conscientious in attempting to master it, and able to progress at an acceptable pace. Students who do not meet this description are going to cause the teacher frustration and problems, even though these students may have very attractive personal and social qualities. This frustration may produce negative emotional responses in teachers, motivating them to try to develop effective ways to cope with the situation.

People can deal with persistent frustrations and problems either by coping or by defending (Murphy, 1962). Coping includes attempts to solve or overcome the problem by redoubling our efforts, getting help, analyzing our approach to try to identify the flaws in it, seeking alternative approaches that might be more successful, and so on. Successful coping involves eliminating the problem.

If we have not been able to cope with the problem despite repeated efforts, we may eventually give up and accept the problem as unsolvable. This will require us to live indefinitely with whatever sense of frustration or failure might be involved. Should these negative feelings be too powerful for us to handle, we may defend against them by attempting to ignore the problem or act as if it did not exist by rationalizing our behavior in an attempt to explain away failure or make the problem seem much less important than it really is; by avoiding responsibility for failure by assigning the blame to someone else or to factors beyond our control; and so on. If frustration or other negative feelings have built up as a result of the experience, we may displace them away from ourselves and ventilate them against someone else, especially if we are blaming someone else for the problem.

As Weiner (1979) and others have noted, teachers' reactions to problems presented by students are likely to depend on their attributions concerning the nature and causes of those problems. Poor achievement attributed to low ability is likely to lead to reduced expectations and probably sympathetic treatment, but poor achievement attributed to lack of effort is likely to lead to criticism of the student and attempts to produce change. Students are likely to be blamed for problem behavior that the teacher sees as controllable, especially if the behavior is also seen as deliberate. When problems are seen as uncontrollable and thus not the fault of the student, however, the teacher is likely to respond with sympathy and help.

The operation of these principles could be seen in the patterns of behavior the teachers showed with students ranked consistently high or low on scales relating to student success in meeting the demands of the student role. The mildest and most limited contrasts in teacher reaction to student differences were seen in connection with students ranked high versus low on achievement and creativity. The adjective description data for these two scales indicated that rankings were based heavily on teacher perceptions of student ability. These differences in ability are seen as innate, or at least as not under the control of the students themselves, so it follows that student differences in achievement and creativity are not under student control, either. Therefore, the high achievers do not deserve special praise, nor do the low achievers deserve special blame.

The contrasting patterns of teacher-student interaction involving students ranked high and low on these scales correspond with these theory-based expectations. Highly achieving or creative students did not have notably positive relationships with teachers, despite their academic success, nor were they especially likely to receive praise or affection from teachers. Similarly, students low in achievement and creativity maintained good general relationships with teachers even though they did not contribute much to public discussions and were not able to cope with work demands as well as their classmates. Teachers tried to help them by providing them with more frequent supervision and assistance, and in the case of the low achievers, also initiated frequent social interactions with them and expressed physical affection toward them.

There were some general differences relating to the differences in ability and achievement between these student groups, however. The higher-achieving and more creative students had more public interactions with teachers, and were especially likely to be called on after volunteering by raising their hands. Students low in achievement and creativity were generally passive in public response opportunity situations, so that teachers often had to call on them as nonvolunteers in order to get them to participate at all. They also had to initiate interactions with these students much more often during seatwork situations, because they required closer supervision and more feedback and structure.

Teachers were more likely to refuse the initiations of low achievers and to criticize the poor work of students low in creativity, but this is most likely due to the probability that low achievers often came at inappropriate times or with inappropriate requests. Also, students low in creativity seemed generally low in maturity and ability, suggesting that their work often left much to be desired. In general, then, large and consistent differences in achievement and creativity do lead to differential patterns of teacher-student interaction, but these differences are concentrated in interactions that involve the teacher operating in the role of instructional leader and the student operating in the role of learner. By and large, they do not extend to more personalized interactions between teachers and students as individuals, apparently because teachers attribute differences in achievement and creativity to differences in ability and not to more personal causes such as intentions, motives, or attitudes.

Data on the students ranked careful versus careless extend the patterns seen for achievement and creativity rankings. Adjective descriptions of careless students mention things like inattentiveness, underachievement, and untrustworthiness, indicating that teachers held the careless students responsible and thus blameworthy for their careless work. Behavioral data indicate that the careless students presented more problems for the teachers than the students low in achievement or creativity. Careless students often came to the teachers for help with their work or to try to tattle on their peers, misbehaved more often (although not more disruptively), and often projected hostility toward the teacher. Teachers responded generally well to this pressure and even gave extra physical affection to the careless students, but they also criticized them frequently for poor work and held them up as bad examples to the class. In general, the data suggest that the careless students were immature and impulsive. Unlike the students ranked low in achievement and creativity, they presented not only learning problems but frequent and often intense behavior problems to the teachers. As a result, the data on teachers indicate frequent teacher frustration and negativism toward careless students, even though the teachers generally were trying to provide them with the kind of individual attention and close supervision that they required.

The contrasts with students described as immature are instructive. Adjective description data indicate that teachers saw immature students as low achievers and poor workers, and as likely to be hyperactive, temperamental, dependent on the teacher, or to have medical problems. Yet, they were not held responsible for their behavior. They were not particularly likely to be described with unflattering adjectives indicating deliberate misbehavior or faulty character traits. Behavioral data show that the immature students, like the careless students, were likely to come to the teacher in attempts to tattle on peers and likely to misbehave frequently and respond sullenly when disciplined. Furthermore, the misbehavior of these students was often disruptive. However, unlike the careless students, the immature students did not project hostility directly toward the teacher by griping, sassing, or defying. Also, they had notably pleasant social contacts with teachers. Thus, blame or rejection was not a factor in the teacher-student relationships involving immature students, even though they presented frequent and often serious problems to the teachers.

Teachers did criticize the poor work of immature students, and criticized or punished their misbehavior. However, they also frequently praised these students' good work (this was the only group for whom this was true), and were likely to give them physical affection. These patterns of interaction with immature students indicate that teachers can tolerate even frequent and disruptive violations of student role expectations and still maintain a basically positive stance toward the students involved if the students do not project hostility toward them personally and if they are able to attribute the students' inappropriate behavior to limited ability, immaturity, or other factors suggesting that the students are not responsible for the problems they present.

Sources of advice to teachers on classroom management and interpersonal relationships regularly exhort them to criticize the behavior but not the person. Teachers apparently are able to do this successfully with immature students and other students whose problem behavior is attributed to factors beyond their control. Teachers can be critical and even punitive with such students when necessary, but without rejecting the students as persons or losing sight of their own role as an adult facilitator who is there to help the students. As a result, interactions with such students during times when the students are behaving appropriately are often quite positive, and negative affect occurring during disciplinary interactions does not seem to carry over to the rest of the relationship, either for the teacher or for the students. This is a very different picture from what is seen with students who are held responsible and blameworthy for their inappropriate behavior, especially if the problems they present are frequent and severe.

This was most obvious with the uncooperative students (discussed in the next chapter), but among the student groups included in the present chapter, it was most clear with those ranked as restless or as low in persistence. Teachers described restless students as having various undesirable personal attributes in addition to mere restlessness in behavior, and the behavioral data indicated that restless students showed hyperactivity, lack of responsibility, frequent initiations with teachers for nonacademic reasons (including tattling), and frequent and disruptive misbehavior that included hostility directed at the teacher. Teachers responded to this with frequent refusals of initiatives, projection of negative affect, withholding of positive affect, and generally unsympathetic treatment.

It was interesting that this negative pattern held even though the restless students showed some indications of concern about how the teachers felt and some tendencies toward dependency on the teachers. Their high rates of personal initiations included not only attempts to tattle but attempts to get teacher approval by showing completed work and attempts to get permission or help from the teachers for meeting personal needs. Thus, these students did not avoid the teachers and did not seem to have generally negative attitudes toward them, despite the hostility they projected during disciplinary contacts. They gave the teachers opportunities to build relationships with them by interacting with them frequently, and gave teachers opportunities to praise them by coming to show their work and seeking approval. Yet, teachers typically did not respond positively even during these student-initiated interactions.

Apparently, the combination of high frequencies of behavior problems caused by these hyperactive students and the direct hostility that these students sometimes projected toward the teachers was too much for most teachers to handle.

Basically, the teachers had given up on many restless students, in the sense that they no longer were seriously trying to change their behavior by building positive relationships with them and reinforcing their appropriate behavior and their academic successes. As Nash (1973) found with respect to disliked students, teachers seemed oriented more toward isolating these students and minimizing the trouble they caused than toward teaching them or bringing about genuine change in their behavior. This was so even though they generally saw these students as theoretically able to control the problem behaviors they presented. This seemingly paradoxical response was also noted by Brophy and Rohrkemper (1980), who found more teacher blame and rejection and fewer teacher attempts to bring about change with students seen as deliberately misbehaving than with students seen as unable to control their behavior. Apparently, the negative emotions aroused in these circumstances were strong enough to dislodge teachers from the helper role and to orient them toward defensiveness and counter-aggressiveness, even though these were not solutions to the problem.

There also was a great deal of mutual negative affect exchanged between the teachers and the students ranked low in persistence. However, unlike the situation with restless students, the generally negative pattern of teacher interactions with students low in persistence was broken by some positive behaviors. The teachers were likely to praise the students low in persistence when these students came to them for help with their work or came to show their completed work and seek approval. Thus, the teachers took advantage of the opportunities to be positive presented to them by the students low in persistence, even though they did not take advantage of similar opportunities offered by the restless students. Also, teachers were likely to display positive affect toward the students low in persistence, even though they expressed a lot of negative affect toward them as well.

In part, these differences in pattern are probably due to differences in teacher perceptions of the two groups of students. The students ranked low in persistence were seen as immature, poorly motivated, lacking in responsibility, and likely to be active or inattentive, but they were not described with more negative labels like aggressive or untrustworthy. Also, the behavior problems they presented to teachers were neither as frequent nor as extreme and disruptive as those presented by the restless students. This gave the teachers more time to work through their own frustrations and resume a facilitative role with the students ranked low in persistence even after hostile interactions with these students. Thus, the generally rejecting and avoiding attitudes seen with the restless students did not develop with the students ranked low in persistence, even though these students were quite hostile toward the teachers during discipline-related interactions.

Taken together, the data on students who failed to meet the demands of the ideal student role suggest that teacher responses varied with both the quantity and quality of behavior problems that students presented and the causal attributions that teachers probably made in interpreting the reasons for these problems. Poor work that teachers probably attributed to limited abilities, immaturity, or other factors beyond the students' control typically elicited sympathy and extra help from the teachers. However, poor work that teachers probably attributed to carelessness or lack of motivation elicited less sympathy, more criticism, and pressure from the teacher for change in behavior. Finally, widespread, inappropriate behavior, especially when it included disruption of the classroom or hostility directed against the teacher, produced negative teacher reactions. Usually these were tempered with attempts to improve relationships with students or at least to reinforce their acceptable behavior, but in the case of restless students, the pressures were strong and consistent enough to dislodge teachers from their role as adult facilitator and cause them to treat the restless students with avoidance, hostility, and rejection.

Students rated toward the more desirable ends of these scales, who were largely successful in fulfilling the ideal student role expectations, enjoyed generally pleasant and rewarding, although not notably affective, relationships with the teachers. Teachers were least notably positive toward the students ranked high in achievement or creativity (which they apparently attributed to high intelligence). These students often volunteered and were called upon in public response opportunity situations, but they were not particularly likely to receive praise, affection, or other overt displays of teacher positive regard or positive affect. Thus, teachers showed respect for these students and had good working relationships with them, but did not otherwise treat them preferentially.

Teachers appeared to be more appreciative of students they saw as calm, careful, persistent, or (especially) mature. Attributions probably were involved in this difference. That is, students apparently were seen as calm, careful, persistent, or mature not merely because of ability or other innate qualities, but because of their own efforts. Thus, these students deserved personal credit for their positive characteristics in a way that the highly achieving and creative students did not.

Perhaps because of this, students rated as calm, careful, persistent, or mature not only were called on frequently for public response opportunities, but also were likely to be held up as positive examples to the rest of the class, to be praised for good conduct, or to receive some form of positive affect from the teachers. Even so, they were not any more likely than other students to be praised for good answers or good work, to be flattered, or to be objects of displays of physical affection by teachers. Thus, teachers' relationships with these students who fulfilled the ideal student role expectations were more notable for the absence of indications of negative affect or communication problems than for widespread and overt teacher favoritism or positive affect. Thus, ideal students got along well with teachers and were treated with respect, but were not necessarily the students that teachers liked best. Strong affective reactions by teachers apparently depended more on students' personal qualities than on their achievement levels or work habits.

16

Students' Personal Attributes

After discussing data relating to aspects of the ideal student role in the previous chapter, we now turn attention to the data on students' more personal attributes: ratings for happy, attractive, noticeable, eye contact, and cooperation.

The data for the happy versus unhappy students illustrate the importance of teachers' direct experiences in interactions with students (as opposed to teachers' observations of students interacting with their peers) in determining teachers' perceptions of students. Students consistently ranked as happy were those who were cheerful and positively responsive in their interactions with teachers, and not necessarily those who were most popular or exuberant on the playground. These students liked school and teachers, participated freely in lessons and discussions, worked productively on assignments, kept the rules, and even came to teachers frequently with offers to run errands or perform chores. Yet, they were not dependent on the teachers, and did not pester them with ill-timed or inappropriate requests, tattling attempts, or other immature behaviors. In general, then, these happy students had smooth and mutually rewarding contacts with the teachers, and apparently got along well in school generally.

Yet, teachers did not react to them strongly. Happy students were no more likely than other students to receive praise or positive affect from teachers. Nor were the teachers especially likely to initiate social contacts with them. Furthermore, when circulating around the room to check seatwork, teachers were likely to merely observe the happy students without stopping to interact with them. Recognition that these students were well adjusted to classroom life did not cause teachers to seek these students out for more frequent interaction or to favor them with more positive treatment. Instead, teachers generally let these students alone when they showed no apparent need for attention or help, and instead spent their time with students who did seem to require their input.

Unhappy students constituted one such group. Teachers recognized that they were troubled and responded sympathetically to them, even though they misbehaved frequently and often directed hostility toward the teacher when doing so. Teachers systematically provided the unhappy students with both more praise and less criticism during academic contacts, and in general went out of their way to respond positively to their initiatives and to try to reinforce their successes. Even when disciplining these students, they seemed to hold back, confining their response to warnings or threats instead of criticism or punishment in situations where other students would ordinarily get less sympathetic treatment. These data on unhappy students again illustrate the importance of teacher attributions concerning the causes underlying student problem behavior. Teachers are likely to be sympathetic to and make allowances for students whom they see as troubled by factors beyond their control (economic hardship, parental conflict, or other severe stress in the home, for example). Teachers typically conclude that students suffering from such pressures "are not themselves," and thus are not personally responsible for their troublesome behavior. These perceptions and attributions help teachers to be able to take misbehavior and even defiance or hostility in stride, perhaps discounting it by concluding that students do not really mean what they say or do not fully realize what they are doing when they are suffering great emotional stress in their home situations. This is of course very different from how teachers are likely to react when they believe that students have no excuse for disruptive or defiant behavior.

These considerations point up the importance of several concepts stressed in attribution theory analyses of when and why people are likely to help other people perceived to have problems: locus of causality of the problem, degree of controllability attributed to the actor who shows the problem, and stability of the problem over time (Weiner, 1979); globality of the problem across situations (Abramson, Seligman, and Teasdale, 1978); and the degree of intentionality attributed to the actor (Rosenbaum, 1972).

A sympathetic response and attempts to help are likely: when the problem behavior is seen as (1) caused by factors in the environment that affect the person rather than by factors internal to the person (such as moral defects or illegitimate goals and motives); (2) not within the person's control; (3) unintentional (an involuntary response to situational pressures rather than a preconceived, deliberate act); (4) temporary due to unusual outside pressures (and not as a stable problem reflecting some kind of character defect); and (5) situational (responsive to particular stress factors, rather than global or generalized across situations such that it constitutes normal or expected behavior for this person). Where these perceptions hold, the person is seen as a victim suffering from powerful pressures beyond his or her control, and thus as deserving of sympathy and help. Where the opposite perceptions hold (the problem is attributed to causes internal to the person and seen as controllable, intentional, stable, and global), the person is likely to be held fully responsible and thus blameworthy, and reactions are likely to include rejection and punishment rather than sympathy and help. The data on unhappy students in this study suggest that teachers tended to see them as victims of outside pressures, and thus to respond with attempts to provide support and assistance.

The data on student attractiveness yielded very little evidence of differential teacher treatment of attractive versus unattractive students, even though many studies have indicated that attractive individuals are perceived more favorably (Dion, Berscheid, and Walster, 1972; Berscheid and Walster, 1972; Rich, 1975;

Marwit, Marwit, and Walker, 1978; Demeis and Turner, 1978), and even expected to achieve at higher levels than unattractive students (Clifford and Walster, 1971; Clifford, 1975). Despite agreement in these and other studies that physical attractiveness enhances positive impressions and behavioral responses in others, the data may not generalize to interactions between teachers and students.

Most studies of physical attractiveness involve ratings of pictures or responses to strangers who are encountered only once and for a brief interaction. Under these circumstances, physical attractiveness is one of the few, if not the only, sources of information available about the other person, and it takes on a much greater importance under these circumstances than it does in ordinary daily interactions among people who know a great deal about one another and who share a past history of interactions. Physical attractiveness may be important in forming first impressions, but these impressions recede in importance as more and more information about other people becomes available to us through continuing interactions with them. Also, physical attractiveness may be especially important in determining the likelihood that individuals will get together on a dance floor or in a social situation, but it is much less important and often irrelevant in determining whether or how often interactions will take place between people who share some kind of formalized relationship with one another. In schools, for example, student physical attractiveness usually has little or nothing to do with assignment to teachers, and once assignments are made, the teacher and students are linked, for better or worse, for the duration of the term or school year. Physical attractiveness is unlikely to play much of a role in determining the nature of teacher-student interaction, relative to such factors as the degree to which the student approaches the ideal student role and the degree to which the teacher and student offer personal qualities that each finds attractive or rewarding.

Thus, despite the great many experiments in social psychology indicating various effects of physical attractiveness, this factor does not seem to be very important in determining the interaction between individuals who share continuing and institutionalized role relationships with one another. This conclusion was reached by Clifford (1975), who found that more attractive subjects elicited better ratings and higher achievement expectations when only pictures were shown, but that these relationships did not hold up after interactions with the real students, and it is supported even more strongly in the present study. Recall that the data on the attractiveness scale in the present study refer to real students who were consistently rated as attractive or unattractive across repeated ratings by two separate teachers. Thus, there were real and noticeable differences in the physical features of these students. Nevertheless, the number of significant relationships involving the attractiveness scale barely exceeded chance expectations, and did not include any of the measures indicating teacher or student affect. Thus, the first impressions generated by physical attractiveness apparently become superceded by more important considerations as teachers and students get to know each other, and physical attractiveness is not an important factor determining the quantity or quality of teacher-student interaction. La Voie and Adams (1974) reached a similar conclusion.

The students ranked low on noticeable in the present study are equivalent in most respects to students labeled indifference students in previous studies by Silberman (1969), Jenkins (1972), Good and Brophy (1972), Evertson, Brophy, and Good (1973b), and Willis and Brophy (1974). These studies agreed in finding that indifference students had low rates of interaction with teachers and a general pattern of passivity in the classroom. However, they left some question as to whether these low rates of interaction were due to the teachers, the students, or both. The present study agrees with the Good and Brophy (1972) finding that the low rates of interaction apparently are due almost entirely to the behavior of the students, not the teachers.

The students ranked low on the noticeable scale in this study (the invisible students) seldom made contributions to public discussions, and when they did, it was because the teachers called on them as nonvolunteers, since they seldom raised their hands or sought opportunities to respond. Furthermore, they seldom initiated private interactions with teachers, and when they did, it was usually because they had to come to teachers for help with their work. Yet, the teachers clearly did not respond to this passivity and avoidance with similar behavior on their part. Instead, they actively reached out to the invisible students, trying to involve them in lessons and discussions, praising them when they did respond or do good work, minimizing criticism, responding positively to the initiatives that did occur, and providing frequent positive affect.

Despite these consistent positive overtures from the teachers, the invisible students were notably unlikely to respond with positive affect to the teachers, and they generally avoided the teachers except when they needed help. This avoidance was passivity and disinterest rather than alienation. The invisible students were actually better behaved than average, and they did not project any hostility or negative affect to teachers even though they also did not express positive affect. Thus, their passivity and detachment appears to be more a matter of personal style and preference than an indication of anything about the affective quality of the teacher-student relationship.

This introduces the second major question raised by the earlier studies of indifference students: were teachers merely indifferent toward these students, or were they subtly rejecting? Different studies gave slightly different answers, but the present study seems to indicate clearly that the teachers did not reject the invisible students and in fact systematically attempted to win them over with positive treatment and outreach behaviors. Perhaps the unusually clear findings in this study indicating that the low rates of interaction between invisible students and the teachers were due mostly to the passivity of these students, and also indicating that teachers did not reject or give up on these students despite the lack of response from them, are due to the methodology of the study.

Recall that students ranked consistently low on the noticeable scale were ranked that way by two separate teachers across repeated measures. This helped insure that the students classified as invisible really were the passive and unresponsive students, and it minimized the likelihood that certain students were included on the list because they did not get along well with teachers or subtly extinguished or punished teacher overtures by responding negatively. Previous studies, which depended on data collected a single time from a single teacher, probably included among the indifference students a subset that were not merely passive and quiet in the classroom but also were negatively responsive (not merely neutral or unresponsive) to their teachers.

In any case, the present study documents that certain students simply do not respond positively to even repeated teacher attempts to build relationships with them through verbal praise, positive affect, and positive treatment generally. This is the case even though these students are generally well behaved and do not show any signs of alienation from teachers or negative feelings toward them. They simply do not respond to teacher overtures. However, this lack of response by the invisible students apparently did not deter the teachers from continuing to try to reach them. Thus, the teachers clearly were not indifferent toward the invisible students, even though these students shared many qualities with students labeled indifference students in earlier studies. It may be that the indifference label is a misnomer, because it pictures teachers as unconcerned about invisible students, when the data from the present study indicate continuing concern about and attempts to reach them, despite lack of response.

The present study (as well as those by Good and Brophy, 1972, and by Evertson, Brophy, and Good, 1973b) illustrates the importance of coding teacher versus student initiation of contacts. If this information had not been recorded, the present study would have agreed with the general finding that invisible students have low rates of interaction with their teachers, but would not have provided any information about why this is so. Because information on teacher versus student initiation of interaction was recorded, however, we are able to state clearly that these low rates of interaction involving invisible students are due to the extremely low rates of initiation by the students themselves, and not to any failure by the teachers to go after these students. In fact, our data indicate that the teachers were systematically reaching out to these students, and yet their interaction totals were below average because their rates of student initiation were extremely low. In summary, then, our data indicate that the low rates of teacher-student interaction for invisible students were due to the behavioral preferences of the students themselves and not to any teacher tendency to ignore these students.

The data on students who avoided eye contact make a nice contrast with the invisible students. These students were not generally passive like the invisible students. Nor were they merely shy and unresponsive to teachers.

The data indicate that they had poor relationships with teachers and responded negatively to the teachers' positive attempts to reach them. This was true even though students who avoided eye contact with teachers were not especially likely to misbehave or to respond with overt hostility toward teachers during disciplinary contacts. Their alienation from teachers took on a more passive and avoiding quality although with negative affect as an observable and continuing part of their response.

Teachers did make some efforts to reach these students by directing questions at them when they did not volunteer and by praising their academic successes. However, they did not show the widespread pattern of outreach that was evident with respect to the invisible students, and in particular there was no indication of positive teacher affect being extended to these students. Thus, even though there was no overt conflict between the teachers and these students, neither the teachers nor the students seemed to like each other much. These students largely avoided the teachers, and they made the teachers sufficiently uncomfortable as to succeed in extinguishing most teacher attempts to reach them. In many ways, these students who avoided eye contact with teachers constituted a true indifference group in the sense that teachers recognized that they had some problems and were somewhat alienated, but did not do much to try to change the situation.

Of the scales considered in this chapter, the ratings of cooperative versus uncooperative student behavior produced the most numerous and sizeable differences in the patterns of teacher-student interaction. Cooperative students had cordial and apparently mutually satisfying relationships with teachers. Negative affect was especially unlikely between the teachers and these students, although there were no indications of favoritism or high frequencies of mutual positive affect, either. Thus, like high achievement, good conduct makes for smooth relationships between students acting within the student role and teachers acting within the teacher role, but it does not by itself elicit teacher favoritism or positive affect.

Sustained lack of cooperation, on the other hand, does produce negative affect in teachers, even when the students involved do not become alienated themselves. The uncooperative students showed frequent and intense disruptive misbehavior, and often projected hostility or other negative affect toward the teacher during disciplinary contacts. They also had to be supervised closely and helped or redirected frequently during seatwork times, because they were not working on their assignments or not doing them carefully. Finally, they frequently had to be called on as nonvolunteers during public response opportunity situations, because they seldom raised their hands (they were likely to call out answers without permission when they were paying attention, however).

The pressures applied by these uncooperative students were sufficient to dislodge teachers from their roles as adult facilitators, even though the students themselves frequently came to the teachers to attempt to get personal needs met or to tattle on their peers when they were not misbehaving. Teachers responded to these students with avoidance and criticism. They often initiated contacts with them to correct their behavior or remind them of their personal responsibilities, but they seldom initiated social contacts with them. They criticized them frequently for poor work and punished them frequently for misbehavior, but were not especially likely to praise them for good work or good conduct. The teachers also frequently refused the initiations of these students, including attempts to get help with their work in addition to attempts to tattle or get permission to do something.

Across all contacts taken together, teachers were more likely to express negative affect toward the uncooperative students than the cooperative students, although there were no significant differences for more specific measures such as impatience during work contacts or making the student a bad example for the rest of the class. Thus, it appears that the behavior of these students made teachers frustrated and unsympathetic, but this did not progress to the point that teachers were picking on these students or responding with hatred, vengeance, or other powerful negative affect. Perhaps this is why the students themselves did not become completely alienated from the teachers, despite their constant conflict with them.

The pattern of interaction involved here is similar to that reported by Nash (1973) and hypothesized by Cooper and Lowe (1977). That is, teachers find interactions with these extremely uncooperative students to be frustrating and perhaps also threatening. During such interactions there is always the danger that the teacher or the student will lose control, and in addition the disruptive behavior and defiance of these students endangers the teacher's general authority over the class as a whole and destroys the academic focus that the teacher has tried to establish. Repeated experiences of this kind will motivate teachers to try to avoid such contacts (if they have not been successful in changing the student's behavior). Theoretically, this should lead to teacher attempts to minimize the frequency of interactions with these students and the duration of the interactions that do occur.

The present study yielded little evidence of teacher attempts to minimize interactions with these students. The teachers did avoid initiating social contacts with them, but they frequently initiated interactions geared to check on their work or see that they were fulfilling their personal responsibilities, and they often called on them in public response situations (frequently as nonvolunteers, because these students usually did not raise their hands). However, as Cooper and Lowe (1977) point out, these are all teacher-initiated interactions during which teachers have a greater sense of control than they do for student-initiated interactions. The data on student initiations do follow the predictions of Cooper and Lowe: teachers minimized these by frequently refusing the initiatives of the uncooperative students, even presumably legitimate initiatives involving attempts to get help with their work. Thus, although frustration with the behavior of uncooperative students does not seem to lead teachers to single these students out for active persecution or vengeful treatment, it does lead them to avoid contact with these students, to withhold positive affect from them, and, in general, to concentrate on controlling their behavior and neutralizing the trouble they cause rather than on teaching and socializing them in a more positive sense. Extremely uncooperative students pressure teachers into dealing with them as behavior problems first and as individual learners and personalities second, if at all.

17

Teacher Attitudes

In this chapter, we will review the findings concerning the teacher attitudes of attachment, rejection, and concern, and relate them to earlier work reviewed in chapter 3. In particular, we will consider how the present findings fit with the general pattern of agreement found concerning attachment students and the discrepancies reported in studies of concern and rejection students.

Studies by Silberman (1969), Good and Brophy (1972), Evertson, Brophy, and Good (1973b), McDonald (1972), Nash (1973), Willis and Brophy (1974), and Power (1971) all agreed in finding that attachment students tended to be conforming high achievers who were trusted and respected by teachers and got along well with teachers, but were not openly favored in easily identifiable ways. Many of these investigators suggested that some subtle favoritism did exist, but all agreed that teacher attachment did not result in clearly positive treatment in the same way that teacher rejection resulted in negative treatment. There were indications that part of the reason for this is that teachers tend to be aware of their positive feelings toward certain students but careful to avoid showing favoritism of these students because they feel it is their duty to treat all students equally.

The data from the present study replicate and support these findings. Teachers described the preferred students whom they ranked highly on the attachment scale as bright, quiet, well motivated, and helpful. They called on these students frequently in public response opportunity situations, apparently because these students frequently volunteered. They were less likely to initiate private academic or personal contacts with them, however, apparently because they did not require close supervision.

Teachers favored these students to the extent that they were unusually open to their initiatives and likely to approve them, and likely to appoint them as classroom monitors. Thus, the teachers treated these students with considerable trust and respect. However, there were no significant tendencies for unusual positive affect on the part of either the teachers or the preferred students. Thus, even though the teachers reported liking these students to the extent that they would like to keep them around for another year, they did not express positive affection toward these students directly in their classroom behavior. As other investigators have reported, any special treatment or favoritism that these preferred students did receive was relatively subtle, and much of it can be attributed to the behavior and personal qualities of the students themselves.

Thus, although teachers treated these students with respect and were particularly unlikely to criticize them or express negative affect toward them, this was due in large part to the fact that the preferred students seldom gave teachers any reason for negative response. They were successful, cooperative, and generally ideal students. Similarly, although teachers were likely to respond positively to the initiatives of these students, to approve their requests, and to assign them special and prestigious responsibilities, this "favoritism" could be defended on objective grounds. That is, the preferred students were generally mature and responsible, so that the majority of the requests they made were likely to be seen as legitimate and appropriate by the teachers. Furthermore, these students kept up with their studies and were the kind of responsible students that teachers felt safe in entrusting with demanding tasks or appointing as classroom monitors.

In summary, then, teachers do not favor preferred or attachment students with overt expressions of positive affect or grossly discriminatory teacher's pet treatment, but they do treat these students with respect and allow them a greater measure of initiative and independence than they allow most other students. This can be labeled as subtle favoritism, but it also can be defended as appropriate individualized treatment based on objective personal characteristics and behavior. In short, the typical attachment student deserves such treatment because he or she has earned it.

The literature on rejected students reviewed in chapter 3 shows somewhat less agreement across studies than the literature on attachment students. All investigators agreed that rejection students tend to misbehave frequently and disruptively, and in particular to project hostility toward the teacher. Studies also agree that teachers tend to respond by keeping these students under surveillance, criticizing them frequently for inattention or poor work, and punishing them often for misbehavior. The main disagreement across studies of rejection students is on the issue of whether teachers form generally negative patterns of attitude and behavior toward these students or instead show a more conflicted pattern in which high rates of criticism and punishment are balanced somewhat by high rates of praise or other indications of attempts to change these students through positive treatment.

Silberman (1969) found such a conflicted pattern, as did Power (1971). However, Good and Brophy (1973a), Evertson, Brophy, and Good (1973b), Nash (1973), Brooks and Wilson (1978), Willis and Brophy (1974), and Evertson, Brophy, and Good (1973b) all reported consistent patterns of mutual negativism and hostility between teachers and rejection students, without any evidence of guilt on the part of teachers or attempts to shape the behavior of the rejection students through positive treatment.

Data from the present study support this pattern. Teacher perceptions of the rejected students were completely negative and included descriptions such as untrustworthy, which indicate character defects and blameworthiness. The teachers apparently saw these rejected students as responsible for their unacceptable behavior, and not as struggling with limitations or pressures beyond their control.

Behavioral data indicate that the rejected students typically did not attend to or participate in classroom activities regularly, and that they misbehaved often, disruptively, and in ways that communicated disrespect for and hostility toward the teacher. Teachers responded by calling on them frequently as nonvolunteers; keeping them under close surveillance when they were supposed to be working on seatwork assignments; frequently reminding them of their personal responsibilities; criticizing their poor answers or poor work; refusing many of their academic, housekeeping, and personal initiations and treating them with impatience during such interactions; holding them up as bad examples to the rest of the class; and criticizing, warning, or punishing them when they misbehaved. Thus, the teachers and the rejection students were locked into a pattern in which each was continually frustrating the other and producing reactions of negative affect and hostility.

The contrast between patterns for these rejected students and patterns for the students ranked as chronically uncooperative are instructive in indicating that hostility breeds hostility, and that this is the key factor in determining why teachers reject certain students. Recall that the uncooperative students as a group continuously pressure teachers by disrupting class, and often compound this by responding with hostility when teachers intervene to discipline them. However, the pattern of negative affect and hostility toward the teacher observed in the uncooperative students was not as widespread and consistent as for the rejected students. Presumably because of this, teacher reactions to the uncooperative students as a group were confined mostly to frustration and lack of positive treatment but did not extend to clear-cut negative treatment and hostility. This was not the case with the rejected students.

Thus, although most if not all rejected students were behavior problems, only a subset of the uncooperative students were rejected. These likely were the students who responded most negatively to the teachers, treating them with hostility, defiance, or aggression. It is possible that teachers withstood this negativism for a time and tried to reach these students by building positive relationships, encouraging them, and reinforcing their progress. However, where this treatment did not work, and where hostility from the student continued or escalated, teachers would tend to gradually give up serious attempts to change the students and switch their orientation from the adult facilitator role toward a more self-protective and authoritarian role. By the end of the year, when the classroom observations were made in this study, the teachers had settled into a completely negative pattern of interactions with rejected students, apparently having abandoned attempts to change them for the better. They had to content themselves with controlling misbehavior and threats to authority by maintaining tight surveillance on these students and intervening with whatever degree of demand, threat, or punishment was necessary to force the student to conform to at least minimal expectations.

In view of the fact that these rejected students generally made life miserable for their teachers, it is tempting to condone the teachers' negative response to them. After all, how much can we expect teachers to put up with? On the other hand, consider the data in perspective: these were elementary (grades two through five) classrooms in stable working class neighborhoods, not junior high schools in the slums. Furthermore, 39 (11 percent) of the 360 target students were consistently classified as rejected by two consecutive teachers. It is true that our ranking method required teachers to place some students at the rejection end of the scale, and thus identified more students as rejected than a question like "Are there students in your room that you simply can't stand?" would have identified. Still the percentage of students who remain rejected across time and teachers seems too high, and suggests the need for much better preservice and inservice training of teachers in classroom management and interpersonal relationships.

Good information and training on these topics was not really available to teachers until fairly recently, but developments over the last 10 or 15 years have produced a great deal of agreement on and even some support for basic principles and methods of organizing groups of students for instruction and socializing them into the student role effectively (Brophy and Putnam, 1979). Widespread dissemination and implementation of approaches advocated by such authors as Good and Brophy (1978, 1980), Krumboltz and Krumboltz (1972), Gordon (1974), or Glasser (1969, 1977) should help teachers to cope more effectively with these problem students and minimize the percentage of the time that relationships deteriorate to the kind of mutual negativism and lack of positive progress observed in the present study and other studies of rejected students.

Previous work on concern students (reviewed in chapter 3) agreed that the major characteristic of this group is difficulty in meeting school demands due to limited intelligence or academic background. Behavior problems are sometimes involved as well, but the major reason that teachers consider in nominating concern students (students with whom the teachers would like to be able to spend a lot more individualized time) is that these students have difficulty making progress on their own and seem to need a lot of teacher guidance and help.

The main source of disagreement in research on concern students is whether teachers tend to respond to their plight primarily by lowering expectations and making things easier for them, or instead by providing not only extra time and attention but extra push and encouragement in an attempt to pressure the concern students into keeping up with their classmates. Silberman (1969) found that teachers gave the concern students a lot of extra time and encouragement, showing a willingness to explain things more fully to these students and even to allow them to interrupt to ask questions. He also suggested that teachers were more likely to praise concern students for relatively minor achievements, and to quickly give them answers if they could not respond to questions on their own. Good and Brophy (1972) also noted teacher willingness to spend extra time with concern students and provide extra explanation and help, but they did not see evidence of overly frequent praise or tendencies to give these students answers instead of waiting them out.

If anything, Good and Brophy suggested, the teachers in the study were working to elicit improved performance from the concern students, perhaps pushing them a little harder than other students rather than treating them with exaggerated sympathy or reduced expectations. However, Evertson, Brophy, and Good (1973b) reported findings more similar to Silberman's (1969) findings for concern students. That is, the teachers in that study did seem to go out of their way to encourage and praise concern students, and did seem to give them answers or call on someone else quickly if they were not able to respond to questions. Power (1971) also found that teachers gave concern students easier tasks and tried to avoid overtaxing them.

The data from the present study do not speak directly to all of these variables. In particular, we did not systematically record information on whether teachers would give the answer or call on someone else versus stick with the student and attempt to elicit an improved response when a student failed to answer the initial question. The general pattern of findings, however, is consistent with the notion (suggested by the majority of studies reviewed) that teachers not only spend more time with concern students but tend to make extra allowances for them and to provide them with extra encouragement. They were more likely to praise the concern students when these students initiated academic or approval-seeking interactions, and they were not especially likely to criticize them, even though they made a great many mistakes. Furthermore, teachers were notably patient in dealing with the concern students when they came for help with their work, where as they were impatient in similar circumstances with immature students, rejected students, or students low in persistence. Thus, the teachers were unusually patient, encouraging, and helpful when the concern students showed difficulty with their work.

They did make demands on these students, however, as indicated by their willingness to call on them as nonvolunteers because they seldom raised their hands seeking to respond in public response opportunity situations. Thus, in general, it appears that the teachers were trying to move the concern students along at whatever pace they seemed to be able to handle, although they apparently avoided pushing them too hard or allowing them to become discouraged. They provided concern students with the extra individualized attention and help that they seemed to need, and they retained a patient and encouraging stance while doing so. This seemed to be quite appropriate for the needs of these students, and it illustrates how teachers are usually willing to go out of their way to meet what they consider to be legitimate special needs in students who are not held personally responsible for their problems.

It is interesting that this occurred even though the concern students did not provide any special reinforcement to the teachers for their help (except in the form of progress in mastering the curriculum). The concern students were not particularly likely to project positive affect toward the teachers, initiate social interactions with them, or otherwise indicate any special liking for or gratitude toward the teachers. Apparently, most of the special interactions that took place between teachers and concern students involved the teachers dealing within the teacher role with students operating within the student role. The teachers apparently saw giving extra and individualized attention to the concern students as part of their job, and they apparently did so for this reason and not because they liked the concern students better than other students or because the concern students regularly rewarded them with gratitude or positive affect. Thus, clear-cut positive affect from students does not seem to be necessary to induce teachers to sustain positive treatment of those students, although clear-cut and continuing negative affect from students apparently will turn off teachers and produce corresponding negative affect on their part.

18

The Meanings of Classroom Interaction Measures

The classroom observation data for the Student Attribute Study were collected with a low inference coding system designed to record the occurrence of specific, discrete observable behaviors. This low inference approach is considered a more objective way to measure teacher behavior than using high inference rating scales, because it involves less judgment and thus less opportunity for biasing of the measurement by the classroom observers. This advantage seems to be real as far as it goes, but it still leaves questions about the reliability of low inference classroom measurement.

Until recently, concern about reliability of measurement has focused on the reliability of the observers: when a particular behavior relevant to the coding system occurs, do the observers regularly record the appropriate code? Investigators typically try to insure this by training observers until they can regularly meet high standards of reliability indicating agreement with one another in coding the same segment of classroom interaction. In the present study, for example, classroom observers were required to meet a criterion of 80 percent agreement with fellow observers, using the following formula: percent agreement = number of codes made and agreed upon by both observers, divided by the same number plus the number of codes made by both observers but disagreed upon, plus the number of codes made by Observer A but not by Observer B, plus the number of codes made by Observer B but not Observer A. This is a high standard, and observers who meet it successfully clearly are using the system appropriately and reliably.

Even where the observers are reliable in their coding, however, there remains the question of the reliability of the behavior itself. For example, suppose that a teacher visited on Tuesday calls on 25 volunteers and only 5 nonvolunteers during a recitation, but then on Thursday is observed to call on 10 volunteers but 20 nonvolunteers during another recitation. This would indicate instability (low reliability) in the frequencies of these two behaviors and in their proportional relationship to each other. Investigations of classroom processes (measures of teacher and student behavior or teacher-student interaction) have revealed that reliabilities in this sense are often quite low, often too low to support attempts to generalize from the data (Shavelson and Dempsey-Atwood, 1976; Erlich and Borich, 1979).

There are ways for investigators to get around this problem, however. One way is to visit each classroom repeatedly and accumulate a great many hours of classroom observation. This allows day-to-day fluctuations to cancel out when data from all of the observations are accumulated and analyzed for general trends. This strategy was used in the present study, where each classroom was observed for ten half-days, or about 20 hours. This is a rather heavy schedule of observations per classroom, and it yielded enough information across enough separate occasions to allow us to identify general trends even in behaviors that fluctuate from day to day.

A second way to control such fluctuations is to limit the contexts within which classroom observations are conducted. We have argued elsewhere (Brophy, 1979a; Brophy and Evertson, 1978) that failure to control context, and not low observer reliability, is the main reason for low reliability and generalizability of classroom process data (assuming that enough data are collected in the first place to provide some reason to expect reliability or generalizability). In any case, it is clear that the rates of occurrence and patterns of relationship among various measures of teacher and student behavior and teacher-student interaction differ according to such factors as time of day (morning versus afternoon) or size of group (whole class versus small group) (Crawford, Brophy, Evertson, and Coulter, 1977). The meanings and qualitative nature of many interactions are also affected by whether they are initiated by the teacher versus the student or whether they occur in public versus private settings (Brophy and Evertson, 1978).

Most of these factors were at least partially controlled in the present study. All data were taken at the same time of the year (spring) in each classroom, and were balanced between morning and afternoon observations. Coding was done only during academic interactions, excluding recess, testing, movies, games, or other activities in which teachers and students did not play their usual classroom roles. Response opportunities were coded separately according to whether they occurred in general class or small group settings, and private interactions were coded separately for teacher versus student initiation. These and other distinctions built into the coding system helped us to retain some of the qualitative distinctions between ostensibly similar behaviors by allowing for separate tabulation of data from separate contexts.

The factors reviewed above helped us to maximize the reliability of measurement of the teacher and student behaviors of interest in this study. Even so, reliability does not by itself insure validity, and ours and others' (Borich, Malitz, and Kugle, 1978) recent experiences indicate that even seemingly clear and simple classroom coding categories may include two or more subtypes that are qualitatively distinct from one another and perhaps should be coded separately.

Brophy (1979b) has addressed these issues in regard to the coding category of teacher praise. Praise can be defined operationally in such a way as to produce very high agreement among observers as to when it exists and when it does not, and thus very high reliability of coding. Typically, however, a great many different teacher behaviors fit this definition and in effect are treated as identical because they all are coded under teacher praise. Among others, these include: expressions of admiration for unusually good conduct or performance (this is what we usually mean by praise); attempts to say something positive or be encouraging even when conduct or performance has not been very good; attempts to be pleasant toward or to try to compensate for previous negative interactions with difficult students; and perfunctory comments made to students who come up and show their completed work (often these comments indicate not so much genuine praise based on careful appraisal of the work as mere certification that the work has been completed and the student now has permission to do something else).

This example indicates how classroom coding categories can subsume behaviors that vary in meaning and perhaps even contrast with the common sense interpretation of the coding category based on its label (for example, praise is usually equated with the concept of reinforcement, but it is clear that some of the types of praise mentioned above are not reinforcing at all). It also points up the need to examine the interrelationships among classroom process measures in order to gather information on their meanings. The meanings implied in the operational definitions of these measures cannot simply be assumed. In the remainder of this chapter, we will consider the meanings of the classroom process measures used in this study, based on their distribution across the types of students identified for study (summarized in Table 7.2) and on their correlations with one another (which were too voluminous to include in this volume).

TYPES OF CONTACT

Frequent public response opportunities, especially in the general class setting, generally have positive implications about the students involved. Students who are called on frequently, especially if called on as volunteers who have raised their hands, tend to be the brighter, more attentive, and generally more successful students in the class. Also, by virtue of the fact that they are willing to volunteer frequently in public response situations, these students tend to be assertive, confident, and healthy in their self-concepts.

The situation is somewhat different for students who have most of their public response opportunities in the small group setting, especially if they are frequently called on as nonvolunteers. It is in small groups that teachers concentrate on working with the slow and more timid students whom they often hesitate to put on the spot in the general class setting. Thus, frequent response opportunities in small groups, especially when the students themselves do not often seek such opportunities through hand raising, have negative implications about the intelligence or confidence of the students involved, although they do indicate that the teacher is trying to work with these students.

Frequent student initiation relative to teacher initiation is generally a good sign in private contacts, as well. Students who initiate actively and comfortably with teachers generally have good relationships with the teacher, although overly frequent initiations might indicate low intelligence (and thus frequent need for help) or immaturity and dependence on the teacher. Proportion scores expressing the frequency of student-initiated contact as a proportion of all private contacts (the total of student- plus teacher-initiated contacts) generally correlate positively with desirable student qualities, although this usually is not so much a direct positive effect of student initiations. It is a result of the fact that good students typically do not have frequent behavior contacts with teachers, and have below average frequencies of teacher-initiated contacts, because they generally do not need as much supervision as other students do.

High frequencies of nonacademic or behavioral contacts have negative implications about students. Those with high frequencies of nonacademic contacts tend to be immature, coming to the teacher overly often and frequently inappropriately to try to initiate social contact, to request opportunities to do housekeeping chores, to attempt to tattle or (especially) to seek permission or help in meeting personal needs. The latter indicates that these students have difficulty meeting the responsibilities built into the student role, and frequently lose track of their belongings, forget to do things when they are supposed to be done and thus have to try to do them later at the "wrong" time, and so on. In addition to these considerations, nonacademic contacts by their very nature indicate that the student is not engaged in academic work, so that high frequencies of such contacts have negative implications about the student's motivation or abilities.

Finally, behavior contacts speak for themselves. In general, the more such contacts, the more frequently and disruptively the student misbehaves. As we have seen in this study, frequent and especially disruptive misbehavior places strain on the teacher and the teacher-student relationship, often bringing about negative teacher affect and behavior.

TYPES OF RESPONSE OPPORTUNITIES

In this study, response opportunities were classified as volunteer, nonvolunteer, hand waving, or calling out. Of these, only volunteer response opportunities have clear positive implications about students. High proportions of volunteer response opportunities relative to total response opportunities indicate that the students raise their hands offering to respond to teacher questions, but wait to be called on before actually making a response. These tend to be cooperative, well-socialized, good students who know most of the answers and yet are willing and able to restrain their enthusiasm for responding.

High frequencies of nonvolunteer response opportunities indicate that the students are not volunteering very often and thus that the teacher must compensate by calling on them when they do not have their hands raised. Many of these are students who show general passivity, alienation, or anxiety in the classroom in general or at least in public response opportunity situations. Teachers usually accommodate to these students to some degree and in particular try to avoid putting them on the spot, but they do not allow these students to simply withdraw from public response opportunity situations, and thus they must call on them sometimes. Even if this is less often than average, these students will still show relatively high percentages of being called on as nonvolunteers simply because they so seldom raise their hands voluntarily.

A subtype of the nonvolunteer response opportunity is what Brophy and Good (1970b) called the discipline question. This occurs when teachers call on nonvolunteers not merely because they do not have their hands raised, but because they are inattentive and calling on them is one way to make them focus on the lesson and pay attention. Needless to say, this also has negative implications about the students involved.

Hand waving in an attempt to get the teacher's attention and gain a response opportunity does indicate attentiveness and interest on the part of the student, but it also suggests immaturity, impulsivity, and perhaps, dependency on the teacher. The problem facing teachers in dealing with hand wavers is to encourage and reinforce their willingness to volunteer, but at the same time to socialize them to simply raise their hands instead of frantically waving their arms or yelling "teacher, teacher!"

High frequencies of calling out responses do not have any single, clear-cut meaning. Calling out often suggests hyperactivity and poor impulse control, but it also signals high interest in the activity and a positive orientation toward the teacher. In the early grades, in fact, the students who call out the most tend to be those who have frequent but relatively minor behavior contacts with teachers because of hyperactivity and difficulty staying within the bounds of the student role, but who are not alienated from teachers. This kind of calling out gradually fades away as children get older, partly because hyperactivity is less frequent and extreme in the higher grades, and partly because older students seldom are eager and teacher oriented to the point that they want to call out answers. Also, growing peer group orientation and concern about making a fool of one's self in public can cause students to inhibit this kind of behavior.

Whereas in the early grades call outs are generally a nuisance, they may become positive factors in the higher grades, where they tend to be more relevant (Evertson, Anderson, Anderson, and Brophy, 1980), and where they often facilitate lesson goals by moving things along at a good pace. Our general experience in coding call outs indicates that, even though they are initiated by students, their frequency in any given classroom is determined by teacher reactions to them. That is, teachers who tolerate or even encourage them will have a lot of call outs, but teachers who insist that students raise their hands and wait to be recognized before responding will minimize them. Thus, the task facing teachers who find call outs facilitative at times is to communicate their perceptions clearly to students and socialize them to recognize what kinds of call outs are acceptable, and under what circumstances they might be appropriate.

TEACHER INITIATIONS

High frequencies of teacher-initiated academic contacts with students are not positive signs, even though they indicate that the teacher is working hard to help the student master the curriculum. The problem is that frequent teacher-initiated academic contact indicates that the student is a slow learner or is insufficiently responsible or persistent and thus needs careful monitoring by the teacher. From the teacher's point of view, of course, these students should have more frequent academic contacts and closer monitoring, because they need it.

In contrast to teacher-initiated academic contacts that involve actual interaction and intervention with the student, teacher initiated academic contacts that involve merely observing the student at work are positive indicators, at least to the extent that they indicate that the student apparently is progressing well and does not need help. It should be noted, however, that correlations of this variable with other variables in the study suggest that high frequencies of mere observation without intervention were especially likely in the case of students that teachers generally did not interact with much, perhaps because they saw them as self-conscious or easily embarrassed. Thus, the meaning of this behavior in a specific case depends upon the reason for it. It is a positive indicator when teachers confine themselves to mere observation because they simply are disinclined to interrupt a good student who is working successfully. There are mixed implications, however, when teachers hesitate to speak to students for fear of embarrassing them. The fact that they do not need to speak or intervene indicates that the students are working successfully, but the teacher inhibition indicates self-consciousness or related problems in the students.

Frequent teacher-initiated housekeeping interactions are a positive sign indicating that the teacher respects and trusts the student. Teachers often mention assigning errands to students or involving them in housekeeping chores as ways to build relationships and reach difficult students, and apparently they do this with some frequency. However, our data indicate that they assign such errands and chores most frequently to the students with whom they have the best relationships, and among these, the brighter and more responsible ones in particular.

High frequencies of teacher-initiated personal contacts have negative implications about students, suggesting that they are irresponsible, forgetful, sloppy in their work, or messy in their personal habits. These are the students who do not, on their own initiative, do the things that they are supposed to do, so that teachers find it necessary to come and remind them or order them to do so. These students are not necessarily alienated from the teachers, however. Also, frequent teacher initiation of personal contacts does not necessarily indicate dislike or rejection of the students.

Prior to this study, we expected that frequent teacher initiation of social contacts with students would be a positive sign, and would be particularly likely with mature and sociable students with whom teachers shared very positive relationships. The data yield a very different picture, however. Frequent teacher initiation of social contact was observed most often with immature, low-achieving, or low persistence students. Apparently, these contacts represent teacher attempts to build relationships with or be (compensatorily?) pleasant toward slow or immature (but usually liked) students. From a larger perspective, this relationship is but one element of a general pattern observed in this study indicating that teachers share smooth and satisfying relationships with liked and successful students, but do not spend disproportionate time with these students or go out of their way to interact with them. Instead, they go after the students whom they perceive as needing closer supervision and more personal relationships.

In general, the rates of teacher-initiated contacts showed more orderly relationships with other variables and with student types than did the proportion measures. This was because teachers initiate more of every type of contact except housekeeping contacts with the less mature and lower-achieving students. This is another example of the general principle noted earlier that high frequencies of teacher-initiated contact are expected when teachers are concerned about students, particularly students who are not achieving at a good rate.

STUDENT INITIATIONS

Student initiation of academic contacts with teachers has mixed implications. On the one hand, it suggests student concern about completing work correctly and indicates that the student feels comfortable in coming to the teacher for help. However, high frequencies of such student initiations may indicate poor persistence or difficulties in independent problem solving, especially in the early grades. Frequent student initiations for help might be more appropriate, however, where the work is difficult and where the teacher expects such help seeking. Thus, a major factor to consider here is the degree to which the teacher approves of and sanctions such help-seeking behavior.

Student approval seeking was another variable for which the data did not match our initial expectations. We thought that such approval seeking would have neutral connotations about the students when it was done routinely to get certification that work was finished and that the student had permission to move on to something else. However, we expected negative implications when approval seeking went beyond this routine version to indicate genuine concern about getting the teacher's approval for accomplishments. We thought that this might be a sign of immaturity, and perhaps even of poor teacher-student rapport (such that the student sought to return to the teacher's good graces by showing completed work). However, inspection of the correlations of student-initiated approval seeking with other variables in the study indicates that high frequencies are not linked with immature dependency, but instead with well-adjusted, confident, sociable show-offs! Apparently, the students who came to the teachers most often to show completed work were cheerful extroverts who were seeking not so much reassurance as validation of their own positive perceptions of their accomplishments. An exception to this pattern were the restless students, who did seem to fit the expectation that approval seeking can represent an attempt to retain contact and improve rapport with teachers on the part of students who have trouble getting along with them. In general, though, approval-seeking contacts were initiated with a positive "Look what I've done now!" rather than a more tentative "See, I can do good things, too."

The data concerning tattling were also surprising, and they contrast nicely with the data for approval seeking. Initially, we thought that high rates of tattling would be associated with "goody two shoes" types who were overly teacher oriented and morally offended by essentially minor misbehavior. We did find that tattling was more frequent in the early grades than in the later grades, and more frequent among students labeled immature than those seen as mature. However, it was most frequent among students labeled restless, careless, low in persistence, or uncooperative. In some students, high frequencies of tattling may constitute an example of "misery seeks company," a defense against frequent teacher criticism and punishment on the part of the students who frequently misbehave. Such tattlers approach the teachers not so much with immature shock and outrage, but with implicit messages of "You punished me, so punish him, too!" or "I'm not so bad—she does it, too!" This is a common defense among students who are frequently in trouble for misbehavior (Redl and Wineman, 1951): if you can't boost yourself by pointing to positive behavior or accomplishments, pull down peers to your level by pointing out their faults.

Such defensiveness does not necessarily characterize all students who tattle frequently, however. Some tattlers may be confused about just what the teacher does or does not expect, and may tattle as a method of testing the rules. Others may tattle for no better reason than to take a break from work or to provide themselves with something to do. In any case, however, high rates of tattling tend to be associated with undesirable student attributes.

High frequencies of student-initiated personal contacts are also negative signs, suggesting immaturity, and perhaps in some cases, a sense of being cheated or picked on. High frequencies of these personal contacts were associated with restless and uncooperative students, especially in the early grades. They suggest forgetfulness, difficulty in keeping track of possessions, and generally poor adjustment to the student role, as well as hyperactivity and frequent desires to move around the room, go get a drink, visit the lavatory, and so forth. In general, then, students who have very high rates of initiation of personal interactions with their teachers are likely to be seen as having too many such interactions, and many of the requests they make are likely to be perceived as inappropriate and thus refused.

High frequencies of student-initiated social contacts with teachers are neutral to positive in their implications about students, but perhaps less positive than we expected them to be. These initiations are not very frequent in the absolute sense, although they are relatively more frequent among girls and in the higher grades. In general, relatively high rates of social initiations with teachers are observed in students who are generally talkative and sociable types, with peers as well as with their teachers. Thus, contrary to our expectations, these social initiations do not so much indicate a strong interest in the teacher as an interest in chatting and socializing generally.

The percentage of misbehavior which is disruptive is of course a very negative indicator, associated with restlessness, immaturity, and lack of cooperation. It is more frequent among boys than girls, and among students who are hyperactive and have difficulty controlling their impulses or their aggression.

High percentages of behavior contacts that involve griping, sassing, or defying the teacher are even worse, indicating authority problems generally and conflict with the teacher specifically. This hostility directed at the teacher tends to generalize to nondisciplinary interactions and induce reciprocal hostility from the teacher if it persists, so that high frequencies of these behaviors were one frequent correlate of placement of students into the rejected category.

High frequencies of noninteractive antisocial behaviors also had negative implications about students, although the category contained a mixture of problems. Of these, the most serious in its implications was lying, something to which teachers are particularly sensitive and negatively responsive. The teacher adjective description variable untrustworthy was regularly associated with types of students with whom teachers had very bad relationships, and in general, teachers (like most people) find lying particularly hard to tolerate or forgive.

Other variables included in this category were cheating and sleeping. Cheating indicates mostly low intelligence and a difficulty in handling classroom work demands, although it also indicates a degree of alienation from the teacher. Thus, low achievers who struggled with their work and tried to do it well were unlikely to cheat and instead likely to come to the teacher for help and become objects of teacher concern, whereas low achievers who were less concerned about mastering the material or pleasing the teacher were more likely to copy answers from someone else than to seek help from the teacher, and thus were less likely to become objects of teacher concern (in the positive sense of the term). This kind of cheating is expected or at least tolerated, however, because it does not lead to the intensely negative reactions that lying does.

Sleeping did not occur often enough to allow us to develop data on its correlates. Presumably, it indicated a poor home situation.

STUDENT AFFECT

Clear-cut positive affect expressed toward teachers by students was seldom observed in our study, and when it did appear it usually was a direct reaction to praise or some positive behavior by the teacher. High frequencies of positive student affect have positive implications about the student in that they indicate good relationships with the teacher, although general patterns of intercorrelation suggest that these students may be overly involved with the teachers. For example, even though they are good students and have many public response opportunities and are often praised, they tend to have many of their academic initiatives refused. Furthermore, many come from single-parent families and have problems with their peers. Thus, the data provide some indication that students who have the most extreme and obvious positive affect toward teachers may be investing emotionally in the teachers at least in part because they have poor social adjustments and peer relationships.

In contrast to the relatively infrequent rate of noteworthy positive affect toward teachers, negative affect was relatively frequent, at least among certain students. It also was a very bad indicator, suggesting student alienation from the teachers and probably leading to reciprocal negative affect on the part of the teachers. Like griping, sassing, and defying, generalized negative affect toward the teacher was one of the surest signs of a bad teacher-student relationship.

In partial contrast, frequent coding of sullenness on the part of students when they were being disciplined for misbehavior was not linked so closely with alienation and rejection. Perhaps teachers considered this to be a natural or at least an expected and tolerated reaction to criticism or punishment. Students who had the highest frequencies of sullenness tended to be hyperactive students with high frequencies of most kinds of contacts with teachers. Thus, they were often in trouble for misbehavior and clearly did not like to be criticized or punished for it, but they usually confined their negative response to pouting or sulking rather than exploding with hostility directed at the teacher.

TEACHER PRAISE AND CRITICISM

The data on praise and criticism from the Student Attribute Study confirmed earlier work by ourselves and others indicating that these variables do not always have the meanings usually assigned to them, and also provided some new surprises. First, teachers were much more likely to praise good answers or good work than to criticize poor answers or poor work, but despite the popularity of behavior modification and the emphasis on "catching students being good," praise of good behavior was rare and criticism of misbehavior was frequent. The teachers may have been intuitively correct here, however, because there are several reasons to believe that praise of good classroom conduct is not particularly reinforcing and may even backfire (Brophy, 1979b). In the first place, such praise typically is delivered not so much to try to reinforce the good conduct of the student being praised, as to motivate other students to follow suit. This is unlikely to be successful because misbehaving students probably would not be misbehaving if they were very concerned about pleasing the teacher in the first place, so that they are unlikely to feel deprived when they see the teacher praise a peer for good conduct and thus unlikely to imitate that peer in an attempt to get similar praise for themselves. If anything, they are likely to taunt or reject the peer, which is why such praise can backfire and may even function as a punishment rather than a reinforcer with respect to that individual's conduct. In any case, the low frequency of praise of good conduct may well represent appropriate teacher behavior.

Another thing to bear in mind about the teacher praise and criticism data is that praise and criticism correlated positively. That is, a particular student who was likely to be praised relative to other students also was likely to be criticized relative to other students. In general, teachers are more evaluative, both positively and negatively, in responding to low achievers and uncooperative students than they are in responding to cooperative high achievers. Thus, praise and criticism are partly automatic responses elicited by student behavior and partly behavior-shaping techniques used selectively by teachers according to their perceptions of need for change in student behavior and likelihood of positive response to the technique.

Praise of good answers or good work (academic praise) was most frequent with students labeled as immature, low in persistence, not noticeable, or high on the concern scale. This indicates that such praise is behavior modification for the needy rather than admiration or reinforcement for the successful. This is why such praise typically does not correlate significantly or even correlates negatively with measures of student learning gains in the early grades (Brophy and Evertson, 1976).

The frequency of teacher academic praise seems to relate not only to teacher perceptions of student need for it but also to teacher perceptions of student response to it. Such praise was directed especially often to students who responded positively by showing positive affect during private work contacts with teachers. Teacher praise during teacher-initiated academic contacts correlated positively with praise during student-initiated academic contacts, with teacher smiles, and with physical affection toward the student, but also with teacher frowns and critical or punishing responses to misbehavior. Thus, in general, teachers were both more evaluative and more emotionally responsive to certain students, apparently at least in part because these students responded more overtly to such teacher behavior.

Teacher criticism of poor answers and poor responses (academic criticism) was associated with students labeled restless, careless, immature, low in persistence, or uncooperative. In general, then, it was associated with poor work due to poor effort or application rather than to poor ability, especially when it occurred in teacher-initiated academic contacts. High frequencies of such criticism indicate that the teacher is blaming the student for poor application, not merely for failure.

However, teacher criticism of poor answers offered during public response opportunity situations was especially likely to be directed to happy, attractive, and noticeable students, and criticism during student-initiated academic or approval-seeking contacts also was associated with happy students. This indicates that certain kinds of criticism may indicate not so much rejection or blame as communication of high expectations for certain students (Brophy and Evertson, 1976). Here, the teacher communicates not so much "you have failed," or "you should be ashamed," as "you have not worked up to your abilities and can do better than this—go back and do so."

The relationships between these types of teacher criticism and other variables or student group categories suggest that communication of high standards and expectations is especially likely with students seen as able to take it. It is also worth noting that these forms of criticism usually are not associated with undesirable teacher behaviors or teacher-student interaction patterns, so that they apparently have positive or desirable implications about the students involved.

CRITICAL TEACHER BEHAVIORS

Appointing the student as a monitor was a rare but very positive sign, showing significant relationships only for attachment students. In general, this indicates that the teacher trusts and respects the student, although the behavior itself is questionable because it may cause peer relationship problems for the student who is appointed as monitor.

Holding up the student as a good example to the rest of the class also was rare. It was more frequent in the higher grades than in the lower grades, but was not significantly associated with any of the student types included in the study. As with appointing the student as a monitor, it indicates teacher respect for the student but may cause peer problems for the student. The data suggest that teachers unfortunately tended to hold up as good examples to the rest of the class students who were well behaved and hard working but were not social leaders. Unfortunately, this would minimize the likelihood that other students would respond positively to this teacher behavior, and maximize the likelihood that the students involved would be taunted with cries of "teacher's pet!"

Teacher flattery of students is generally a negative indicator. Flattery correlated positively with praise, positive teacher adjective descriptions, and positive teacher treatment of students, but also with tattling, frequent misbehavior, hand waving, and other indications of immaturity and dependency on the teacher. Furthermore, the data suggest that flattery is part of a cluster of teacher behavior modification strategies rather than an indication of genuine teacher liking or affection for the students involved.

Similarly, teacher expressions of physical affection toward students also had negative implications. Such physical affection was particularly likely with students labeled careless, immature, or low in achievement or persistence. Like flattery, it is part of a general pattern of positive treatment of the students involved, but the students themselves tend to be somewhat immature and likely to have difficulty playing the student role. Interestingly, such physical affection correlates mostly with measures of verbal praise and behavior modification techniques rather than with other measures indicating genuine teacher positive affect. Thus, open displays of affection toward students are more likely to be calculated teacher attempts to build relationships with the students or to modify their behavior than to be spontaneous or credible expressions of liking or affection for the students involved. This is a particularly instructive example of how even seemingly clear-cut classroom behavior does not always mean what we assume it to mean. One wonders what students perceive and feel when they receive such displays of affection from teachers or when they observe them being directed toward their peers (c.f. Weinstein and Middlestadt, 1979).

Another variable in this vein is the awarding of errands, housekeeping chores, or special personal privileges to students, either at the teacher's initiative or in response to student requests. In these situations, the teacher does not merely make an assignment or approve a request, but makes a point of indicating that the action is being taken in recognition of some good conduct or achievement by the student, and thus constitutes a reward. This behavior was relatively rare, being more frequent with boys than girls and more frequent in the early grades. The latter is probably appropriate, because the data suggest that this is a rather condescending and somewhat transparent attempt by teachers to manipulate the students involved. In any case, it is clear that the awarding of chores and privileges has a different and much less positive implication about the student than the spontaneous assignment of these things to students or approval of student requests for them.

In contrast to physical affection, teacher positive affect as communicated through smiles and pleasantness is more positive in its implications about students and more credible as an indicator of the teacher's true feelings. Positive affect of this kind was especially likely for students labeled calm and for those ranked low on noticeable. Thus, noteworthy positive affect by the teacher was most likely to be seen with shy and quiet students, presumably those who responded well to it. Note, however, that it was not particularly likely to be observed with attachment students, reinforcing the repeated finding that teachers do not tend to overtly display their positive feelings toward such students.

Praise of good conduct or behavior (behavioral praise) is associated with objectively good conduct by the students and with high regard of the students by the teacher. Unfortunately, however, teachers tend to praise the good conduct of quiet and studious types who are not peer leaders, thus inviting "teacher's pet" problems and minimizing the likelihood that such behavioral praise will lead to the hoped for results. Fortunately, such praise is mostly confined to the early grades, and is rare in the higher grades.

Making the student a bad example to the class is a particularly negative indicator, associated with students labeled restless, careless, low in persistence, and (especially) rejected by the teacher. Teacher rejection seems to be the key here. The data suggest that students high on this variable are poorly behaved but no worse than many others who do not tend to get singled out publicly as bad examples.

Teacher impatience during academic interactions is another very negative indicator. It is associated with students labeled immature, low in persistence, low on teacher concern, and high on teacher rejection. Apparently, teachers find these students irritating and blame them for their problems, including their difficulties in mastering the curriculum. Impatience correlates with a broad range of measures of criticism and negative affect, as well, and in general indicates that teachers not only dislike these students but have difficulty masking their negative feelings. Thus, like making the student a bad example to the class, impatience during academic interactions is an especially diagnostic teacher behavior, much more so than the frequency or even the intensity of criticism and punishment.

Refusals of student-initiated academic and housekeeping contacts also have negative implications, being especially frequent with students labeled restless, immature, uncooperative, or rejected. Here, teachers are turning down opportunities to be nice or helpful when students present them. Even so, this is not quite so negative an indicator as making the student a bad example or showing impatience. The data indicate that students particularly likely to show up on these variables are those who have high rates of all kinds of interactions with teachers and are generally hyperactive, suggesting that the reasons for refusals often have to do with poor timing or illegitimacy of requests rather than with a rejecting or punitive attitude toward the students. Still, teachers tend not to refuse such initiatives by low achievers who fit into the concern group, indicating that blame and rejection do play a part here as well.

Refusal of student-initiated personal requests are especially likely with students labeled noticeable, uncooperative, or rejected. Obviously this has bad implications, because it applies only to the most disliked and alienated students. To the extent that these refusals occur when student requests are legitimate and likely to be approved for other students, high frequencies on this variable suggest that the teachers may be getting even with students they resent by refusing to let them meet their personal needs or do the things that they want to do.

Refusal of tattling is also a negative indicator associated with students labeled restless, noticeable, or uncooperative (but not necessarily rejected). This indicates that refusals are due more to illegitimate tattle demands on teachers than to teacher rejection of the students or desires to get even with them. The generally negative teacher response to tattling is understandable in view of the findings reported earlier indicating that tattlers tend to be hyperactive misbehavers. In addition, Brophy and Rohrkemper (1980) found that teachers tend to respond to tattling as an unwelcome placing of demands on themselves rather than as a helpful or praiseworthy action by a concerned student. This occurred even though the tattling vignette in their study depicted a student who was apparently upset by the bad language used by peers on the playground, and did not suggest any misbehavior on the part of the tattler. Apparently, the fact that most tattling that teachers experience in their classrooms comes from students who do not behave well themselves has conditioned the average teacher to respond negatively to tattling and assume negative qualities on the part of an individual who tattles.

Teacher refusals of student-initiated social contact also had negative implications, although this did not happen often and there were relatively few correlations with other measures to suggest what was going on. Such refusals were associated with high rankings on noticeable and eye contact, which do not indicate much about the students involved. Perhaps most such refusals occurred simply because the students came at bad times or came too often and were starting to bug the teachers. It is interesting, though, that refusal of social initiations was associated with frequent teacher criticism and negative affect, suggesting a degree of dislike for such students as well.

Negative teacher affect as expressed through frowns and other nonverbal indicators was a very bad sign, associated with students labeled restless, immature, low in persistence, uncooperative, and rejected. This negative pattern seems to speak for itself. It is worth noting that negative affect correlates much more consistently with other nonverbal indicators of teacher affect than it does with teacher praise or criticism, suggesting that it is a credible index of the teachers' real feelings and not merely part of a behavior modification attempt.

Finally, teacher responses to misbehavior followed the expected pattern. Confining of response to mere management messages or to warnings was associated with respect for the student or with kid gloves treatment of students seen as particularly vulnerable or in need of encouragement. In contrast, threats, criticism, and punishment were seen with students who were blamed and held personally responsible for their misbehavior and rejected because of it. To a large degree, the differences in teacher reactions to misbehavior can be attributed to the frequency and intensity of the misbehavior itself: students who get more negative treatment ask for it by misbehaving often and intensively. Still, as noted periodically throughout the book, teacher feelings about the students are involved here, as well. Teachers will be more tolerant and will make more allowances for students when they believe that the students are trying to change their behavior or that the students are suffering from powerful external trauma beyond their control. They are much quicker to blame, reject, or punish when they see the students as acting deliberately and without an excuse.

CONCLUSION

Looking back on the data from the study as a whole, we note that many of the findings were predictable, but that many surprises were revealed. These occurred at two levels. First, patterns of teacher-student relationship were not completely predictable from knowledge about the students themselves: teachers sometimes were surprisingly tolerant and positive toward difficult students or surprisingly unresponsive and even negative toward students that might have been expected to provoke more positive treatment. A second set of surprises occurred in the relationships of various classroom process measures to one another or to the types of students under study. Most of these conformed to expectations, but some indicated that the classroom process measures did not have the meanings that most observers typically ascribe to them. These kinds of data underscore the need for more such investigation of the linkages among process variables themselves, in addition to the more popularly emphasized attempts to link process variables to outcome variables, particularly student learning. Also, there is a need for information about how students perceive and interpret teachers' classroom behavior. Weinstein and Middlestadt (1979) have made a good start in this direction, but much more such research is needed.

References

Abramson, L., Seligman, M., and Teasdale, J. Learned helplessness in humans: Critique and reformulation. *Journal of Abnormal Psychology*, 1978, *87*, 49–74.

Ames, R. Teachers' attributions of responsibility: Some unexpected nondefensive effects. *Journal of Educational Psychology*, 1975, *67*, 668–676.

Anderson, L., Brophy, J., Evertson, C., Baum, M., and Crawford, J. Relationships between teacher and observer adjective descriptions and teacher perceptions of student characteristics. Report No. 4035, Research and Development Center for Teacher Education, University of Texas, Austin, 1975 (ERIC ED 147 015).

Anderson, L., Evertson, C., and Brophy, J. An experimental study of effective teaching in first-grade reading groups. *Elementary School Journal*, 1979, *79*, 193–233.

Austin, D., Clark, V., and Fitchett, G. *Reading rights for boys*. New York: Appleton-Century-Crofts, 1971.

Bandura, A. *Principles of behavior modification*. New York: Holt, Rinehart and Winston, 1969.

Banks, B., Biddle, B., and Good, T. Sex roles, classroom instruction, and reading achievement. *Journal of Educational Psychology*, 1980, *72*, 119–132.

Bates, J. Effects of children's nonverbal behavior upon adults. *Child Development*, 1976, *47*, 1079–1088.

Baum, M., Brophy, J., Evertson, C., Anderson, L., and Crawford, J. Grade and sex differences in adjective descriptions of elementary school children given by their teachers and by classroom observers. Report No. 4033, Research and Development Center for Teacher Education, University of Texas, Austin, 1975 (ERIC ED 146 154).

Becker, J. *A study of differential treatment of females and males in mathematics classes*. Unpublished doctoral dissertation, University of Maryland, 1979.

Beckman, L. Teachers' and observers' perception of causality for a child's performance. Final Report, Grant No. OEG-9-70-0065-0-1-031, HEW, Office of Education, 1972.

Beez, W. Influence of biased psychological reports on teacher behavior and pupil performance. *Proceedings of the 76th Annual Convention of the American Psychological Association*, 1968, *3*, 605–606.

Bell, R. A reinterpretation of the direction of effects in studies of socialization. *Psychological Review*, 1968, *75*, 81–95.

Bem, D. *Beliefs, attitudes, and human affairs*. Belmont, California: Brooks/Cole, 1970.

Berscheid, E. and Walster, E. Effects of physical attractiveness. *Psychology Today*, 1972, *74*, 43–46.

Biber, H., Miller, L., and Dyer, J. Feminization in preschool. *Developmental Psychology*, 1972, *7*, 86.

Borich, G., Malitz, D., and Kugle, C. Convergent and discriminant validity of five classroom observation systems: Testing a model. *Journal of Educational Psychology*, 1978, *70*, 119–128.

Borko, H., Cone, R., Russo, N., and Shavelson, R. Teachers' decision making. In P. Peterson and H. Walberg (Eds.) *Research on teaching: Concepts, findings, and implications*. Berkeley: McCutchan, 1979.

Brandt, L., Hayden, M., and Brophy, J. Teachers' attitudes and ascription of causation. *Journal of Educational Psychology*, 1975, *67*, 677–682.

Braun, C. Teacher expectation: Socio-psychological dynamics. *Review of Educational Research*, 1976, *46*, 185–213.

Brooks, D. and Wilson, B. Teacher verbal and nonverbal behavioral expression toward selected pupils. *Journal of Educational Psychology*, 1978, *70*, 147–153.

Brophy, J. Teacher behavior and its effects. *Journal of Educational Psychology*, 1979a, *71*, 733–750.

Brophy, J. Teacher praise: A functional analysis. Occasional Paper No. 28, Institute for Research on Teaching, Michigan State University, East Lansing, 1979b.

Brophy, J. and Evertson, C. *Learning from teaching: A developmental perspective*. Boston: Allyn and Bacon, 1976.

Brophy, J. and Evertson, C. Context variables in teaching. *Educational Psychologist*, 1978, *12*, 310–316.

Brophy, J., Evertson, C., Baum, M., Anderson, L., and Crawford, J. Grade level and sex of student as context variables in elementary school. *Journal of Classroom Interaction*, 1979, *14*, 11–17.

Brophy, J., Evertson, C., Anderson, L., Baum, M., and Crawford, J. Student personality and teaching. Final report of the Student Attribute Study, 1980 (ERIC ED 121 799).

Brophy, J. and Good, T. The Brophy-Good dyadic interaction system. In A. Simon and E. Boyer (Eds.) *Mirrors for behavior: An anthology of observation instruments continued, 1970 supplement*, Volume A. Philadelphia: Research for Better Schools, Inc., 1970a.

Brophy, J. and Good, T. Teachers' communication of differential expectations for children's classroom performance: Some behavioral data. *Journal of Educational Psychology*, 1970b, *61*, 365–374.

Brophy, J. and Good, T. *Teacher-student relationships: Causes and consequences*. New York: Holt, Rinehart and Winston, 1974.

Brophy, J., King, C., Evertson, C., Baum, M., Crawford, J., Mahaffey, L., and Sherman, G. Manual for the student attributes coding system. Report No. 4002, Research and Development Center for Teacher Education, University of Texas, Austin, 1974 (ERIC ED 150 156).

Brophy, J. and Laosa, L. Effect of a male teacher on the sex-typing of kindergarten children. *Proceedings of the 79th Annual Convention of the American Psychological Association*, 1971, 169–170.

Brophy, J. and Putnam, J. Classroom management in the elementary grades. In D. Duke (Ed.) *Classroom Management. The 78th Yearbook of the National Society for the Study of Education, Part II*. Chicago: University of Chicago Press, 1979.

Brophy, J. and Rohrkemper, M. Teachers' thinking about problem students. Research Series No. 68, Institute for Research on Teaching, Michigan State University, East Lansing, 1980.

Cantor, N. and Gelfand, D. Effects of responsiveness and sex of children on adults' behavior. *Child Development*, 1977, *48*, 232–238.

Clarizio, H. and McCoy, G. *Behavior disorders in children*, 2nd Edition. New York: Thomas Y. Crowell, 1976.

Clifford, M. Physical attractiveness and academic performance. Paper presented at the annual meeting of the American Educational Research Association, 1975.

Clifford, M. and Walster, E. The effect of physical attractiveness on teacher expectation. Mimeographed research report, University of Minnesota, 1975.

Clift, P. and Sexton, B. . . . And all things nice. *Educational Research*, 1979, *21*, 194–198.

Cooper, H. and Lowe, C. Task information and attributions for academic performance by professional teachers and role players. *Journal of Personality*, 1977, *45*, 469–483.

Crawford, J., Brophy, J., Evertson, C., and Coulter, C. Classroom dyadic interaction: Factor structure of process variables and achievement correlates. *Journal of Educational Psychology*, 1977, *69*, 761–772.

Crawford, J. and Washington, W. A computer tallying system for data collected by the student attributes coding system. Report No. 74–3, Research and Development Center for Teacher Education, University of Texas, Austin, 1974.

Demeis, D. and Turner, R. Effects of students' race, physical attractiveness, and dialect on teachers' evaluations. *Contemporary Educational Psychology*, 1978, *3*, 77–86.

Dion, K., Berscheid, E., and Walster, E. What is beautiful is good. *Journal of Personality and Social Psychology*, 1972, *24*, 285–290.

Doyle, W., Hancock, G., and Kifer, E. Teachers' perceptions: Do they make a difference? *Journal of the Association for the Study of Perception*, 1972, *7* (Fall), 21–30.

Efran, M. *Visual interaction and interpersonal attraction*. Unpublished doctoral dissertation, University of Texas, Austin, 1969.

Elashoff, J. and Snow, R. *Pygmalion reconsidered*. Worthington, Ohio: Charles A. Jones, 1971.

Erlich, O. and Borich, G. Occurrence and a generalizability of scores on a classroom interaction instrument. *Journal of Educational Measurement*, 1979, *16*, 11–18.

Evertson, C., Anderson, C., Anderson, L., and Brophy, J. Relationships between classroom behaviors and student outcomes in junior high mathematics and English classes. *American Educational Research Journal*, 1980, *17*, 43–60.

Evertson, C., Brophy, J., and Good, T. Communication of teacher expectations: First grade. *Catalog of Selected Documents in Psychology*, 1973a, *3* (No. 374), 60.

Evertson, C., Brophy, J., and Good, T. Communication of teacher expectations: Second grade. *Catalog of Selected Documents in Psychology*, 1973b, *3* (No. 375), 60.

Fagot, B. and Patterson, G. An *in vivo* analysis of reinforcing contingencies for sex-role behaviors in the preschool child. *Developmental Psychology*, 1969, *1*, 563–568.

Feldman, R. and Prohaska, T. The student as Pygmalion: Effect of student expectation on the teacher. *Journal of Educational Psychology*, 1979, *71*, 485–493.

Festinger, L. *A theory of cognitive dissonance*. Evanston, Illinois: Row, Peterson, 1957.

Flanders, N. *Analyzing teaching behavior*. Reading, Massachusetts: Addison-Wesley, 1970.

Fleming, E. and Anttonen, R. Teacher expectancy or My Fair Lady. *American Educational Research Journal*, 1971, *8*, 241–252.

Friedman, P. Comparisons of teacher reinforcement schedules for students with different social class backgrounds. *Journal of Educational Psychology*, 1976, *68*, 286–292.

Fuller, F. Concerns of teachers: A developmental conceptualization. *American Educational Research Journal*, 1969, *6*, 207–226.

Garner, J. and Bing, M. The elusiveness of Pygmalion and differences in teacher-pupil contacts. *Interchange*, 1973, *4*, 34–42.

Getzels, J. and Jackson, P. *Creativity and intelligence*. New York: John Wiley and Sons, 1962.

Glasser, W. *Schools without failure*. New York: Harper and Row, 1969.

Glasser, W. Ten steps to good discipline. *Today's Education*, 1977, *66* (November-December), 61–63.

Good, T. Teacher effectiveness in the elementary school: What we know about it now. *Journal of Teacher Education*, 1979, *30*, 52–64.

Good, T. Classroom expectations: Teacher-pupil interactions. In J. McMillan (Ed.) *The social psychology of school learning*. New York: Academic Press, 1980 (in press).

Good, T. Biddle, B. and Brophy, J. *Teachers make a difference*. New York: Holt, Rinehart and Winston, 1975.

Good, T. and Brophy, J. Behavioral expression of teacher attitudes. *Journal of Educational Psychology*, 1972, *63*, 617–624.

Good, T. and Brophy, J. *Looking in classrooms,* 2nd Edition. New York: Harper and Row, 1978.

Good, T. and Brophy, J. *Educational psychology: A realistic approach,* 2nd Edition. New York: Holt, Rinehart and Winston, 1980.

Good, T., Cooper, H., and Blakey, S. Classroom interaction as a function of teacher expectations, student sex, and time of year. *Journal of Educational Psychology*, 1980, *72*, 378–385.

Good, T. and Grouws, D. Reactions of male and female teacher trainees to descriptions of elementary school pupils. Technical Rept. 62, Center for Research in Social Behavior, University of Missouri-Columbia, 1972.

Good, T., Sikes, J., and Brophy, J. Effects of teacher sex and student sex on classroom interaction. *Journal of Educational Psychology*, 1973, *65*, 74–87.

Gordon, T. *T.E.T., Teacher Effectiveness Training*. New York: Wyden, 1974.

Greenberg, S. and Peck, L. An experimental curriculum designed to modify children's sex role perceptions and aspiration levels. Paper presented at the annual meeting of the American Educational Research Association, 1973.

Hartley, D. Sex and social class: A case study of an infant school. *British Educational Research Journal*, 1978, *4*, 75–81.

Herrill, J. Galatea in the classroom: Student expectations affect teacher behavior. Paper presented at the annual meeting of the American Psychological Association, 1971.

Hillman, S. and Davenport, G. Teacher-student interactions in desegregated schools. *Journal of Educational Psychology*, 1978, *70*, 545–553.

Jackson, P. *Life in classrooms*. New York: Holt, Rinehart and Winston, 1968.

Jackson, G. and Cosca, C. The inequality of educational opportunity in the Southwest: An observational study of ethnically mixed classrooms. *American Educational Research Journal*, 1974, *11*, 219–229.

Jackson, P., Silberman, M., and Wolfson, B. Signs of personal involvement in teachers' descriptions of their students. *Journal of Educational Psychology*, 1969, *60*, 22–27.

Jenkins, B. *Teachers' views of particular students and their behavior in the classroom.* Unpublished doctoral dissertation, University of Chicago, 1972.

Kedar-Voivodas, G. and Tannenbaum, A. Teachers' attitudes toward young deviant children. *Journal of Educational Psychology*, 1979, *71*, 800–808.

Kester, S. and Letchworth, G. Communication of teacher expectations and their effects on achievement and attitudes of secondary school students. *Journal of Educational Psychology*, 1972, *66*, 51–55.

Klein, S. Student influence on teacher behavior. *American Educational Research Journal*, 1971, *8*, 403–421.

Krumboltz, J. and Krumboltz, H. *Changing children's behavior*. Englewood Cliffs, New Jersey: Prentice-Hall, 1972.

Lahaderne, H. and Cohen, S. Freedom and fairness: A comparison of male and female teachers in elementary classrooms. Paper presented at the annual meeting of the American Educational Research Association, 1972.

La Voie, J. and Adams, G. Teacher expectancy and its relation to physical and interpersonal characteristics of the child. *Alberta Journal of Educational Research*, 1974, *20*, 122–132.

Leinhardt, G., Seewald, A., and Engel, M. Learning what's taught: Sex differences in instruction. *Journal of Educational Psychology*, 1979, *71*, 432–439.

Maccoby, E. and Jacklin, C. *The psychology of sex differences*. Stanford, California: Stanford University Press, 1974.

Marland, P. A study of teachers' interactive thoughts. Unpublished doctoral dissertation, University of Alberta, 1977.

Martin, R. Student sex and behavior as determinants of the type and frequency of teacher-student contacts. *Journal of School Psychology*, 1972, *10*, 339–347.

Marwit, K., Marwit, S., and Walker, E. Effects of student race and physical attractiveness on teachers' judgments of transgressions. *Journal of Educational Psychology*, 1978, *70*, 911–915.

McDonald, C. *The influence of pupil liking of teacher, pupil perceptions of being liked, and pupil socio-economic status on classroom behavior.* Unpublished doctoral dissertation, University of Texas, Austin, 1972.

Medway, F. Causal attributions for school-related problems: Teacher perceptions and teacher feedback. *Journal of Educational Psychology*, 1979, *71*, 809–818.

Merton, R. The self-fulfilling prophecy. *Antioch Review*, 1948, *8*, 193–210.

Moles, O. and Perry, E. Sources of teacher expectations early in first grade. Paper presented at the annual meeting of the American Educational Research Association, 1975.

Morrison, A. and McIntyre, D. *Teachers and teaching*. Baltimore: Penguin Books, 1969.

Murphy, L. *The widening world of childhood*. New York: Basic Books, 1962.

Nash, R. *Classrooms observed: The teacher's perception and the pupil's performance*. Boston: Routledge and Kegan Paul, 1973.

Noble, C. and Nolan, J. Effect of student verbal behavior on classroom teacher behavior. *Journal of Educational Psychology*, 1976, *68*, 342–346.

Palardy, J. What teachers believe—what children achieve. *Elementary School Journal*, 1969, *69*, 370–374.

Power, C. *The effects of communication patterns on student sociometric status, attitudes, and achievement in science*. Unpublished doctoral dissertation, University of Queensland, 1971.

Rankin, K. What teachers say may not be what students hear: Non-verbal communication in the classroom. *Oregon School Study Council Bulletin*, 1978, *21* (No. 5).

Redl, F. and Wineman, D. *Children who hate*. New York: Free Press, 1951.

Rich, J. Effects of children's physical attractiveness on teachers' evaluations. *Journal of Educational Psychology*, 1975, *67*, 599–609.

Rutter, M. *Helping troubled children*. New York: Plenum, 1975.

Rosenbaum, R. M. *A dimensional analysis of the perceived causes of success and failure*. Unpublished doctoral dissertation, University of California, Los Angeles, 1972.

Rosenthal, R. The Pygmalion effect lives. *Psychology Today*, 1973, *7* (September), 46–63.

Rosenthal, R. and Jacobson, L. *Pygmalion in the classroom*. New York: Holt, Rinehart and Winston, 1968.

Ryan, F. Trait ratings of high school students by teachers. *Journal of Educational Psychology*, 1958, *49*, 124–128.

Serbin, L. and O'Leary, K. D. How nursery schools teach girls to shut up. *Psychology Today*, 1975, *9* (No. 7), December, 56–58, 102–103.

Serbin, L., O'Leary, D., Kent, R., and Tonick, I. A comparison of teacher response to the preacademic and problem behavior of boys and girls. *Child Development*, 1973, *44*, 796–804.

Sexton, P. *The feminized male: Classrooms, white collars, and the decline of manliness*. New York: Random House, 1969.

Shavelson, R., Cadwell, J., and Izu, T. Teachers' sensitivity to the reliability of information in making pedagogical decisions. *American Educational Research Journal*, 1977, *14*, 83–97.

Shavelson, R. and Dempsey-Atwood, N. Generalizability of measures of teaching behavior. *Review of Educational Research*, 1976, *46*, 553–611.

Silberman, M. Behavioral expression of teachers' attitudes toward elementary school students. *Journal of Educational Psychology*, 1969, *60*, 402–407.

Silberman, M. Teachers' actions and attitudes toward their students. In M. Silberman (Ed.) *The experience of schooling*. New York: Holt, Rinehart and Winston, 1971.

Stevenson, H., Parker, P., Wilkinson, A., Hegion, A., and Fish, E. Predictive value of teachers' ratings of young children. *Journal of Educational Psychology*, 1976, *68*, 507–517.

Thomas, A., Chess, S., and Birch, H. The origin of personality. *Scientific American,* 1970, *223,* 102–109.

Weiner, B. A theory of motivation for some classroom experiences. *Journal of Educational Psychology,* 1979, *71,* 3–25.

Weinstein, R. and Middlestadt, S. Student perceptions of teacher interactions with male high and low achievers. *Journal of Educational Psychology,* 1979, *71,* 421–431.

Willis, S. *Formation of teachers' expectations of students' academic performance.* Unpublished doctoral dissertation, University of Texas, Austin, 1972.

Willis, S. and Brophy, J. Origins of teachers' attitudes toward young children. *Journal of Educational Psychology,* 1974, *66,* 520–529.

Yarrow, M., Waxler, C., and Scott, P. Child effects on adult behavior. *Developmental Psychology,* 1971, *5,* 300–311.

Zajonc, R. Attitudinal effects of mere exposure. *Journal of Personality and Social Psychology Monograph Supplement,* 1968, *9,* 1–27.

Author Index

Subject Index